Externalism, Self-Knowledge, and Skepticism

Written by an international team of leading scholars, this collection of thirteen new essays explores the implications of semantic externalism for self-knowledge and skepticism, bringing recent developments in the philosophy of mind, the philosophy of language, and epistemology to bear on the issue. Structured in three parts, the collection looks at self-knowledge, content transparency, and then metasemantics and the nature of mental content. The chapters examine a wide range of topics in the philosophy of mind and the philosophy of language, including 2D semantics, transparency views of self-knowledge, and theories of linguistic understanding, as well as epistemological debates on contextualism, contrastivism, pragmatic encroachment, anti-luminosity arguments, and testimony. The scope of the volume will appeal to graduate students and researchers in epistemology, philosophy of mind, philosophy of language, cognitive science, psychology, and linguistics.

Sanford C. Goldberg is Professor and Chair of the Department of Philosophy at Northwestern University. His publications include *Anti-Individualism* (Cambridge, 2007), *Relying on Others: An Essay in Epistemology* (2010), and *Assertion: On the Philosophical Significance of Assertoric Speech* (2015).

Externalism, Self-Knowledge, and Skepticism

New Essays

Edited by

Sanford C. Goldberg

Northwestern University

CAMBRIDGE UNIVERSITY PRESS

CAMBRIDGE
UNIVERSITY PRESS

University Printing House, Cambridge CB2 8BS, United Kingdom

One Liberty Plaza, 20th Floor, New York, NY 10006, USA

477 Williamstown Road, Port Melbourne, VIC 3207, Australia

314-321, 3rd Floor, Plot 3, Splendor Forum, Jasola District Centre, New Delhi-110025, India

79 Anson Road, #06-04/06, Singapore 079906

Cambridge University Press is part of the University of Cambridge.

It furthers the University's mission by disseminating knowledge in the pursuit of education, learning and research at the highest international levels of excellence.

www.cambridge.org
Information on this title: www.cambridge.org/9781107636736

© Cambridge University Press 2015

This publication is in copyright. Subject to statutory exception and to the provisions of relevant collective licensing agreements, no reproduction of any part may take place without the written permission of Cambridge University Press.

First published 2015
First paperback edition 2018

A catalogue record for this publication is available from the British Library

Library of Congress Cataloging in Publication data
Externalism, self-knowledge, and skepticism : new essays / edited by Sanford C. Goldberg, Northwestern University.
　pages　cm
Includes bibliographical references and index.
ISBN 978-1-107-06350-1
1. Reference (Philosophy)　2. Externalism (Philosophy of mind)
3. Self-knowledge, Theory of.　I. Goldberg, Sanford, 1967 – editor.
B105.R25E98　2015
121´.68–dc23
　　　　　　　　　　　　　　　　　　　　2015014008

ISBN　978-1-107-06350-1　Hardback
ISBN　978-1-107-63673-6　Paperback

Cambridge University Press has no responsibility for the persistence or accuracy of URLs for external or third-party internet websites referred to in this publication, and does not guarantee that any content on such websites is, or will remain, accurate or appropriate.

This book is dedicated, with deep affection, to the memory of Tony Brueckner – friend, colleague, teacher, and all-around *mensch*, who taught so many of us about these topics and so much more.

Contents

List of contributors	ix
Acknowledgements	xi
Introduction SANFORD C. GOLDBERG	1
Part 1 Foundations of Self-Knowledge	17
1 Luminosity and the KK thesis ROBERT STALNAKER	19
2 Some questions about Burge's "self-verifying judgments" TONY BRUECKNER	41
3 Self-knowledge: the reality of privileged access CRISPIN WRIGHT	49
4 Contrastive self-knowledge and the McKinsey paradox SARAH SAWYER	75
Part 2 Content Transparency	95
5 Further thoughts on the transparency of mental content PAUL BOGHOSSIAN	97
6 Counting concepts: response to Paul Boghossian MARK SAINSBURY AND MICHAEL TYE	113
7 Internalism, externalism, and accessibilism BRIE GERTLER	119
8 The insignificance of transparency ÅSA WIKFORSS	142

9	On knowing what thoughts one's utterances express GARY EBBS	165
10	Anti-individualism, comprehension, and self-knowledge SANFORD C. GOLDBERG	184

Part 3 Metasemantics and the Nature of Mental Content 195

11	Externalism, self-knowledge, and memory JORDI FERNANDEZ	197
12	Externalism, metainternalism, and self-knowledge JUSSI HAUKIOJA	214
13	Externalism, metasemantic contextualism, and self-knowledge HENRY JACKMAN	228
	Bibliography	248
	Index	260

Contributors

PAUL BOGHOSSIAN is Silver Professor of Philosophy at New York University. He is the author of *Content and Justification: Philosophical Papers* (2008) and *Fear of Knowledge: Against Relativism and Constructivism* (2006).

TONY BRUECKNER passed away in 2014. He was Professor of Philosophy at the University of California-Santa Barbara, and was the author of *Essays on Skepticism* (2012) and co-author of *Debating Self-Knowledge* (with Gary Ebbs, Cambridge, 2012).

GARY EBBS is Professor and Chair of Philosophy at Indiana University. He is the co-author of *Debating Self-Knowledge* (with Tony Brueckner, Cambridge, 2012), and is the author of *Truth and Words* (2009) and *Rule-Following and Realism* (1997).

JORDI FERNANDEZ is Lecturer in Philosophy at the University of Adelaide. He is the author of *Transparent Minds: A Study of Self-Knowledge* (2012) and is co-editor of *Delusion and Self-Deception: Affective Influences on Belief-Formation* (with Tim Bayne, 2009).

BRIE GERTLER is Commonwealth Professor of Philosophy at the University of Virginia. She is the author of *Self-Knowledge* (2011), the editor of *Privileged Access: Philosophical Accounts of Self-Knowledge* (2003), and co-editor of *Arguing about the Mind* (with Lawrence Shapiro, 2007).

SANFORD C. GOLDBERG is Professor and Chair of Philosophy at Northwestern University. He is the author of *Anti-Individualism: Mind and Language, Knowledge and Justification* (Cambridge, 2007), *Relying on Others: An Essay in Epistemology* (2010), and *Assertion: On the Philosophical Significance of Assertoric Speech* (2015).

JUSSI HAUKIOJA is Professor of Philosophy at Norwegian University of Science and Technology. He is the editor of *Advances in Experimental Philosophy of Language* (2015) and has published many articles in the philosophy of mind and the philosophy of language.

HENRY JACKMAN is Associate Professor of Philosophy at York University. He is the author of many articles in the philosophy of mind, the philosophy of language, epistemology, and pragmatism.

MARK SAINSBURY is Professor of Philosophy at the University of Texas at Austin. He is the author of many books, most recently *Seven Puzzles of Thought and How to Solve Them: An Originalist Theory of Concepts* (with Michael Tye, 2012), *Fiction and Fictionalism* (2009), and *Reference Without Referents* (2005).

SARAH SAWYER is Senior Lecturer in Philosophy at the University of Sussex. She is the author of many articles in the philosophy of mind, the philosophy of language, metaphysics, and epistemology.

ROBERT STALNAKER is Professor of Philosophy at Massachusetts Institute of Technology. He is the author of many books, including *Our Knowledge of the Internal World* (2008), *Ways a World Might Be: Metaphysical and Anti-Metaphysical Essays* (2003), and *Context and Content: Essays on Intentionality in Speech and Thought* (1999).

MICHAEL TYE is Professor of Philosophy at the University of Texas at Austin. He is the author of *Seven Puzzles of Thought and How to Solve Them: An Originalist Theory of Concepts* (with Mark Sainsbury, 2012), *Consciousness and Persons: Unity and Identity* (2003), and *Color, Consciousness, and Content* (2000).

ÅSA WIKFORSS is Professor of Philosophy at the University of Stockholm. She is the author of many articles in the philosophy of mind, the philosophy of language, and epistemology.

CRISPIN WRIGHT is Professor of Philosophy at New York University and Professor of Philosophical Research, University of Stirling. He is the author of many books, including *Saving the Differences* (2003), *Rails to Infinity* (2001), and *The Reason's Proper Study* (with Bob Hale, 2001).

Acknowledgements

I have thought about these topics with a great number of people over many years. My own thinking has been helped enormously by them. They include Kent Bach, Dorit Bar-On, Paul Boghossian, Larry Bonjour, Jessica Brown, Tony Brueckner, Tyler Burge, Earl Conee, Fabrizio Cariani, Dave Chalmers, Gary Ebbs, Ray Elugardo, Kati Farkas, Rich Feldman, Carrie Figdor, Bryan Frances, Richard Fumerton, Mikkel Gerken, Brie Gertler, John Gibbons, Michael Glanzberg, Katrin Glüer, Peter Graham, Thomas Grundmann, John Hawthorne, Henry Jackman, Jesper Kallestrup, Igal Kvart, Jennifer Lackey, Peter Ludlow, Matt McGrath, Sidney Morgenbesser, Peter Pagin, Nikolaj Pederson, Ted Poston, Duncan Pritchard, Hilary Putnam, Baron Reed, Sarah Sawyer, Laura Schroeter, Barry Smith, David Sosa, Ernie Sosa, Rob Stainton, Tim Sundell, Åsa Wikforss, Timothy Williamson, and Crispin Wright.

I would like to thank my home university, Northwestern, as well as the University of Edinburgh, where I was a Professorial Fellow from 2013 to 2015, for their generous support over the duration of this project.

Introduction

Sanford C. Goldberg

1

In the nineteen sixties and seventies a new view began to emerge, first in the philosophy of language, then subsequently in the philosophy of mind, having to do originally with the theory of reference. Prior to this time, and in accordance with a particular (not uncontested) reading of Frege, it had been common to assume that who or what one was referring to, when one used a linguistic expression to refer to someone or something, was determined by *the satisfaction of certain criteria*. The criteria in question were assumed to derive either from the meanings of one's expression, or from the cognitive significance that speakers attached to that expression, or perhaps from the referential intentions speakers have in mind as they purported to refer.[1]

But in the sixties and seventies various authors began to question this *satisfaction-theoretic conception of reference determination*.

There were two main sources of dissatisfaction. One is a dissatisfaction with the implications of the satisfaction-theoretic conception for modal logic. As both Ruth Barcan Marcus and Saul Kripke were to recognize, the view that reference proceeds by satisfaction appears to have unacceptable implications for the semantics of sentences involving proper names (and other referring expressions). The other source of dissatisfaction has to do with the overly intellectualist (and individualistic) assumptions of the satisfaction-theoretic conception. If that conception were correct, using an expression to refer would require a

---

[1] Admittedly, this is not an entirely happy way to put the point, for two reasons. First, I am ignoring the distinction between speaker reference and semantic reference. Second, I am assuming something that many theorists will resist, namely, that it makes sense to speak of reference in connection with e.g. predicates. Still, in the interest of brevity I persist in this highly informal way of speaking, trusting that the more technical uses of 'refers' as well as the various distinctions that can be drawn will be irrelevant to the contrasts I am hoping to bring out, and that in any case the technicalities will be well known to the readers who are most involved in these debates.

speaker to have identifying knowledge of the referent, and to be disposed to express this knowledge by using the referring expression itself. Many theorists argued that these conditions are not jointly satisfied in some cases; illustrations included cases in which the expressions themselves were common names with standard references (Kripke 1972, Evans 1973), natural kind terms (Putnam 1975), definite descriptions used in a referential way (Donnellan 1966), or demonstratives (Kaplan 1975, 1979; Evans 1975, 1979).

Thus began the so-called "externalist" revolution in the philosophy of language. In place of the satisfaction-theoretic conception of reference determination, various authors proposed "causal" or "historical" theories of reference, on which reference determination proceeds by way of the causal or historical antecedents of the use of a given expression. (Early versions were proposed by Chastain (1975) and Stampe (1977), though Barcan Marcus (1961, 1971, 1972), Putnam (1975), Kripke (1972, 1977), Donnellan (1966, 1968, 1979), Evans (1973, 1975, 1979), and others published influential relevant early work on this as well.) What these views have in common is the idea that in specifying who or what the expression refers to – alternatively, in specifying who or what the speaker refers to when she uses that expression on an occasion – the theorist must ineliminably appeal to items or properties in the speaker's "external" environment. Where the satisfaction-theoretic account had it that the reference is determined by way of the satisfaction of criteria, the "externalist" account has it that the reference is determined in some more or less complicated way by appeal to the environmental object or property that plays the relevant role in the history of the use of that expression. In some cases, the relevant role is the history of the use of that expression in the linguistic community itself: a name, for example, might be thought to refer in virtue of its being part of a name-using practice that can be traced back to an original baptismal act, where the person or thing named in the original act is the referent of the name as it is used by anyone participating in this practice; or a predicate might be thought to refer in virtue of its being part of a sophisticated practice of the "division of linguistic labor" on which ordinary speakers defer to experts, where the experts themselves employ the predicate in scientific theorizing (in which case the reference might be the most salient natural property responsible for their use of the predicate). In other cases, the relevant role is simply the object or property that elicited this referring use by the speaker on this occasion: a demonstrative such as 'this' or 'that' will refer to whatever object or property the speaker was attending to as her target (whatever properties she happened to think that object satisfied). These views require further refinement, of course; but it has

Introduction 3

struck many that this is the sort of project one ought to embrace in the theory of reference.

Not long after "externalist" views about linguistic reference began to emerge, a number of authors extended the "externalist" analysis from language and linguistic (or speech act) reference to thought. In retrospect, the extension from language to thought is natural. Many mental states, such as thoughts, have representational content. It is natural to think of the content of a mental representation as how the mind, when in that state, represents the world to be. It is also natural to think that how the mind represents the world to be depends on at least two things:[2] *who* or *what* is being thought about, and what is being attributed to who or what is being thought about. An externalist account of both dimensions is natural. Consider for example perceptual thought. In perceptual thought, who or what is being thought about will be determined in part by one's causal-perceptual relations to one's environment; and (there will be cases in which) what properties one ascribes to that item in thought is determined in part by the "external" properties with which one oneself has been in causal-perceptual contact in the past. Nor is the externalist analysis limited to perceptual thought. For insofar as one expresses one's thoughts in language, it would seem that an "externalist" account of the content of one's thought is appropriate whenever an "externalist" account of the reference of one's linguistic items is appropriate. If so, externalist analyses are relevant far beyond the case of perceptual thought. Views of these kinds, which we might label "attitude externalism," were developed by Burge (1979), McGinn (1982), and McDowell (1986).

Even as attitude externalism was being developed, various authors had a suspicion that the epistemic implications of this doctrine might be far-reaching. Here I highlight two potential problems, both of which purport to bring out these implications in connection with a subject's self-knowledge of her thoughts. Following the taxonomy first introduced by Martin Davies (2000) and subsequently developed by Jessica Brown (2004a), I will call these problems the "achievement problem" and the "consequence problem." Both assume that a thinker's judgments regarding her own occurrent thoughts enjoy a special ('first-personal') authority: one can know from the armchair what one is thinking merely by reflecting on one's thoughts. If this is so, then the assumption of attitude externalism appears to give rise to two problems,

---

[2] "At least": there may be more that goes into this. Perhaps there is the "how": *how* what is being thought about is being thought about. What I say above is consistent with the relevance of the "how."

both of which are nicely summarized by Sarah Sawyer in her contribution to this volume:

> According to the achievement problem, if [attitude externalism] were true, then we could not achieve the kind of privileged access to the contents of our psychological states that we think we have. According to the consequence problem, the hypothesis that we do have privileged access to the contents of our [externalistically] individuated psychological states apparently has the prima facie absurd consequence that we can have broadly a priori knowledge of the environmental conditions which serve in part to individuate those states. (*Chapter 4, this volume*)

A good deal of the early work developing attitude externalism attempted to respond to these worries.

Burge's influential 1988 aimed to show that, at least when it came to a certain range of thoughts, the achievement problem was not a problem at all, owing to the self-verifying nature of a class of judgments he called "*cogito*-like" judgments. These were self-ascriptions of the form '(With the very thought) I am thinking that p' or '(In this very judgment) I hereby judge that p'. Burge noted that these judgments will invariably be true simply in virtue of being made; and he noted that the assumption of attitude externalism does not jeopardize them, for the simple reason that the very content being self-ascribed is a constituent in the thought or judgment itself, so whatever conditions individuate the first-order thought or judgment – the thought or judgment *that p* – will also individuate the higher-order (self-ascriptive) thought or judgment – the thought or judgment that *I myself am thinking/judging that p*. The result is an account of a class of judgments that manifested what Burge called our "basic self-knowledge." While I think it is fair to say that most people in the debate thought that Burge's account of basic self-knowledge was sound, not everyone agrees. Several chapters in this volume address the soundness, scope, and details of this account. (See for example those by Brueckner, Fernandez, and Haukioja.)

Two claims underlie Burge's account of basic self-knowledge. These claims (which Burge defended at some length) pertain to the nature of our knowledge of our thoughts. First, he claimed that to know one's thought, when one is thinking that p, is to know that one is thinking that p. Second, he claimed that one can know that one is thinking that p, even though one can't distinguish the thought that p from other thoughts that one would have had, if one had grown up in some counterfactual situation. This combination of claims has been challenged, in ways that go to the heart of our conception of self-knowledge. To begin, several authors have questioned the significance of the sort of knowledge one has when one (merely) knows that one is thinking that p. Following the influential work of Paul Boghossian, these authors have begun to think that we should expect more from an account of self-knowledge of one's thought. Such authors have argued that we should expect a theory of self-knowledge of thoughts to vindicate *the transparency of thought content*: the idea that, for every thought a thinker can think, she can tell from the armchair when she is thinking a thought with that content, and so can discriminate that thought from all other thoughts with distinct contents. Boghossian (1992a, 1994, 2011) had argued that any theory that violates transparency will represent subjects as not always in a position to tell from the armchair whether their reasoning is valid, and so will jeopardize the "*a priori* of logical ability" (in Boghossian's words). Others, following Boghossian, had argued that the violation of transparency will give rise to an inability to capture the agent's point of view (see Wikforss 2006, 2008a; but see Goldberg 2002 for a contrary view). Since it is widely acknowledged that attitude externalism is incompatible with this principle of transparency, Boghossian draws the lesson that such theories are not acceptable; and his paper has generated a lively debate regarding the status of the demand for transparency. Many of the chapters in this volume address this question. (See for example the chapters by Boghossian, Sainsbury and Tye, Wikforss, Gertler, Jackman, Ebbs, and Goldberg.)

It is also worth remarking that, even if it is sound, Burge's account of basic self-knowledge only covers a restricted domain of the phenomenon of self-knowledge. (Burge himself was under no illusions on this score.) We might want to know how to extend an account of "externalist" self-knowledge beyond the knowledge manifested in the class of cogito-like judgments. Burge himself (1996) sought to do so; and several of the chapters in this volume also seek to ask about the nature of first-person authority more generally. (See for example those by Ebbs, Wright, Stalnaker, and Jackman.)

Turning next to the consequence problem, this problem was first developed by Michael McKinsey in his influential 1994. (For this reason the problem is sometimes labeled "McKinsey's paradox," and the recipe for generating the so-called paradox is sometimes called "McKinsey's recipe.") When it is presented as a 'paradox', the problem consists in the fact that three propositions, all of which are thought (at least by proponents of attitude externalism) to be plausible, appear jointly inconsistent. The first is the principle of first-person authority itself, according to which, for all thoughts that p, whenever S thinks that p, S knows from the armchair that she thinks that p. The second is the doctrine of attitude externalism itself: for some attitudes, being in that attitude (bearing an attitude to that particular content) requires the existence of some "external" condition. The third is an anti-skeptical thesis, to the effect that one can't tell from the armchair that external-world skepticism is false. These three propositions are thought to be jointly inconsistent on the assumption that, as a philosophical thesis, attitude externalism itself can be known from the armchair (if it can be known at all). Thus it would appear that a subject who thinks that water is wet is in a position to deduce from the armchair that external-world skepticism is false: she can combine her knowledge of her thought, together with her knowledge of the truth of attitude externalism, to derive the existence of some "external" condition – of which the falsity of external-world skepticism is a trivial implication.

Various replies to this worry have been presented in the literature. Of these, two types are prominent. One allows that the reasoning behind the paradox is both valid and involves premises knowable from the armchair, but it denies that epistemic warrant can be "transmitted" across this sort of inference (Wright 1986, 2000, 2003; Davies 2000, 2003a, 2004; and Sawyer 2001, 2006; see also Brown 2004a for a critical discussion). The other denies that the premises are all knowable from the armchair. Most replies of this type argue that one cannot tell from the armchair, regarding one's thought, that it is a thought whose availability requires the existence of some "external" condition (see McLaughlin and Tye 1998a, 1998b; Goldberg 2003a, 2003b, 2003c, 2007). In this volume, several authors suggest other replies to the McKinsey paradox (see the chapters by Sawyer and Haukioja).

2

The foregoing characterization of the debate enables us to situate many of the chapters in this volume in the discussion of externalism's epistemic implications. But what motivated this volume was not merely the hope that there are new things to say about these topics. I hope that these contributions make interesting and novel contributions to those older discussions. But this hope is not groundless; there are reasons to think that there should be new things to say about these older debates. In particular, in the last two decades several developments in the philosophy of mind, the philosophy of language, and epistemology make it worthwhile to reconsider semantic externalism's implications for self-knowledge and skepticism. In the philosophy of mind and language, these developments include various versions of 2D semantics, the emerging popularity of so-called transparency views of self-knowledge (owed originally to Gareth Evans, and defended more recently by Alex Byrne

(2003, 2010, 2011)), the development of a new theory of concepts (the originalist account in Sainsbury and Tye 2014), and recent developments in the theory of understanding. In epistemology, these include various doctrines pertaining to the semantics of 'knows' (such as contextualism, contrastivism, and pragmatic encroachment), a renewed focus on anti-luminosity arguments (deriving from the work of Williamson (2000)), and developments in the epistemology of testimony as well as in the epistemology of understanding. These contributions bring these novel developments to bear on the older debates.

In this respect, this volume aims to contribute to the literature in two ways. First, it aims to update the literature pertaining to the (semantic and epistemic) implications of "externalist" views of mind and language. Second, it aims to bring these debates regarding the implications of the "externalist" views in mind and language to other issues in contemporary philosophy of mind and language. I will now describe the individual contributions themselves.

3

I have grouped the chapters in this volume into three main groups corresponding to their main thematic orientation. In the first part are those focusing on the mechanisms of self-knowledge and the semantics of ascriptions of self-knowledge. In the second are those focusing on issues of transparency and the nature of one's grasp of one's own concepts. In the third part are those focusing on metasemantics and the nature of content itself.

3.1

The volume begins with the four chapters focusing on the mechanisms of self-knowledge and/or the semantics of ascriptions of such knowledge.

In "Luminosity and the KK Thesis," Bob Stalnaker explores the scope of Williamson's anti-luminosity argument. After arguing that phenomenal properties are not the best place to challenge Williamson's (2000) anti-luminosity argument, Stalnaker argues that purely epistemic or doxastic properties fare better. In this he follows Selim Berker, who had argued (in Berker 2008) that the anti-luminosity argument succeeds only regarding conditions that are constitutively independent of thought and judgment. In the light of this idea, Stalnaker considers a KK thesis, according to which knowing that p puts one in a position to know that one knows that p. Such a principle renders knowledge that p luminous in Williamson's sense, and so this

KK principle should be susceptible if Williamson's anti-luminosity argument is fully general. And yet, Stalnaker argues, Williamson's anti-luminosity argument does not undermine such a KK thesis – Williamson's own claim to the contrary notwithstanding. Whereas Berker's argument against the generality of the anti-luminosity argument lead him to reject that safety (as Williamson construes it) can be captured in terms of a margin-for-error principle, Stalnaker's argument calls into question both Williamson's margin-for-error principle as well as Williamson's safety condition on knowledge. Although Stalnaker himself does not put the point this way, the significance of his argument for those with an interest in externalism and self-knowledge is straightforward: Stalnaker's argument paves the way for externalists to continue to insist on a limited form of luminosity in the sort of *cogito*-like judgments Burge had highlighted in his account of basic self-knowledge. After all, according to Burge's account of basic self-knowledge, the conditions judged to obtain in *cogito*-like judgments are not constitutively independent of the judgments themselves.

In "Some Questions about Burge's 'Self-Verifying Judgments'," Tony Brueckner takes up Burge's account of basic self-knowledge and defends it against a recent objection presented by Finn Spicer. Spicer (2009) had sought to show that Burge's argument for the doctrine of basic self-knowledge, and by extension his case for the compatibility of attitude externalism and first-person authority, both fail for failing to square with a necessary condition on substitution within propositional attitude contexts. In response, Bruckner (2011) sought to show that Spicer's (2009) objection posed no threat to Burge's account. In his contribution to this volume, Brueckner seeks to further advance that debate, as well as our understanding of the *cogito*-like thoughts on which Burge's account had focused. Brueckner's aims are two: first, to show that Spicer's (2009) objection had rested on an unacceptably strong construal of sameness of truth conditions in propositional attitudes; and second, to explore several possible mechanisms by which the *cogito*-like thoughts Burge explored might be self-verifying.

In "Self-knowledge: the Reality of Privileged Access," Crispin Wright aims to address several criticisms (presented in Snowdon 2012) of his earlier account of first-person authority. Wright's view is that first-person judgments regarding's one's occurrent states of mind have three features that need to be accounted for: they are *immediate* (in the sense that they are not based on any evidence), *authoritative* (in the sense that they presumed to be epistemically secure, and enjoy this status so long as there are no reasons for doubt on this score), and *salient* (in the sense that they cover the whole range of the mind's occurrent states – no mental state "eludes awareness"). Wright agrees with Snowdon in two criticisms: first, that Wright's earlier taxonomy of the states regarding which we have authoritative self-knowledge – the phenomenal and the propositional – oversimplifies matters; and second, that his earlier claim to the effect that first-person judgments of the relevant sort are "groundless" was itself confusing (and in some respects confused). Even so, Wright argues that his earlier account of such self-knowledge, as largely an artifact of our language game, remains defensible. If he is right in this, he has paved the way for externalists in the philosophy of mind to endorse an "avowability" conception of self-knowledge that goes beyond what Burge had offered in accounting for what he had called basic self-knowledge. (Wright himself does not draw this conclusion, but it seems clear from what he does say that he would endorse it.)

In "Contrastive Self-Knowledge and the McKinsey Paradox," Sarah Sawyer argues that the contrastive account of knowledge provides the basis for a response to the McKinsey argument for incompatibilism, and makes clear how it is that we can have authoritative self-knowledge of our own thoughts. After developing a contrastive account of self-knowledge, she goes on to diagnose the failure of McKinsey's argument as a failure to appreciate the relevant contrasts. The basic point is that a subject who has the relevant sort of self-knowledge knows that (for example) she herself is thinking that water is wet as opposed to thinking that grass is green; but this is compatible with it's being false that she knows that she herself is thinking that water is wet as opposed to thinking that q (where 'that q' is the BIV-analogue proposition). Since the success of the McKinsey argument trades on the subject's having the latter sort of knowledge, the contrastive account of self-knowledge thus provides a way to endorse the compatibility of externalism and self-knowledge, without having to embrace the unacceptably strong anti-skeptical implications of the McKinsey argument.

3.2

The next part of the book groups together the chapters that focus mainly on the topic of transparency and/or the nature of a thinker's grasp of her own concepts and thoughts.

In his "Further Thoughts on the Transparency of Mental Content," Paul Boghossian returns to the doctrine of transparency, according to which "When our faculty of introspection is working normally, we can know a priori via introspection with respect to any two present, occurrent thoughts whether they exercise the same or different concepts" (p. 98). It has long been acknowledged that externalism about mental content is incompatible with transparency in this sense. Following Tyler Burge, many authors (including Falvey and Owens (1994), Schroeter (2007, 2013), and Goldberg (1999)) have embraced this implication and have tried to argue on independent grounds that the doctrine of transparency is false. In their recent book *Seven Puzzles of Thought* (2014), Sainsbury and Tye defend a view of concept individuation which similarly has the implication that transparency is false, and they offer their defense of this implication. Boghossian examines their defense and finds it wanting. His main concern, anticipated in several of his earlier seminal papers on this topic (1992a, 1994, 2011), is that without transparency we appear to have no way to construe what it is for a thinker to be rational in the inferences she draws. Sainsbury and Tye (2014) had proposed that we do so by appeal to the reasonableness of higher-order belief and judgment (regarding e.g. the validity of one's own inferences). Boghossian points out, first, that such a view is only applicable, if at all, to creatures who can have higher-order beliefs, and second, that issues of the reasonableness of second-order beliefs appear to raise precisely the same questions all over again. While Sainsbury and Tye had anticipated this worry and tried to spell out how we might assess this reasonableness in terms of how inferences "strike" subjects, where this need not involve explicit belief or judgment at all, Boghossian concludes that such a view needs to be fleshed out before it can be assessed. The conclusion is that work remains for any externalist who hopes to live with the rejection of transparency.

In their reply to Boghossian's contribution, "Counting Concepts: Response to Paul Boghossian," Mark Sainsbury and Michael Tye respond to Boghossian's concerns. They acknowledge that their (2014) "originalist" theory of concepts implies that there can be cases in which thinkers "behave as if they were mistaken about how many concepts their thoughts involve; or about whether a pair of thoughts is contradictory; or about whether an argument fails to be valid through equivocation." But they respond that originalism has the resources to construe such thinkers as rational nevertheless. For, they contend, it "can be *rational* to so behave." Their explanation is by way of the principle (R), according to which "Thinkers who believe contradictions, or who incorrectly assess the validity-status of simple arguments, or who make fallacious inferences from simple arguments, are irrational, unless they have an excuse." And Sainsbury and Tye go on to say that the sorts of cases to which Boghossian appeals are cases in which the subject does have an excuse. In the Paderewski case, given the subject's background (justified) beliefs, the subject is rational in believing that there are two Paderewskis (even though in fact there is only one). In the 'water' case, the subject is rational in *not* having the belief that his word form 'water' picks out two distinct kinds of liquid (even though it does in fact pick out two distinct kinds). In both cases, the rationality of the subject's perspective – whether in the presence of a rational though false belief, or the rational absence of a true belief – both explains, and so excuses, the very actions that lead to the errors of reasoning to which Boghossian had drawn our attention.

In "Internalism, Externalism, and Accessibilism," Brie Gertler advances the idea that the best case from self-knowledge against externalism is not the case involving the incompatibility of externalism with basic self-knowledge, but rather the case involving the incompatibility of externalism with what she calls explicational self-knowledge of one's thoughts. While Burge and other externalists have argued that in fact we have no such self-knowledge, Gertler argues that such self-knowledge appears to be a precondition on our best account of rationality – that embodied by Frege's differential dubitability test. In the course of marking out her position, she argues that Burge's attempt to square externalism with a modified version of the differential dubitability test fails. She also points out that, contrary to what many internalists appear to think, internalism about attitude individuation itself need not be committed to the idea that a subject can always correctly and fully explicate all of her concepts through reflection alone.

In "The Insignificance of Transparency," Åsa Wikforss argues that the issue of transparency is irrelevant to the assessment of externalism's implications for self-knowledge. In making this point, she aims to criticize *any* argument that hangs much on the would-be implications of externalism for transparency – whether the argument is critical, or in support, of externalism itself. To this end, Wikforss distinguishes two ways of spelling out the notion of transparency: according to the metalinguistic notion, transparency amounts to higher-order knowledge regarding the sameness and difference of one's mental states and their contents; according to the functional notion, transparency amounts (roughly) to the notion that one who is rational and in good cognitive health invariably treats one's mental states as same and different (in reasoning with them and acting on them) when in fact they are as one treats them to be. Wikforss argues that either way transparency is too higher-order a phenomenon to capture what is wrong with externalism. The real problem facing externalism, rather, is its implication that a subject's believing the contents she does might nevertheless fail to make sense of why she reasons and acts as she does.

In "On Knowing What Thoughts One's Utterances Express," Gary Ebbs considers the self-knowledge that is manifested in the *cogito*-like judgments Burge had highlighted. But Ebbs puts a decidedly metalinguistic construal on the topic of his interest: he is interested in the conditions on *knowing what thought one's own utterance expresses*. In a series of previous papers, Ebbs has defended the view that such self-knowledge – which he calls 'minimal self-knowledge' – is had whenever one is "able to use one's words competently in discourse – to raise and address questions, evaluate one's own and others' claims, answer challenges to one's claims, express one's conjectures, and so on" (Chapter 9, p. 165). Such self-knowledge is minimal, according to Ebbs's account, as it can be had even when one's metalinguistic self-knowledge of the thought one expressed does not go beyond the purely disquotational knowledge expressed in judgments like this:

(D) The thought I express with 'Water is wet' is the thought that water is wet.

In his contribution to this volume, Ebbs addresses two questions that arise regarding his account of minimal self-knowledge. First, assuming that the minimal self-knowledge Ebbs discusses is compatible with having no substantial (nondisquotational) self-knowledge of one's thought, how does one acquire such substantial self-knowledge in the first place? Second, how does this account square with the sorts of cases Gareth Evans described, in which one expresses thoughts without having the sort of understanding that is required for Ebbs-style minimal self-knowledge? Ebbs's reply is to formulate more carefully what is involved in minimal self-knowledge, and then to go on to argue that, so understood, there is no way to have this sort of self-knowledge without at the same time having the sort of understanding that is required for it.

In "Anti-individualism, Comprehension, and Self-Knowledge," I argue for two claims. The first is a claim about comprehending the contents of *others' speech*: a doctrine pertaining to the conditions on testimonial knowledge, together with plausible assumptions about the prevalence and ease of transmission of such knowledge, yields a 'minimalist' account of what is involved in understanding others' speech. The second is a claim about comprehending the contents of *one's own thoughts*: I argue that this first result, together with the claim that much of what we think is shaped by our accepting the say-so of our colinguals, supports a 'minimalist' account of what is involved in grasping one's own concepts and thoughts. In this way, I purport to link the epistemology of linguistic comprehension with the epistemology of self-knowledge. In so doing, I develop a suggestion that Tyler Burge made some time ago, to the effect that "comprehending standing, conceptual aspects of one's own thought and idiolect is itself, as a matter of psychological and sociological fact, normally dependent on having

Introduction

comprehended thoughts (one's own) that were shaped and expressed through the words of others" (Burge 1999, p. 243).

3.3

I move now to the final part of the book and to the chapters that raise issues in metasemantics about the nature of mental content itself. In "Externalism, Self-Knowledge, and Memory," Jordi Fernandez draws on the tools of 2D semantics to reconsider Boghossian's 'Memory Argument' for the incompatibility of externalism and self-knowledge. Fernandez argues that Boghossian's argument trades on an ambiguity between two notions of mental content. He begins by distinguishing between the "objective" content of a belief – roughly, the truth conditions it has in the actual world, applied to any possible world – and the "subjective" content of a belief – roughly, the truth conditions that a belief expressed by the same form of words would have had in a given world, had it been believed there. He then diagnoses Boghossian's argument as vacillating on the notion of content in play in the memory argument: while memory preserves the objective content of a belief (and need not preserve the subjective content), the plausibility of the premises of the Memory Argument itself, according to Fernandez, trade on reading them as pertaining to the subjective content of belief.

In "Externalism, Metainternalism, and Self-Knowledge," Jussi Haukioja argues that we should distinguish between two questions – What factors individuate content? and What makes it the case that such factors individuate content? – and that once we do so we will have paved the way to responding to McKinsey's argument for incompatibilism. The two questions themselves correspond roughly to a distinction (first developed in Cohnitz and Haukioja 2013) between first-order and second-order views on the internalism–externalism dispute. First-order externalism is the view that (there are cases in which) factors external to the thinker's mind individuate the contents of her attitudes. Haukioja argues that while standard arguments give us good reason to endorse such a view, they do not give us reasons to endorse *second-order externalism*, according to which external factors partly determine what *makes it the case that* first-order externalism is true (i.e., that external factors sometimes individuate the contents of her attitudes). And once we reject second-order externalism in favor of second-order internalism, Haukioja contends, we will be in a position to see McKinsey's argument for incompatibilism as flawed. Where McKinsey had argued that if externalism is true then a thinker who thinks a water thought can know through introspection some empirical proposition E (e.g. that water exists, or that she is a member of some linguistic community), if the sort of externalism that is in view is first-order externalism (combined with second-order internalism), the best such a thinker can know through introspection is that *if* her linguistic intentions were satisfied and her water thought picks out anything, *then* E.

In "Externalism, Metasemantic Contextualism, and Self-Knowledge," Henry Jackman argues that the broadly Davidsonian metasemantic view he favors underwrites an account of self-knowledge that is compatible not only with first-person authority, but also with the doctrine of transparency. According to that metasemantic view, what a speaker means by her words is fixed by the best methodology of interpretation, where this will involve a function that maximizes the true beliefs that would be ascribed to the interpretee, albeit in a way that reflects the relative importance she herself assigns to matters. (The idea is that those beliefs that have a higher relative importance to the subject have priority, in the sense that in cases of trade-off, interpretations which preserve *their* truth at the expense of the truth of other, less important beliefs are to be preferred.) The result is that insofar as either the subject's background beliefs or her relative importance assignments change over time, so too will the proper interpretation of her words. Such an account, Jackman argues, will best capture the agent's point of view as it evolves over time. What is more, the resulting semantic theory (he goes on to argue) will be one on which the ascription of meaning to an utterance will be a context-sensitive matter – a sort of 'semantic contextualism', albeit one that is importantly different from standard versions of contextualism in the philosophy of language. Jackman concludes by noting that, while his account (following Davidson's) embraces semantic holism, the account itself does not suffer from the sort of difficulties from which holist accounts generally are thought to suffer, and so it is significantly more plausible than critics of holism might think at first glance.

4

Although I have organized the chapters so as to highlight several of the themes that are most salient in them, it is perhaps not remiss to conclude here by quickly highlighting the main themes and the chapters that address them, as not all of this information can be captured in the volume's organization. Perhaps the most salient theme is the relevance (or not) of the issue of transparency to capturing the agent's point of view; in addition to the chapters in Part 2, on transparency, this theme is also addressed in Chapter 13. Related to this is the sort of expectation we ought to have of a theory of self-knowledge of one's thoughts. Some

(Sainsbury and Tye in Chapter 6, Ebbs in Chapter 9, and Goldberg in Chapter 10) defend rather austere or 'minimalist' views, while others (Boghossian in Chapter 5, Gertler in Chapter 7, Wikforss in Chapter 8, and Jackman in Chapter 13) hold out for more. Another theme concerns the role of content in communication, and the relevance of this role to questions of the compatibility of externalism and authoritative self-knowledge; this theme plays out in the chapters by Ebbs, Goldberg, and Haukioja. Yet another theme concerns the semantics of knowledge ascriptions and their relevance to issues of self-knowledge; this theme is played out, in different ways, in the chapters by Jackman, Stalnaker, and Sawyer. One final theme concerns the mechanisms of self-knowledge: how it is that we know our own thoughts. In addition to the chapters in Part 1, this theme is also developed in Chapter 9 by Ebbs.

Part 1

Foundations of Self-Knowledge

1 Luminosity and the KK thesis

Robert Stalnaker

Introduction

"The mind," according to a Cartesian picture, "is transparent to itself. It is of the essence of mental entities, of whatever kind, to be conscious, where a mental entity's being conscious involves its revealing its existence and nature to its possessor in an immediate way. This conception involves a strong form of the doctrine that mental entities are 'self-intimating', and usually goes with a strong form of the view that judgments about our own mental states are incorrigible or infallible, expressing a super-certain kind of knowledge which is suited for being an epistemological foundation for the rest of what we know."[1] This is Sydney Shoemaker's characterization of a picture that he, along with most epistemologists and philosophers of mind of the twentieth century, rejected. Timothy Williamson, writing at the end of the twentieth century, summed up the general idea of the Cartesian picture this way: "There is a constant temptation in philosophy to postulate a realm of phenomena in which nothing is hidden from us," "a cognitive home in which everything lies open to our view."[2] These impressionistic descriptions obviously need to be pinned down to a specific thesis if one is to give an argument against the Cartesian picture of the mind and of our knowledge of its contents, and different anti-Cartesian philosophers have done this in different ways. At least some critics of the picture, including Shoemaker, want to allow for distinctive epistemic relations of some kind that a subject bears to his or her mind – to one's own experiences and thoughts – even while rejecting the kind of transparency that Shoemaker's and Williamson's Cartesian assumes. The challenge is to spell out, explain, and defend the distinctive kind of epistemic relations.

---

[1] Shoemaker 1994, p. 271. [2] Williamson 2000, p. 93.

Shoemaker, in the lectures from which this characterization of the Cartesian picture is taken, focuses on the notion of introspection, and his main target was not the Cartesian picture, but what he called "the perceptual model" of introspection, a view that holds that "the existence of mental entities and mental facts is, logically speaking, as independent of our knowing about them introspectively as the existence of physical entities and physical facts is of our knowing about them perceptually." His aim was to find a middle ground between the Cartesian view and this perceptual model, a view according to which there are constitutive conceptual connections between our experience and thought and our introspective knowledge of it. He argues, for example, that a certain kind of "self-blindness," a condition in which a rational, reflective, and conceptually competent agent is ignorant of his or her beliefs, is incoherent.

While there is a sense in which Shoemaker's own view falls between the Cartesian picture and the perceptual model, there is also a way to understand the Cartesian view so that it is a version of the perceptual model. One can interpret the Cartesian as holding that it is right to say that we perceive the contents of our minds, which are conceptually independent of our perceiving them, but we do so with a special perceptual capacity that is direct and infallible. Whether or not this is the right way to think of the Cartesian view, it does seem that some versions of this picture at least exploit the metaphors of perception to describe the way we know what we feel and think. For example, in saying that we are directly *acquainted* with the contents of our mind, the Cartesian is co-opting what is, in its more ordinary use, a causal relation between distinct things. Williamson's choice of the term "luminous" for characterizing the kind of access to the mind that the Cartesian tempts us to postulate also suggests this way of thinking of the Cartesian picture: a luminous state (according to the metaphor) is one that emits a special light that renders it essentially perceptible. But Williamson does not rely on the metaphor; he defines luminosity in more sober terms: a state or condition is *luminous* if and only if a person who is in that state or condition is thereby in a position to know that he or she is in it. Williamson's rejection of the Cartesian picture is more uncompromising that Shoemaker's, whose rejection of the perceptual model allows for mental states that are luminous in this sense. But Williamson argues that there are no nontrivial states or conditions that are luminous.

Williamson's general picture of knowledge and the mind is thoroughly externalist. "Externalism" (like the contrasting "Cartesian picture") can be pinned down in various ways, but the general idea is that we should understand subjects – those who are able to experience, think, and know about the world – from the outside.³ We should formulate the philosophical questions about knowledge and intentionality as questions about the relations that hold between one kind of object in the world (those capable of experience and thought) and the environments they find themselves in. More specific externalist theses, such as reliabilist accounts of knowledge, and anti-individualist accounts of the intentional content of thought, are developed in the context of such a general picture. There are tensions between the externalist theses and the possibility of mental states that are luminous in Williamson's sense, but there are many attempts to resolve the tensions. Tyler Burge, for example, argues that his anti-individualism about mental content is compatible with the thesis (to put it roughly) that a thinker knows the content of his or her thought in virtue of thinking it.⁴ The general strategy of those who aim to reconcile an externalist, anti-Cartesian conception of knowledge and the mind with a limited kind of luminosity is to argue, as Shoemaker does, for constitutive conceptual connections between some mental states and our knowledge of them. Selim Berker follows this strategy in his critique of Williamson's anti-luminosity argument. His claim is that Williamson "presupposes that there does not exist a constitutive connection between the obtaining of a given fact and our *beliefs* about the obtaining of those facts," and that his anti-luminosity argument succeeds only with this presupposition.⁵ I agree with this general strategy, but one has to look at the details.

My plan in this chapter is first to sketch Williamson's master argument against the possibility of luminous states or conditions, looking first at a version of the argument aimed at the thesis that phenomenal states are luminous, and then at a version applied to knowledge itself: an argument against the thesis that *x knows that P* implies that *x knows that x knows that P* (or at least that knowing that P puts one in a position to know that one knows that P). While I have some sympathy with the argument as applied to phenomenal states, I will try to show that the refutation of the KK thesis does not work. I will argue this by giving a simplified and idealized model of knowledge – one that is thoroughly externalist – in which the KK thesis holds, and then considering where the anti-luminosity argument goes wrong for that idealized concept of knowledge. While the model I will

---

³ See chapter 1 of Stalnaker 2008 for my attempt to characterize the general externalist perspective. In chapter 6 of that book, I address the tension between an externalist account of mental content and the thesis that the content of a thinker's thoughts are, in a sense, transparent to the thinker. Though I don't put it this way, one can see the arguments of that chapter as an attempt to reconcile a certain kind of luminosity with an externalist and anti-Cartesian picture.
⁴ Burge 1988. ⁵ Berker 2008.

Safety and margins of error

Williamson's anti-luminosity arguments are given for particular examples of concepts that are the most favorable cases for luminosity, but the arguments all take the same generalizable form, and they are all based on a "margin of error" principle, which is in turn motivated by a safety principle for the concept of knowledge. The safety principle is that knowledge that φ implies, not only that φ is true, but that it is *safely* true. Safety, as Williamson explains it, is one of a family of concepts that include reliability, robustness, and stability. He illustrates the general notion with an example of a contrast between a ball balanced on the tip of a cone in a state of *unstable* equilibrium, and a ball sitting at the bottom of a hole in a state of *stable* equilibrium. In the former case, the ball falls out of equilibrium in "nearby" possible situations where, for example, the surrounding air currents are very slightly different, while in the latter case minor variations in the environment would have no such effect.[6] Safety for knowledge implies that the truth of the proposition known must be stable in this sense: true not only in the actual situation, but also in all "nearby" possible situations. But the unstable equilibrium example brings out the fact that the kind of "nearness" of possible situations that is relevant to a safety condition for knowledge is distinctive, and not exactly the same as the kind of "nearness" that is relevant to the equilibrium example. One observing the ball in unstable equilibrium can know that it is not falling since even if the ball is not safe from falling, the observer is safe from falsely believing that the ball is falling. This is because if it were to fall, the observer would see that it did, and so no longer believe that it is not falling. Williamson puts the safety condition this way: "In case α one is safe from error in believing that C obtains if and only if there is no case close to α in which one falsely believes that C obtains."[7]

The anti-luminosity arguments do not give any general characterization of the notion of nearness of possible situations that is relevant to safety for knowledge. Instead, they describe for the particular examples a sequence of possible situations each of which is assumed to be similar in the relevant respects to its neighbors. The specific "margin of error" premises of the anti-luminosity arguments are motivated by the idea of

---

[6] Williamson 2000, p. 123.   [7] Ibid., pp. 126–27.

Luminosity and the KK thesis

safety, but they are stated for the particular example for which the argument is given.

Phenomenal states

Williamson begins with the example of the condition that one *feels cold*. He imagines a person who feels freezing cold at dawn, and then slowly warms up until, at noon, he feels hot. It is supposed, plausibly, "that one's feelings of heat and cold change so slowly during this process that one is not aware of any change in them over one millisecond." He then considers a sequence of times, one millisecond apart, from dawn until noon. If t_i is one of the times, then α_i is the situation of the subject at t_i. The margin of error principle, for this example, is that for each time t_i,

(Ii) If in α_i one knows that one feels cold, then in α_{i+1} one feels cold.[8]

If we assume, for reductio, that 'feeling cold' is luminous – that one who feels cold is thereby in a position to know that he feels cold – and also assume that the person is throughout the time period actively considering whether he feels cold, we will have for each time t_i,

(IIi) If in α_i one feels cold, then in α_i one knows that one feels cold.

From all of the premises of these forms, one can derive that the subject still feels cold at noon, contrary to the stipulation that he then feels hot. To break the chain of inferences to this conclusion, we must assume that at least one of the premises (IIi), is false, which implies that 'feeling cold' is not a luminous condition.

More cautiously, we might say that one must reject either one of the premises (IIi) or one of the premises (Ii). If there is a tight enough conceptual connection between feeling cold and believing that one feels cold, then one might assume that the point at which one stops feeling cold is, more or less by definition, the same as the point at which one stops believing it. If this is true, then Williamson's safety condition might be satisfied, even though one of the margin-of-error premises of the argument is false. Let α_i be the last point in the sequence at which the subject feels cold, and also the last point in the sequence at which the subject believes that he feels cold. So at α_{i+1}, the subject neither feels cold nor believes that he does. If we assume that at α_i, he knows that he feels cold, then one of the margin-of-error premises is false, but there is no violation of the safety condition, since in the very similar situations in

---

[8] Ibid., p. 97.

which it is false that the subject feels cold, he no longer believes it. So the case is like the case where the ball in unstable equilibrium falls out of equilibrium in very similar situations, even though this does not prevent the observer from knowing that it is in equilibrium, since she would no longer believe it was in equilibrium in those nearby situations. (This is Berker's diagnosis.)

One might try to avoid this problem by reformulating the safety condition for knowledge in a way that avoids mentioning belief. Let us say that two types of states or conditions that a person could be in are *robustly indistinguishable* to the person if the following is true: were an experimenter to put the subject into one of the states, and then shift it to the other, and back, the subject, even when attending carefully, would be completely unable to tell when the shifts took place. The subject might be told, when in one of the states that it is state A, and when in the other that it is state B, and then do no better than chance at identifying one of the two states as A, or as B. Using a notion like this, one might characterize a safety condition like this:

> In case α one is safe from error in believing that C obtains if and only if there is no case β close to α, and robustly indistinguishable from it, such that C does not obtain in β.

Since, in defining the series of times in the anti-luminosity argument for feeling cold, Williamson specifies that the times, one millisecond apart, are indistinguishable in something like this sense, it seems that this version of a safety requirement would suffice to imply the margin of error premises.

We have bypassed the notion of belief in stating our safety condition, but it seems that we might also bypass belief in stating a thesis that is motivated by the plausible assumption that there is some kind of constitutive connection between being in a phenomenal state like feeling cold and being aware that one is. It seems reasonable to hold that if states A and B are robustly indistinguishable, then if the subject feels cold in state A, then he or she also feels cold in state B. But if one accepts this assumption, then the kind of sorites sequence that Williamson uses to argue against the luminosity of the state of feeling cold will pose a problem that is independent of any assumptions about knowledge, safety, or margins of error. Our assumption will license the following variations on the luminosity premises:

(I*i) If in $α_i$ one feels cold, then in $α_{i+1}$ one feels cold.

Given that the subject feels cold at dawn, and not at noon, this is enough for a contradiction.

This argument is a version of what Michael Dummett called "Wang's paradox."[9] In his discussion of this paradox, Dummett considered both phenomenal concepts and what he called "observational predicates" such as being red or green. If the relevant predicates apply to things in the world, as "red" and "green" do, then one may respond to the paradox by denying the indistinguishability assumption for such predicates. I think it is reasonable to hold that even if observation plays a role in fixing the reference of color terms, it is still possible for things to differ in color in cases where observers cannot tell them apart. But it is harder to make this move in cases where the predicate characterizes a phenomenal state, since it is at least arguable that distinct but subjectively indistinguishable states cannot be phenomenal states. Dummett took one upshot of the argument to be that "there are no phenomenal qualities, as these have been traditionally understood."[10]

Wang's paradox is of course a version of the sorites paradox, which is problem about vagueness. While Williamson agrees that states such as *feeling cold* are vague, he argues that his anti-luminosity arguments are not dependent on the vagueness of the relevant predicates, and not dependent on his own controversial epistemic account of vagueness. Specifically, he argues that the anti-luminosity argument will still work even for artificially sharpened versions of the predicates for such states. But it matters how one sharpens the predicates. Berker's argument is that there may be a constitutive conceptual connection between *feeling cold* and *believing that one feels cold*, and a connection of this kind seems to motivate the thesis that situations indistinguishable to the subject cannot differ with respect whether he feels cold. If there is a connection of this kind between these two vague notions, than one must be sure to sharpen them together in a way that preserve the connection. Williamson suggests that we might "sharpen 'feels cold' by using a physiological condition to resolve borderline cases."[11] But this would be to leave out a constitutive connection between *feeling cold* and any doxastic state, and I think one should agree, independently of the sorites-style anti-luminosity argument, that states explained this way are not luminous.

Here is one kind of story one might tell about the acquisition and character of phenomenal concepts for states such as *feeling cold*,[12] a story on which Williamson's way of sharpening the vague concept would be appropriate: first, one learns that under certain favorable conditions one is able to tell, by the way one feels, that one is in a cold environment.

---

[9] Dummett 1975. [10] Ibid., p. 232. [11] Williamson 2000, p. 103.
[12] Wilfred Sellars told a story like this in his 1956/1997.

('Cold' here is both vague and context-dependent, but it refers to an objective state of the environment.) One then hypothesizes that there is an internal state type that one is in when one is inclined to report, on the basis of how one feels, that it is cold in one's environment – a state that one calls '*feeling cold*'. This hypothesized state is what explains one's ability to tell, by the way one feels, something about the temperature of the environment. Sometimes one judges that one is in the hypothesized internal state even when one knows that it is not actually cold in the environment, and one also recognizes that one may fail to feel cold, even when it is in fact cold. Scientists might confirm the hypothesis by identifying a state of the nervous system that explains one's capacity to know, in the right conditions, about the temperature in the environment. It is this physiological state (according to this way of thinking about phenomenal states) that is the realization of the functional property of feeling cold.

On this kind of story, the inclination to judge that one's environment is in a certain state plays a reference-fixing role in determining the relevant internal state, but the state itself has no necessary connection, either with the actual state of the environment, or with the inclination to form a belief about it. The story suggests that the following might happen: one goes to the doctor with the complaint that one is always feeling cold, even when the weather is unusually warm. After a thorough neurological examination, the doctor reports that you do not in fact feel cold in these situations; you are suffering from a persistent illusion that you do. Or alternatively, you go to the doctor with a more mystifying complaint: you find that you can no longer tell how cold it is. You report that if you go out in your shirtsleeves on a frigid winter day, it feels just as warm as when you were inside before the fire. After a thorough neurological examination, the doctor reports that the good news is that you *do* in fact feel cold when you go out. The bad news is that you suffer from a condition that blocks your cognitive access to this feeling so that you can't tell that you have it.

Even granting that the doctor has got the physiology right, you might be inclined to resist her description of your situation in either of these scenarios. You might insist (in the first case) that even if the explanation for your feeling is an abnormal one, if it seems to you that you feel a certain way, then you do. In the second case, you might insist that you don't have the feeling if you don't feel it, and you don't feel it you are not at least in a position to recognize that you are feeling it. But the phenomenology may be complicated in abnormal cases, and the subject may be unsure or ambivalent about how such situations should be described.

Suppose that instead of following Williamson's suggestion to sharpen artificially the notion of *feeling cold* by identifying it with a physiological condition, we sharpen it in a way that preserves a constitutive doxastic connection. Suppose we take *feeling cold* to be something like the state of being inclined to believe, based on how one feels, that one is in a cold environment. Now what happens when one goes through the sorites sequence? It is reasonable to suppose, as Williamson does, that the subject's answers to the question, "Do you feel cold?" will be firmly positive at the start, but at a certain point will begin to be hesitant and qualified, perhaps with some backtracking ("I guess I didn't really feel cold a moment ago either"). Suppose one sharpens the concept by saying that at the first sign of hesitation, the subject no longer qualifies as feeling cold, since he is no longer inclined to report, unequivocally, that he feels cold. At that same point, he no longer counts as believing that he feels cold. There is some distortion in this sharpening, and in the assumption of a tight link between the phenomenal state and the disposition to report, since the hesitation and qualification might take an epistemic form ("I'm not quite sure whether I still feel cold"), and the backtracking suggests that the subject is allowing for the possibility that his judgments about whether he feels cold might be mistaken. Furthermore, if we sharpen our revisionary stipulation about what it means to feel cold, and to believe it, in this way, we can expect that there will be some randomness in the determination of the exact point where hesitation begins. There will be points at which the subject does not have a stable *disposition* to report that he feels cold (as contrasted with a more hesitant answer). Sometimes, when in an otherwise indistinguishable state, he will express hesitation, and sometimes not.

It seems that either way of sharpening the vague phenomenal concept will yield an artificial concept that lacks something that seems essential to phenomenal concepts. The explanation may be that there is some incoherence in a notion of a phenomenal state that combined an essentially epistemic or doxastic dimension with the assumption that the state is an intrinsic, nonintentional internal state that one is judging oneself to be in when one reports that one feels cold, or is in pain, or is having a sensation of red. The vagueness of such phenomenal concepts helps to obscure the incoherence, and the attempt to sharpen them artificially brings the incoherence to the surface. If something like this is right, then phenomenal concepts do not offer the best place to challenge Williamson's antiluminosity thesis and argument. But purely epistemic and doxastic concepts may be better cases.

In defense of the KK principle

The KK principle, in its unvarnished form, says that the proposition *that x knows that P* entails the proposition *that x knows that x knows that P*. Jaacko

Hintikka endorsed this principle in his early formulation of epistemic logic,[13] and it is accepted in many developments and applications of this kind of formal semantic theory. As acknowledged from the start, by Hintikka and others, epistemic logic is an idealized and schematic model of knowledge, and not a realistic description. The most that could plausibly be said about a notion of knowledge that applies to real human agents is that knowledge that P puts one in a position to know that one knows that P. But this is enough to imply that knowledge is a luminous concept, in Williamson's sense, and Williamson applies his signature anti-luminosity argument to rebut the thesis that the principle holds. I will question the soundness of the argument by questioning the relevant margin of error principles, and also the more general safety condition on knowledge. I will begin with a simple model of knowledge that validates the KK principle, and a simple example to illustrate it. After seeing where the anti-luminosity argument breaks down for this simple case, I will consider some of the similarities and differences between the simple model and a notion of knowledge that might apply to ourselves.

Knowledge, whatever else it may be, is a state of registering or carrying information, where information is understood in terms that Fred Dretske, among others, has developed.[14] According to the general picture, an object or system registers information about some aspect of its environment if it is causally sensitive in a systematic way to a range of facts. Specifically, a system functions to carry information if it is capable of being in a range of internal states, $S_1, \ldots S_n$ which correspond to a range of states of the environment, $E_1, \ldots E_n$ in the following way: under certain favorable conditions, the object is in states S_i, for each i, if and only if the environment is in the corresponding state E_i. The object or system then carries the information that ϕ if and only if the conditions are favorable in the relevant sense, it is in state S_i, and the environment being in states E_i entails that ϕ. Strictly, the object or system "knows" or carries the information that ϕ only if ϕ is a proposition that distinguishes between the possible situations that satisfy the favorable conditions. Trivially, propositions that state those conditions will be propositions that are entailed by all of the states E_i, but these propositions are presupposed by the system, or by the interpreter of the system.

This abstract framework can allow for misinformation by removing the qualification that the conditions are favorable in the relevant sense. That is, a system that functions to carry information might be said to "believe" that ϕ whether or not conditions are favorable, provided it is in a state S_i

---

[13] Hintikka 1962.
[14] The classic development of this way of understanding knowledge is Dretske 1981.

that is such that, if conditions were favorable, it would carry the information that ϕ.

This simple story will apply to a wide range of objects and systems that are not rational agents – to artifacts such as thermostats and fuel gauges, to impersonal and subpersonal biological systems such as immune systems, and to suprapersonal entities such as economic systems. And there are even simpler cases of information registration: to repeat some often cited examples, the reflection on the lake carries information about the sky above, and the rings on a tree trunk carry information about the age of the tree. But even if information registration is ubiquitous, manifested in things very different from the beings that are of interest to epistemologists, we do naturally use epistemological language metaphorically to describe simpler cases of information carrying. A coil that returns to a certain shape after being deformed has a "memory," since it retains the information about its default shape. The immune system can "recognize" foreign invaders, though it may also "mistake" the body's own tissue for a foreign invader (in cases of auto-immune disease). These metaphors reflect the fact that the simple cases share an abstract structure with the kind of complex and sophisticated information-carrying devices that rational agents are, and I think it helps to understand our own knowledge and belief to start with simpler cases that share the structure, and that may face simpler versions of the epistemological problems that human knowers face. The appeal to this abstract structure to throw some light on philosophical problems about knowledge and intentionality need not be part of any reductive project, either the search for an analytic definition of knowledge, or an attempt to give a materialist reduction of intentionality.

So my examination of the anti-luminosity argument against the KK principle will begin with a simple artifact whose function is to carry information – a measuring device.[15] I want my device to be understood, not just as something that provides information to its users, but as itself a knower, or a simple model of a knower. My device is a digital kitchen scale that I use to weigh the coffee beans before I grind them for our morning coffee. It weighs them in grams, and my target weight is 42 grams. Sometimes, when I am thinking about Williamson's anti-luminosity argument, I add the beans slowly, one at a time, after the scale registers 41. At a certain point sometimes it will flicker a bit between 41 and 42, and a bean or two later it will settle at 42. I don't

---

[15] My discussion is influenced by unpublished work by Damien Rochford, who develops the analogy between rational agents and systems of measuring instruments in illuminating detail.

then take my scale to "know" that the bowl of coffee beans weighs *exactly* 42 grams – it is not that accurate. But it is pretty accurate, so I think I can reasonably assume that it "knows" that the beans weigh 42 ± 1 grams. What this "margin of error" assumption shows, in terms of the abstract structure described, is that while the alternative states of the information-carrying device, $S_1, \ldots S_n$ (the numbers registered on the scale's screen), are pairwise disjoint states, the corresponding states of the external environment (the ranges of weights) need not be disjoint. So, for example, S_{42} and S_{43} (42 and 43 on the screen) will correspond to the ranges 41–43 and 42–44 respectively for the weight in grams of the beans. But taking account of *all* the information carried by a state of the system, the alternative states of the world corresponding to the states *will* be disjoint. This is because the state S_i trivially carries information about itself – specifically, that it is in state S_i. It will always be true that the scale reads 42 only if it reads 42, under favorable (or unfavorable) conditions. So the state of the world corresponding to S_{42} (under favorable conditions) will be the state in which the scale is in state S_{42}, and the actual weight is in the range 41–43 grams.

The description of the abstract structure includes the crucial qualification "under certain favorable conditions," and we pin down a particular application of the information-carrying story only when we specify (explicitly or implicitly) those conditions (*channel conditions*, to use an information-theoretic term, or what Dennis Stampe called "fidelity conditions" in an early paper on this kind of approach to intentional content).[16] In general, the channel conditions will include two different kinds of restriction: first, the correlation will be required to hold only conditional on the proper functioning of the internal workings of the information-carrying device; second, the correlation is conditional on certain features of the external environment. My scale, if it malfunctions, may register a number that fails to correspond, even within the margin of error, to the actual weight. Perhaps, because of a low battery, it sticks on a certain number, or perhaps the zero point is off so that weights are systematically too high by two or three grams. But the registration might also diverge from the actual value because some anomalous atmospheric or gravitational phenomenon creates an environment in which even a well-functioning scale will fail to give an accurate measurement. Maybe it is steel balls rather than coffee beans we are weighing, and there is a magnet below the scale that distorts the measurement. The scale "knows" the weight of what is on the scale only when the channel conditions of both kinds are satisfied. These conditions will be constitutively connected with the margin of

[16] Stampe 1977.

error that fixes the specific content of the information that is registered. If the channel conditions are such that they may be satisfied when the actual weight is 41 and the scale registers 42, then this must be reflected in the specification of the content of the information that the number 42 registers, where this specification is given by the margin of error. And if under the specified channel conditions, the scale measures 42 *only* when the actual weight is between 41 and 43, then the measurement carries the information that the actual weight is within that range.

While the channel conditions and the margin of error are tightly connected, there is some flexibility, and perhaps some arbitrariness, in exactly what the conditions and the corresponding margin of error each are. The line between normal fluctuation and malfunction might be drawn, by an interpreter of a system that functions to carry information, in alternative ways. Some differences between an internal malfunction and the proper functioning of a device may be relatively sharp and inflexible, but at least some of the channel conditions may involve continuities that will require arbitrary cutoffs, at least if we are to avoid vagueness. Consider a slightly different measuring device, an oven thermometer that is designed to measure the average temperature inside the oven. We can be reasonably sure that the molecular energy within the oven is approximately uniform: the temperature of the air in the small part of the space near the sensor will normally be close to the average temperature within the whole oven. But there is a small probability that it will be very different, and when it is, the thermometer will sometimes register a temperature that diverges significantly from the average temperature that it is ostensibly measuring. Thermodynamics will tell us, for each margin of error, how probable it will be that the difference between the average temperature and the temperature in the space close to the sensor will remain within that margin. But how improbable must a distribution be to count as abnormal? The answer to that question will contribute to determining the margin of error, but we should expect the right answer to be both vague and context-dependent. As with the infamous bank cases, used to motivate contextualist and subject-sensitive invariantist accounts of knowledge, this kind of choice may be constrained by the decision-making role that the information-registering device is playing, and on the importance of accuracy for making the right decision.

But who sets these numbers; who specifies the channel conditions, and the resulting margins of error? Remember, we are thinking of our devices, not as things we use to acquire knowledge, but as themselves models of knowers. But knowers (real ones, as well as such artificial models) are also devices that other knowers use to acquire knowledge, and it is the attributors of knowledge (including epistemological theorists) who specify, or presuppose, the conditions that determine the content of the knowledge attributed. The information-theoretic story about knowledge is a thoroughly external one that characterizes the state from the outside, as a feature of things in the world that are sensitive to facts about their environment. Sensitivity to facts about the environment is essentially contrastive: knowers represent things as being *this* way rather than *that* way, and what the contrast is will depend on the background facts that are presupposed by the attributor. There is no escaping the context-dependence of such attributions (on this way of understanding knowledge), since things carry information only relative to facts about the causal relations between those things and other things in their world. They don't carry information *about* those facts, but carry information in virtue of the facts being the way they are. This dependence of information registration on a factual background will be uncontroversial for our simple measuring devices, but I think it is also an unavoidable feature of the more sophisticated measuring devices that we ourselves are.[17]

I want now to look at a version of Williamson's argument against the KK principle that is applied to the schematic account I have given of a system that functions to carry information. His argument is a reductio of the KK principle, and we know that it cannot be sound when applied to this schematic account since the KK principle holds on this account, and it will be clear exactly where the argument goes wrong. Just to be clear on the dialectic of my argument: the critique of this application of the anti-luminosity argument should not be controversial, and does not, by itself, have force against Williamson's anti-KK argument as applied to the ordinary notion of knowledge that is his target. The controversy will be about the extent to which the structure of the schematic account of systems like measuring devices that function to carry information is reflected in an adequate account of real knowledge. But the critique of this variant of the argument does accomplish two things: first, it illustrates the fact that there is a thoroughly externalist, anti-Cartesian conception of something like knowledge that allows for luminosity, in Williamson's sense. Second, by pinpointing the place at which this version of the argument fails, it focuses attention on the corresponding point in Williamson's actual argument, so that we can consider whether the differences between simple systems that function to carry information and real knowers makes a difference for the soundness of the argument.

---

[17] I used the information story about knowledge in Stalnaker 1993 to give a theoretical rationale both for an anti-individualist account of the content of knowledge and belief, and for an essentially contextualist account of knowledge.

Luminosity and the KK thesis

As with the anti-luminosity argument applied to phenomenal states like *feeling cold*, the central premises of Williamson's argument against the KK thesis are margin-of-error (ME) principles that say that one can know that ϕ in situation α only if ϕ is true, not only in α, but also in situations that are very similar to α. Our kitchen scale weighs things with a margin of error $\pm$ 1 gram, so we can assume that two situations where the item being weighed differs in weight by less than this margin of error are sufficiently similar for the purposes of Williamson's ME premises. So consider a sequence of propositions, $\phi_0, \phi_1, \phi_2, \ldots$ defined as follows: ϕ_i is the proposition that the beans in the bowl weigh no less than $40 + i \times (.1)$. For example, ϕ_0 is the proposition that the weight of the beans ≥ 40 grams, and ϕ_{23} is the proposition that the weight of the beans in the bowl ≥ 42.3 grams. The number .1 is well within the margin of error, so the ME principles for this example are the sentences of the following form:

$$(K\phi_i \to \phi_{i+1}).$$

(If it is *known* that the beans weigh no less than x, then it is *true* that they weigh no less than x+.1.)

Williamson's argument assumes that the margin of error principles are not only true, but also known by the knower. Unlike Mr. Magoo (the estimator of the height of a tree in the example used in Williamson's actual argument), our humble scale is not a reflective agent, but the knowledge operator, as interpreted in the semantics for our schematic model, represents what is true in all possible situations compatible with the information carried by the scale. So it includes the channel conditions that are presupposed, as well as other features of the system that are presupposed to hold. So let us assume that if the ME principles are true, then they are "known" in this sense. So we have

$$(ME) K(K\phi_i \to \phi_{i+1}).$$

Along with these premises, we have the KK principle

$$(KK)(K\phi \to KK\phi).$$

For Williamson, the KK principle is a hypothesis assumed for a reductio, but in our model the KK principle is true. Here is an argument for this claim. Suppose the system is in a state S_i such that the corresponding state is E_i, and that E_i is a state that obtains (assuming that the channel conditions are satisfied) only if ϕ. Suppose further that $K\phi$ is true, which presupposes that the channel conditions obtain. Then since E_i is a state in which S_i obtains, it follows that E_i obtains (assuming that the channel conditions are satisfied) only if $K\phi$. So since the channel conditions do obtain, it follows that $KK\phi$ is true.

Now here is the reductio argument, modeled on Williamson's argument. Since the KK principle holds, this will be a reductio of one of the ME premises.

Assume that the scale registers 42, and that channel conditions are satisfied, so that the scale "knows" that the weight is between 41 and 43, inclusive. It follows that it "knows" that the weight is no less than 40, so we have

$$K\phi_0. \tag{1}$$

It also follows that it "knows" that the actual weight is *not* greater than 43, from which it follows that it is false that the weight is no less than 43.1, and so false that the scale "knows" this. So we have

$$\sim K\phi_{31}. \tag{2}$$

Now from each of the (ME) premises, $K(K\phi_i \rightarrow \phi_{i+1})$, we get, by distributing the K,

$$KK\phi_i \rightarrow K\phi_{i+1} \tag{3}$$

(Following Williamson, and standard epistemic logic, we are assuming deductive closure for knowledge.)

From (3) and (KK), we deduce, by the transitivity of the material conditional arrow,

$$K\phi_i \rightarrow K\phi_{i+1} \tag{4}$$

for each i. Then by a sequence of 31 *modus ponens* steps, using 31 instances of (4), and starting with (1), we get

$$K\phi_{31} \tag{5}$$

which contradicts (2).

The argument is obviously valid, so which of the premises is false? Since (KK) and deductive closure for K are true in this simple idealized model, and since the stipulations of the case ensure that premises (1) and (2) are true, we know that at least one instance of (ME) is false. It is easy to see that the culprit is $K(K\phi_{10} \to \phi_{11})$. Our assumptions about the case imply that the scale knows that the weight is no less than 41, but it might be, for all it knows, that the weight is *exactly* 41, in which case ϕ_{11} would be false. So it is compatible with what the scale knows (together with our presuppositions about it) that it knows ϕ_{10}, while ϕ_{11} is false.

Note that this critique of the anti-luminosity argument takes a different form from Berker's, although both critiques are based on a claim of a constitutive connection between the candidate for a luminous condition and knowledge or belief that that condition obtains. Berker's argument was that the safety requirement for knowledge did not imply the margin-of-error premises, while my argument involves a rejection of Williamson's safety requirement itself. In the artificial example, the device "knows" a proposition even though in very similar situations in which it still "believes" the proposition, it is false, violating Williamson's safety condition. But while it is clear that this safety condition fails on the assumption of the schematic account, if we are to extend this critique to the case of human knowers it must be argued that the rejection of this safety condition is intuitively plausible.

First note that it will be very unlikely that the actual value should be at the limit of the scale's range of accuracy. If the scale is *always*, when it is functioning normally and atmospheric conditions are also normal, within the range ± 1, then it will *almost* always be within a narrower range. If we were to learn that the scale registered 42 when the actual weight was within a milligram of being out of range, we would think that *probably* conditions were abnormal. But still, it is *possible* that conditions are normal when the actual weight is 41.0 and the scale registers 42. In this case, according to our model, the scale knows that the weight is 42 ± 1.

So suppose our scale is actually in a situation like this. There are exactly 41.00 grams of coffee beans in the bowl, the scale registers 42, and the relevant normal conditions are satisfied. We now remove one small fragment of a bean from the bowl – just enough to take the actual weight down to 40.99. It could happen that the reading on the scale then drops to 41, but suppose it stays at 42. We can then conclude that the channel conditions are no longer satisfied, since there is a constitutive connection between the channel conditions and the margin of error that defines the content of the information registered, a connection that guarantees that *if* the conditions are satisfied, the actual weight is within the range. The "belief" that the weight was 42 ± 1 was *true* before we removed the fragment of the bean, but because the belief persists and is false in the very similar situation that results from removing the small bean fragment, the belief was not *safe* in the prior situation, in the sense defined by Williamson. Should we take this as a sign that our artificial model leaves out something that is essential to a more realistic conception of knowledge? I will argue that it does not; that Williamson's safety condition does not capture an intuitive notion of safety that it is reasonable to impose on an account of knowledge.

We can grant that there is some artificiality in the precise cutoff point, but whether or not knowledge must satisfy a safety condition, there will inevitably be a sharp and somewhat arbitrary line (in an artificial sharpening of a vague and context-dependent notion of knowledge) between the situation in which the knowledge claim is true and a very similar situation in which it is false. The question is whether it helps – whether it somehow makes the knowledge safer, in a situation on the cusp of this cutoff point – to require that the belief still be true on the other side of the line when it is no longer knowledge. No matter how we understand knowledge, any case just on the other side of the line will be a case in which the agent has a belief, and presumably a justified belief, that is not knowledge. If we assume Williamson's safety condition, then the situation, just on the other side of the line, will be one in which the agent has a *true* belief that is justified, but that is not knowledge. Does it make a belief safer, in a sense of safety that has epistemic merit, if all the very similar situations that are not cases of knowledge are Gettier cases (case of justified true belief without knowledge) rather than cases of false belief? Gettier cases (on one natural diagnosis) are cases where the fact that the proposition believed is true does not play an appropriate role in bringing about or sustaining the belief. In Gettier cases, it is just a coincidence that the justified belief is true. However the relevant nearness relation is spelled out, it does not seem reasonable to think that a belief being true by coincidence in a nearby situation should contribute to the robustness and stability of the belief in the actual situation.

The threshold cases in the sorites-like series used in Williamson's anti-luminosity arguments might not seem like Gettier cases, but in the case of the simple measuring instruments, it is, in a sense, accidental whether the "believed" proposition remains true just on the other side of the threshold point. Consider the case of the oven thermometer. If the distribution of kinetic energy within the oven is sufficiently uneven, and so improbable, then conditions are abnormal. In abnormal conditions, the temperature reading is unreliable, since the temperature in the space near the sensor might easily diverge from the average. But however we draw the cutoff line between normal and abnormal, the reading *might*, by chance, be correct even when conditions are abnormal: it might be that, by chance, the average of the uneven temperatures in the different parts of the oven balance out to be the same (within the margin of error) as the temperature at the point of the sensor. At the point at which the thermodynamical conditions shift from being normal to abnormal, the shift could at the same time bring about a divergence between the instrument's reading and the actual average temperature, or it could leave it within range. But this should not matter for the reliability of the thermometer just before the threshold point. It is, at that point, just barely reliable, either way, and there must be a point (on any artificial sharpening of the notion of reliability) at which a reliable instrument is just barely reliable.

The arbitrariness of the cutoff point is particularly salient in this case, and it will presumably be true in cases of the knowledge of real agents that there will be some continuous gradations relevant to distinguishing what is known from what is not. With both simple artificial examples, and with realistic situations involving real human knowers, the line might be drawn in different places in different contexts. It might be that when the theorist or attributor focuses her attention on threshold cases, there is some temptation to shift to stricter channel conditions, and a narrower margin of error results.[18] But doing so changes the interpretation of the content of what information is registered by the knower. The context change changes not only the second-order claim about what is known about what is known, but also the first-order knowledge claim.

In rejecting Williamson's safety and margin-of-error principles, I am not rejecting the idea that knowledge must be safe. Knowledge, on the kind of account I am promoting, is attributed relative to background conditions that are presupposed to hold (by both the attributor and the agent) when knowledge is attributed or expressed. It is correct to say, on this kind of account, that when a person has knowledge, that knowledge is perfectly safe, *conditional on those presupposed conditions*. Under those conditions, the knowledge claims are *guaranteed* to be correct when the agent is in the relevant internal state. Of course, the presuppositions might be false, and then all bets are off. But that is the situation that we poor cognitively homeless people face, as Williamson has taught us.[19]

The background conditions must be *true*, for the knowledge claimed to be true, but they need not be *known* to be true by the agent. The idea that

---

[18] Cf. Graff-Fara 2000.
[19] "We must ... accept the consequences of our unfortunate epistemic situation with what composure we can find. Life is hard" (Williamson 2000, p. 237).

there are conditions that are necessary for a knower to have knowledge, but that need not themselves be known, is not just a feature of our simple artificial examples of information-carrying instruments. It is a familiar claim, for example, that acquiring knowledge by perception requires that the relevant perceptual systems are functioning normally, but does not require that the person with perceptual knowledge knows that this condition is satisfied.

Still, there are crucial differences between the measuring instruments that I have used as simple models of knowers and the more sophisticated devices that we are, and the differences are relevant to the KK thesis. The simple measuring instruments have a single fixed channel for the receipt of information, and a limited range of facts that they are capable of carrying information about. My humble scale cannot ask itself whether it really knows what our external account says that it knows; it can't ask whether it is functioning normally, whether the weight that it registers is the actual weight of the beans. While it is not required, with either simple measuring devices or real knowers, that the knower knows that the background conditions obtain, it is still true that reflective human knowers, unlike simple devices, can raise the question of whether or not these conditions do obtain. That is, a human knower can consider whether she has reason to believe the propositions she was presupposing when she represented herself as knowing something. One can ask, for example, whether one's perceptual systems are functioning properly, whether one is reasoning correctly in assessing the evidence, whether what one takes to be evidence is evidence that one really has.

The fact that we, unlike the simple information-registering devices, can ask these questions does not imply that we are not information-carrying systems to which a version of the schematic model applies. A human knower, unlike my scale, acquires its knowledge through multiple channels, and has devices for integrating the information received from different sources, and for assessing the reliability of some of its sources with the help of others. This is what makes it possible for it to raise questions about its own reliability, and to go some way toward answering them. Even the scale takes a small step in this direction: it sends a flashing signal when the battery is low – in effect, registering information about the reliability of its basic measurement. So the fact that the low-battery signal is *not* received carries the information (when *its* conditions are normal) that the conditions for the basic measurement are, in one respect, normal. But of course the low-battery indicator might malfunction as well. One cannot draw too much comfort from the fact that a witness assures you that he is a reliable witness, or that your tests of your visual system assure you that it is working well.

The complexity that allows an information-registering device to register information about its own reliability is relevant to the KK thesis since it is natural to take the question whether one knows that one knows some fact as a question of this kind. But to raise a question of this kind – to question the presupposed background conditions relative to which a knowledge claim was made – is to change the context, and when the context is changed in this way, it brings into question the original knowledge claim. Consider any intuitively natural situation in which an agent raises the question, about some proposition he was representing himself as knowing, "Do I really know that?" If on reflection the answer is, "I'm not sure" or "Probably not," then the agent will retract the original claim. It is not just that he will refrain from asserting that he knows it; he will refrain from making the first-order assertion. The argument I gave for the KK principle, in the context of the schematic model of a device that functions to carry information, assumed that the context remained fixed in the following sense: the KK proposition was assessed relative to the same presupposed channel conditions as the first-order K proposition. With real knowers there is much more scope for contextual variation, many more dimensions on which the context for a knowledge claim may vary, but I think it is reasonable to assume that the argument for KK should work, on this assumption, even when we are talking about much more sophisticated measuring devices such as ourselves.

So my defense of the KK principle can allow for cases where the presupposed channel conditions for a first-order knowledge claim are different from those presupposed for a second-order claim about what one knows, and so can allow that the first might be true, in its context, while the second is false in its different context.[20] But the conclusion that the KK principle holds on the assumption that the background presuppositions are held fixed is still a significant thesis, and is a thesis that is incompatible with the premises of Williamson's anti-luminosity argument. On the conception of knowledge that Williamson is defending – one that satisfies his safety and margin-of-error principles – the claim that one knows that one knows that ϕ requires stronger evidence *about* ϕ (and not just about the conditions necessary for knowing ϕ). On this view, a reflective and self-aware person might rationally judge that her evidence is sufficiently strong to assert that ϕ, but not sufficiently strong to assert that she knows that ϕ. So the assertion, "ϕ, but I am not sure that I know that ϕ" or even "ϕ, but it is highly probable that I don't

---

[20] Dan Greco in his 2014 emphasizes the context shift involved in apparent counterexamples to the KK principle.

know that φ" might be appropriate assertions that are in conformity with a knowledge norm of assertion (the norm, defended by Williamson, that is violated by an assertion of a proposition that is not known by the speaker). But one might think that a reflective and self-aware knower could reason this way when she finds herself prepared to assert that φ: "I *could* be in a situation where φ is false, or one in which it is true, but I don't know it." (I'm not infallible. It has on occasion happened that I took myself to be in a position to make an assertion, but it turned out that I was mistaken.) But while I recognize that this theoretical possibility is always there, I am not a skeptic, and I don't take this theoretical possibility to imply that not φ is an *epistemic* possibility for me, in my present situation. My considered judgment is that I am now in an evidential position that justifies an assertion that φ. Am I also in a position to assert that I know that φ? Well, in a sense, I would be *as* safe in asserting that I know that φ as I am in asserting that φ, since if I don't know that φ, then the first-order assertion by itself is in violation of the norm. But if my first-order assertion is in conformity with the norm, then the second-order claim about my knowledge is *true*. Why isn't this enough to make that second-order assertion a *safe* assertion, and why isn't it enough to justify me in claiming that if I indeed do know that φ, then I know that I do? While my defense of the KK principle rested on an analogy with simple artificial information-registering devices, and a highly contentious theoretical hypothesis that a schematic model for such devices generalizes to real human knowers, I am also inclined to think on more intuitive grounds that this reflective, self-aware (if perhaps slightly neurotic) knower is making perfectly good sense.[21]

---

[21] Thanks to Dan Greco and Damien Rochford for helpful discussion of these issues.

2 Some questions about Burge's "self-verifying judgments"

Tony Brueckner

Self-verifying judgments and their background

In "On Always Being Right (about What One is Thinking)," Finn Spicer criticizes Tyler Burge's well-known claim that certain *cogito*-like judgments are self-verifying.[1] I responded in defense of Burge in "A Defense of Burge's 'Self-Verifying Judgments'," and Spicer in turn answered that response in "Two Ways to be Right about What One is Thinking."[2] The issues are so delicate, and Burge's views about self-verification are so well known and influential, that I think that an extension of the exchange between Spicer and me is worthwhile.

The skeptical context of Burge's discussion of self-verifying judgments concerns the consistency of (i) the existence of privileged access to the contents of one's intentional mental states, and (ii) Burge's *anti-individualism* about the contents of such states. According to (ii), the contents of one's intentional mental states are determined, in part, by states of affairs in one's external, causal environment. For example, the thought expressed by my Twin Earthian twin's utterance of 'Water is wet' is *twater is wet*, where 'twater' refers to all and only samples of XYZ, the "watery," nonwater liquid found on Twin Earth. 'Twater' expresses a concept that applies to all and only samples of the XYZ-constituted "watery," nonwater stuff. According to (i), I can know, without any empirical investigation, that I am now thinking that water is wet. But given anti-individualism, how is such privileged access possible? Don't I need to know, by empirical investigation, the character of my external, causal environment (XYZ? H_2O?) in order to know that I am now thinking that water is wet, rather than that twater is wet?

Much has been said in the literature regarding the motivation for the foregoing epistemological worry, a worry about knowledge of content.

---
[1] See Spicer 2009, pp. 137–60. The *locus classicus* for Burge is Burge 1988, pp. 649–63.
[2] Both papers appear in *International Journal for the Study of Skepticism* 1 (2011).

For example, there are variations of the notorious switching scenario that was first described in Burge's "Individualism and Self-Knowledge," in which I am shuttled between Earth and Twin Earth without realizing that this is happening. After dwelling on Twin Earth and interacting with twater and with speakers who speak of twater by using 'water', my own utterances of 'Water is a liquid' come to express, at least on some occasions, twater thoughts. How do I know that, right now, I am not involved in such a switching scenario, now thinking that twater is a liquid, rather than that water is a liquid? If I cannot, without empiricial investigation, rule out the possibility that I myself am now involved in such a switching scenario, now thinking that twater is a liquid, then how can I know, without empirical investigation, that I am now thinking that water is a liquid?

But such scenarios are not the focus of this chapter. Our starting point will be as follows: Burge wants to offer a partial solution to the prima facie problem of inconsistency involving (i) and (ii) by considering a special class of mental states. These are *cogito*-like judgments: not judgments that I exist, but, instead, judgments such as that I am thinking that water is a liquid. According to Burge, regardless of the switching possibililty, when I think a thought expressed in my current language by tokening 'I am thinking that water is a liquid', that thought is guaranteed to be true. Such judgments are *self-verifying*. Given the mechanism of self-verification, the switching possibility poses no threat to privileged access to Burge's *cogito*-like judgments. But how does the mechanism of self-verification work, exactly?

Some preliminaries are in order. I take a judgment to be the mental counterpart to an assertion. *Thinking*, in Burge's extended Cartesian sense, is entertaining a proposition. Believing that it is snowing, hoping that it will stop snowing, desiring warmer clothing, and so on, all involve the entertaining of a proposition. So they are all cases of thinking. Judging that p entails thinking that p, since judging that p entails that one entertains p.

Suppose that I judge

(4) Water is a liquid.

This judging makes

(6) I am thinking that water is a liquid

true. This is because if I judge (4), then I think (4), by the above principle that judging that p entails thinking that p. Thus, when I judge true or endorse (4), it follows that (6) is true, since (6) is just the statement that I am thinking the content of (4). Spicer also notes that if I *believe* (4), then I think (4). Again (6) will then be true. If I doubt (4), then I think (4). Again (6) will then be true, and so on. So Spicer notes that there are *many* ways for me to make (6) true: judging (4) is obviously not the *only* way. According to Burge, there is a rather special way to make (6) true. Burge proceeds from the assumption (quoted by Spicer)

(PC) ... one 'thinks' all propositional components of any thought one thinks.[3]

This is why my *judging (6)* is a way to make (6) true: when I judge (6), I also think (4). This is so, by PC, because (4) is a propositional component of the thought I think when I judge (so think) (6). As just noted, when I think (4), this makes (6) true. This is Burge's understanding of self-verification: when I judge (6), I think (4) and thereby make (6) true.

The argument from truth conditions

Before we turn to Spicer's argument against the Burgean mechanism of self-verification, we must discuss his *Truth Condition Principle*:

(TCP) Propositional attitude ascriptions specify the content of the ascribed attitude at least to the grain of sameness of truth condition.[4]

TCP is intended by Spicer to capture the common ground between Fregeans, Russellians, and defenders of unstructured propositions (like Lewis and Stalnaker): all camps agree that contents ascribed in propositional attitude ascription are *at least as coarse-grained* as TCP requires. The Fregean requires a finer grain. If I judge

(4) Water is a liquid

then the propositional attitude ascription (6) above is true of me on both the Fregean and the Russellian view. But on the Fregean view, if I judge

(7) H_2O is a liquid

then it does not follow that (6) is true of me, even though (4) and (7) have the same truth conditions.

TCP seems to be a principle that lays down a *necessary* condition on substitutivity *salva veritate* in propositional attitude contexts that both a Fregean and a Russellian can agree upon, whatever might be their disagreements about *sufficient* conditions for such substitutivity. Suppose that two propositional attitude ascriptions specify the same thought content. Then TCP lays down the following necessary condition on substitution within the pertinent propositional attitude contexts:

---

[3] See Burge 1996.   [4] See Spicer 2009, p. 143.

(*) If SubTr('S is thinking that Q'/'S is thinking that P'), then necessarily, Prop('P') is true iff Prop('Q') is true.

The antecedent of (*) is meant to say that substitution of 'Q' for 'P' in the second sentence (yielding the first sentence) is logically guaranteed to be truth-preserving; the consequent says that the pertinent propositions have the same truth conditions. Fregeans and Russellians agree on (*). But they disagree on a variant of (*) in which its overall logical form is that of a biconditional. According to the Fregean, there are cases in which (a) the RHS of such a biconditional is true (sameness of truth conditions for the pertinent propositions), but (b) the LHS is false (substitutivity *salva veritate* fails; see (4) and (7) above).

Let us now look at Spicer's original *Argument from Truth Conditions* (hereafter ATCO), which is meant to show that, contra Burge, (6) is not self-verifying:

	(I)	(4) and (6) differ in truth conditions
	(II)	My judging (4) makes (6) true
	(III)	(6) satisfies TCP
So	(IV)	My judging (6) does not make (6) true
So	(V)	(6) is not self-verifying[5]

The key problem in understanding ATCO is to understand how TCP is supposed to move us from the true (I)–(III) to (IV). Unfortunately, in "On Always Being Right (about What One is Thinking)," Spicer gives us no help on this key point. In my response to that paper, I argued that a principle that is *far different* from ⋆ (a principle that is the natural interpretation of TCP, I thought) is a natural candidate for making the (enthymematic) argument valid. The principle that I thought was needed to make the argument valid was both implausible and independent of ⋆.

To save the reader some pain, let me sum up Spicer's overall assessment of the situation, in "Two Ways to be Right about What One is Thinking."[6] Spicer did not intend that TCP, which drives ATCO, be read as ⋆, a principle about substitutivity *salva veritate* within propositional attitude contexts (though certainly, we must admit, a time-honored locus of semantic reflection on grainedness and Frege–Russell disagreements about propositional attitudes). Spicer in fact intended that TCP be read differently (though his intended reading is not to be found in "On Always Being Right (About What One is Thinking)"). Here is Spicer's intended reading of TCP (first version):

---

[5] See ibid., p. 144.
[6] I will not discuss the principle I proposed, since Spicer 2011 rejects it.

Some questions about Burge's "self-verifying judgments"   45

(TCP1) If two propositional attitudes a(c1) and a(c2) both make true the same propositional attitude ascription, then a(c1) and a(c2) share the same truth-conditions.[7]

Here is a revised version of ATCO – call it ATC1 – that is meant to make use of TCP1 (where 'j(p)' stands for 'judging that p')

Ass. for reductio:	0	j(6) makes (6) true
	1	(4) and (6) differ in truth-conditions
	2	j(4) makes (6) true
	3	if j(c1) makes (6) true, and j(c2) makes (6) true, then (c1) has the same truth conditions as (c2)
So	3.5	(6) has the same truth conditions as (4)
So	4	j(6) does not make (6) true

Premise 3 is meant to be an instance of TCP1, but it is not. The suppressed premise that we need instead for ATC1 is provided later by Spicer:

(TCP2) If two propositional attitudes a(c1) and a(c2) both make true the same propositional attitude ascription, then (c1) and (c2) share the same truth conditions.

Premise 3 *is* an instance of TCP2. The key question for ATC1 is whether TCP2 is true. If so, then the argument is a successful reductio of its self-verification assumption, viz. 0.

It is obvious that TCP2 is quite different from the straightforward, innocuous reading of TCP0 as *. The first thing to note about TCP2 is that it gives us a flat, unmotivated denial of Burge's view that j(6) (as well as j(4), believe(4), desire(4), doubt(4), and so on) makes (6) true, owing to the obvious difference in truth conditions between (4) and (6).

But why accept TCP2, whose corresponding *rule of inference* can be formalized as follows:

	Nec	[{a1(S,c1)} → {a'(S,c3)}]
	Nec	[{a2(S,c2)} → {a'(S,c3)}]
So	Nec	[c1 is true iff c2 is true]

The rule of inference says that from the premises that two propositional attitudes of Ss – a1(c1) and a2(c2) – make true the same propositional attitude ascription to S – a'(c3), we can infer the conclusion that the contents of the attitudes in the premises have the same truth conditions. Here is an instance of the foregoing TCP2 rule:

---
[7] See Spicer 2011, p. 6.

Nec [{j(S,P&Q)} → {t(S,P)}]
Nec [{j(S,P)} → {t(S,P)}]
So Nec [P&Q is true iff P is true]

where 'j(S,–)' stands for 'S judges that—', and 't(S,–)' stands for 'S thinks that—'

Here is another instance of the rule:

Nec [{j(S,BP)} → {t(S,tP)}]
Nec [{j(S,tP)} → {t(S,tP)}]
So Nec [BP is true iff tP is true]

where 'j(S,BP)' stands for 'S judges that S believes that P', 'j(S,tP)' stands for 'S judges that S thinks that P', and 't(S,tP' stands for 'S thinks that S thinks that P'.

We also have the following instance of the rule:

Nec [{j(S,BP)} → {t(S, there is some x and some y such that (xBy)}]
Nec [{j(S,BQ)} → {t(S, there is some x and some y such that (xBy)}]
So Nec [BP is true iff BQ is true]

The foregoing instances of the TCP2 rule all seem arguably invalid. Clearly, at the least, TCP2 is not an innocuous principle like the substitutivity principle *.

Two models of self-verification

There is an important subtlety addressed in both of Spicer's papers which I failed to address in my defense of Burge.[8] Spicer claims that there are *two* ways of being self-verifying. The first is *being self-verifying by instantiation*. Spicer characterizes this way as follows: "the *cogito*-like judgment [such as j(6)] instantiates the very property it predicates."[9] Which property is that? Presumably, j(6), on Spicer's current conception, is supposed to instantiate the property it predicates of the judger: thinking that water is a liquid. This cannot be, even prima facie, quite right, because the *judging of (6)*, is, unlike the *judger*, not an entity that is *doing something*, such as thinking. However, the idea Spicer seems to have in mind is that j(6), in being self-verifying by instantiation, predicates of itself that it is *a thinking that water is a liquid* and thereby makes itself true.

---

[8] Brueckner 2011.   [9] See Spicer 2011, p. 3.

By contrast, the second way of being self-verifying is captured by the *Two Event Model*:

the process leading to j(6) involves an earlier mental event t(4) [thinking that water is a liquid]. This event is a necessary part of the process of judging (6), and it satisfies the property predicated by (6) [viz., being a thinking that water is wet]. Hence necessarily, whenever on judges (6), one judges truly.[10]

Spicer holds that of these two models, "only the second ... is viable." Spicer holds that the Argument from Truth Conditions was *only* meant to show that the *first* model of self-verification (self-verification by instantiation) is untenable.[11] But this does not come through clearly in "On Always Being Right (about What One is Thinking)." For example, the conclusion of ATCO in that paper is

VI (6) is not self-verifying

and Spicer declares that "if sound, this argument shows that Burge's thesis is false" (where that thesis is "judgments that constitute subjects' knowledge of their own thoughts ... are self-verifying").[12]

Clearly, though, Spicer's beef is with self-verification by instantiation (the "first model"). This means that both the original ATCO and the new version ATC1 have misstated their conclusions. ATCO's conclusion VI should read '(6) is not self-verifying *by instantiation*'; ATC1's conclusion should read 'j(6) does not make (6) true *in the way in which a judgment that is self-verifying by instantiation would make (6) true*'. Unfortunately, neither conclusion follows from the corresponding premises.

It would seem that in order to accommodate his views about the Argument from Truth Conditions and the Two Models, Spicer needs to go back to the drawing board. The antecedent of the principle that powers his considered ATC1 says nothing in its antecedent about *how* the two propositional attitudes a(c1) and a(c2) make true the same propositional attitude ascription. On Spicer's view, there are *two* ways in which this double making-true can happen, corresponding to his Two Models. Spicer would need to restrict TCP2 accordingly, so that the emended principle only applies to makings-true that conform to the self-verification by instantiation model. The argument needs to be rewritten in the light of the distinction that Spicer has drawn.

I will conclude by considering Spicer's notion of being self-verifying by instantiation (the *bad* form of self-verification, as opposed to the Two Event Model). First, we might ask: why is the Two Event Model kosher, whereas the self-verification by instantiation model is not? There

---

[10] See ibid., pp. 3–4.   [11] See ibid., pp. 1, 10.   [12] See Spicer 2009, pp. 144, 138.

is no readily obvious answer except that (the suspect) TCP2 applies to the latter but not to the former. Second, what is the connection between (i) a judgment's instantiating the very property it predicates of something, and (ii) the judgment's being guaranteed to be true? This alleged connection is not discussed by Burge, just by Spicer. To see a problem for the alleged connection between (i) and (ii), consider the judgment

j*(for all j [F(j)])

This is the judgment that all judgments are false. Judgment j* instantiates the property it predicates of all judgments: being a false judgment. Judgment j* is a false judgment because there are some true judgments. This shows that it is not sufficient for a judgment to be self-*verifying* that it instantiate the property that it predicates of things: j* instantiates the property that it predicates of things and yet is a false judgment.

It seems, then, that we are left with no clear understanding of the alleged connection between (i) and (ii).

Conclusion

In the end, Spicer has not provided an effective critique of Burge on self-verifying judgments.

3 Self-knowledge: the reality of privileged access

Crispin Wright

Paul Snowdon (2012) develops a range of careful and interesting criticisms of ideas about the problem of self-knowledge, and about what I interpreted as the broad contribution to it made by Wittgenstein's later work, that I presented in the Whitehead Lectures at Harvard almost twenty years ago.[1] Snowdon questions whether Wittgenstein's characteristic focus upon the *linguistic expressions* of self-knowledge holds out any real prospect of philosophical progress, and charges that my discussion is guilty in any case of distortion and oversimplification of the 'data', whether conceived as linguistic or otherwise, that set the problem of self-knowledge in the first place. In this chapter, I take the opportunity to respond.

1

Although some philosophers have preferred to think otherwise,[2] it is not philosophy but part of the ordinary folk notion of the mental, enshrined in literature and drama, that each of us stands in a special relationship, denied to others, to our own mental lives – that a significant range of our mental states and attributes are directly available to us and only indirectly available to others, that "You cannot really know what another is thinking," for instance, whereas of one's own occurrent thoughts one cannot but be aware. This special relationship seems to embrace each of sensation, mood, emotion, belief, desire, fear, intention, action (what I am doing), memory (what I am remembering), perception (what I am seeing), thought (what I am thinking), imagination, (idiolectic) meaning ... the list goes on.

Grateful thanks for comments and criticisms to participants at the "Self and Self-Knowledge" conference held at the Institute of Philosophy in London in 2008, at which a prototype of this material was presented, to members of the pilot project on self-knowledge that ran at the Northern Institute of Philosophy from 2009 to 2012, to Sandy Goldberg, and especially to Paul Snowdon.

[1] The lectures, entitled "The Problem of Self-Knowledge," were delivered at Harvard University in the spring of 1996. Since they were first published as chapters 10 and 11 of Wright 2001, I shall so refer to them throughout.
[2] See for example the introductory remarks in McDowell 1991.

Since the furore provoked by Michael McKinsey's 1991, it has often, though not always, been accepted that this *privileged access* we seem to have to our mental states – specifically, our privileged access to a wide class of our *attitudinal* states – collides with the forms of externalism about mental content championed by Burge, Putnam and others,[3] whose acceptance has recently become something like orthodoxy. It is notable, though, that the case for collision – the "McKinsey Paradox" – exploits only a very spare conception of privileged access: merely, that someone can know 'in the armchair' that they, for example, believe a proposition whose content is externally determined by matters like the nature of their physical environment or the history and practices of their speech community, yet know this by means involving no investigation of such matters. That we have privileged access to a wide class of our attitudinal states according to so spare a conception of privileged access may seem ungainsayable. So it is understandable that much of the literature has focused on the externalist component in the resulting aporia.[4] I myself am one of those who are unpersuaded that there is actually any collision in the first place.[5] However I do believe, as Snowdon's discussion indeed brings out, that a more extended and attentive investigation of the other putative component – the nature and extent of privileged access – is long overdue.

As an initial approximation, and setting aside certain differences occasioned by the types of mental attribute concerned, privileged access seems to involve three separable features. First, much of the knowledge we possess of our own mental states is seemingly *immediate*: we do not in general, in coming to knowledge of our own psychological attributes, need to rely on the kind of evidence – what they say, how they act, how they look – on which we need to rely in coming to knowledge of others' or on which, *mutatis mutandis*, they have to rely in coming to know of ours. Immediacy here is at least *noninferentiality*; whether it is something more is something that we will need to consider further below. However that may be, immediacy doesn't of itself imply the second feature: that our opinions about our own psychological attributes often carry a distinctive *authority*: that selves not only know differently to others, as follows from immediacy, but also generally know *better*. And the third feature – *salience* – reverses the direction of fit: selves tend to know what there is to know – selves' mental attributes do not, in general, elude their awareness.

---

[3] The *loci classici* are Putnam 1975 and Burge 1979.
[4] An excellent overview of the debate is provided in Ted Parent's article "Externalism and Self-Knowledge," *The Stanford Encyclopaedia of Philosophy*, http://plato.stanford.edu/entries/self-knowledge-externalism/
[5] My most recent thoughts about this are in Wright 2011. I won't go further into the issue here.

These generalizations are, as I say, an initial approximation. Yet granting that they are even approximately true, and that privileged access, so outlined, is not chimerical, they set a philosophical challenge: to give an account of the self–other asymmetries that they characterize – to explain their source, or ground. Of course it is not transparent what a distinctively *philosophical* explanation should here accomplish. There is, however, a venerable – but deeply problematic – response to the prima facie asymmetries that springs to mind so naturally that it can seem constitutive of the subject matter. This is the idea, associated (perhaps erroneously) by much modern thought with Descartes, that each one's mental life constitutes a totally transparent *inner theatre*, with an audience, necessarily, of one. Others will thus need indirect evidence to suppose that something is happening on your inner stage, but you can just observe it. So of course you know best. And since there is total transparency, you will observe what is there to be observed.

The venerable idea is, of course, deeply problematic for several familiar reasons. To begin with, the appeal to a kind of inner observation involves some degree of distortion of the phenomenology of certain of the attributes concerned – for example, when you recognize that you believe something, there need be no distinctive state of consciousness involved, as there is with, say, a toothache or an itch. But more theoretically, the model plays a villain's part in generating the other minds problem. And its very coherence is put in serious question by the concerns about 'private language' – really, private conceptualization – originated by Wittgenstein in the *Philosophical Investigations*.

The cardinal philosophical problem of self-knowledge, as conceived in the modern debates, has been to do better than the venerable response: to achieve a satisfactory perspective on what is correct about the idea of privileged access – what is special about a subject's self-impressions – which can head off the aporia of what (for convenience) we may call *Cartesianism*, while at the same time finding a place for (perhaps refined versions of) the seemingly undeniable asymmetries that motivate the venerable notion.

2

The trio of *immediacy, authority*, and *salience* allow of two quite different directions of interpretation. On the one hand, each of the three can, obviously, be viewed as a feature of the *cognitive relationship* in which a subject stands to her own mental attributes. On the other hand, and perhaps less obviously, they can be viewed as primarily *features of the discourse* in which we speak of our own and others' mental attributes.

Following Ryle's example in *The Concept of Mind*, I shall use the term 'avowal' to denote the kind of psychological self-ascription whose properties suggest privileged access. Since Ryle – and Wittgenstein – wrote, one tendency of analytical philosophical discussion of psychological self-knowledge has been to focus on its linguistic expression and on the first-person–third-person asymmetries as reflected in characteristics of the competent use of avowals and the competent ascription of mental states to others. So conceived, as a phenomenon of psychological discourse, immediacy will have to do, for example, with the inappropriateness of requesting grounds for a subject's avowals, authority with the propriety of deference to what she has to avow, and salience will be located in the inappropriateness of professions of ignorance of one's own avowable states. And these points – no doubt needing refinement to accommodate details of context and variations in the kinds of mental attribute concerned – are, when viewed from the standpoint of the 'linguistic turn', points not about epistemology but about the 'language-game', about our practices of ordinary psychological ascription.

So the would-be theorist of self-knowledge confronts a fork. What comes first here in the order of explanation: the linguistic practice, or the thoughts of the thinkers manifested in that practice? The problem of self-knowledge will look very different depending on how we choose. On the first option, we will tend to think of matters very much as recent writers such as Bar-On and Finkelstein[6] have continued to do, as centred upon explaining the distinctive marks of avowals. Our problem will be viewed as that of accounting for the "grammar" of avowals, in the respects in which it contrasts with that of the competent other-ascription of mental states; and a range of candidate explanations will then enter the fray, for instance those falling under the broad rubric of *Expressivism*, which are otherwise excluded. On the latter option, by contrast, the relevant features of avowals will, from the outset, be seen as reflections of aspects of the *epistemic character* of the self-directed thoughts they express. And it will seem overwhelmingly natural to suppose just what pre-philosophically we naturally do suppose: that selves characteristically know of the states that give rise to avowals in a way that involves no inference from independent reasons, and which is characteristically very secure; and that the states of the relevant kind are typically salient to their subjects. The problem will then be to account for these apparent epistemic advantages in a way that guards against a slide into Cartesian privacy and its associated nemeses.

---

[6] Bar-On 2004 and Finkelstein 2003.

3

So much for stage setting. Snowdon's principal critical contentions are, in summary, the following three.

First, he is skeptical about the linguistic turn in the modern discussion sponsored by Ryle and Wittgenstein, holding that its value stands unproven and presents "an as yet undecided but very important question." Indeed, his discussion reads, more strongly, as arguing that the Wittgensteinian focus upon language is a misdirection, and that we should consider features of psychological self-knowledge, or features of beliefs about one's own psychological attributes, in their own right rather than concentrate on aspects of the discourse in which such knowledge and beliefs are apparently expressed.

Second, Snowdon makes complications for the taxonomy of avowals that informed my earlier treatment – the broad division between what I termed *phenomenal* avowals (typified by "I have a headache" and "There is a ringing in my ears") and *attitudinal* avowals (typified by "I believe that my printer is ready" and "I fear he may not have survived"). I think there is justice in his criticisms here and will have more to say below about how better we might organize the 'data'.

Third, Snowdon argues that, when interpreted as being on the linguistic side of the fork – that is, as properties of competent practice in the language game of self- and other- psychological ascription – immediacy, authority, and salience do in any case not in fact hold good and involve confusions. Moreover, he continues, even after we correct for this and revert to more purely epistemic construals of the trio, they still emerge as incorrect and/or needing qualification.

I will elaborate on and assess these contentions in turn.

4

The term 'avowal', employed with the sense, roughly, of: authoritative, noninferential psychological self-ascription, is used as if familiar in *The Concept of Mind*, and was evidently a term of art in debates in the philosophy of mind for some time before that work. Now, the problems posed by self-knowledge surely can be raised in a fashion that focuses on avowals without begging any important questions. We can ask, for example, why there are no correspondingly authoritative, noninferential psychological *other*-ascriptions, and in posing that question, we leave open what the explanation might be – whether it might be centred on issues in epistemology and on the cognitive relationship that thinkers bear to their own mental states, or whether we might rather here have to do with an aspect of our linguistic practice that is, say, primitive and fundamental. Snowdon, however, is uneasy about the preoccupation with avowals. Why, he wonders, this focus on features of the way in which we *give expression to* self-knowledge – why engage the problem in this way, rather than attend directly to "the phenomenon itself"? In the discussion of mine to which he is responding, it is true that the trio of properties of immediacy, authority, and salience[7] are for the most part all interpreted as characteristics of speech acts – as pertaining to the conditions of propriety and impropriety of certain utterances and of reactions to them. Thus it is said to be inappropriate to question avowals in certain ways, absurd to profess certain kinds of doubt, required that other kinds of doubt assume a certain shape, and so on. Why, other than because in the grip of a certain post-Wittgensteinian dogma about philosophical method, should we engage the issues about self-knowledge by reflection on such normative claims about proper linguistic practice?

Well, I can only speak for myself. The explanation of the prominence of this type of mode of presentation of the data in my own work was less any commitment to a certain Wittgensteinian conception of philosophical method than a desire to bring out the choice point – the fork – noted above. If the explanandum is that selves' opinions about themselves have a certain kind of characteristic immediacy and cognitive supremacy, the only admissible form of explanation is going to seem to be that selves do enjoy some kind of cognitive advantage, of which it then behoves us to give a model, or an account. But if the datum for explanation consists rather in the operation of a range of distinctive asymmetries within and normative constraints on psychological discourse, then although an explanation in terms of cognitive advantage is *by no means thereby ruled out*, the possibility of other kinds of explanation – and indeed the 'primitivist' suggestion, which I take to be Wittgenstein's, that there is in the end no explanation to give – becomes salient. Snowdon is quite right when he suggests that what I take to be Wittgenstein's proposal – that the relevant features of avowals may be "grammatical" – fits naturally with a preoccupation with speech acts as a starting point, and is much less natural, or relevant-seeming otherwise. So far from skewing the discussion, however, I think that this way of setting it up makes for a much better understanding of Wittgenstein's view than otherwise. That is not to admit that it should in any way predispose one *toward* Wittgenstein's view. All the options remain on the table.

I do think it vital that, in attempting to evaluate Wittgenstein's contribution to these questions, we keep in mind his later explicit

---

[7] There characterized as goundlessness, authority, and transparency.

conception of philosophical problems and philosophical method. His central idea, familiarly, is that philosophical puzzles are driven by misunderstandings of our discourse. In the present case, I take it that the key "misunderstanding" is, as suggested above, that certain superficial analogies between the ways that avowals are made and received and the way that reports of observation are made and received motivate a construction of our epistemic relation to the subject matter of the former on the model of a (variously idealized) version of our epistemic relation to the subject matter of the latter. This provides the shape of a diagnosis about where the Cartesian conception of the mind comes from. It represents it as an artifact of an anyway inappropriate form of theorizing: that of fashioning conceptions of the subject matter of a discourse, and of our relationship to that subject matter, in order to explain and underwrite aspects of its 'grammar'. While it is of course an open issue whether this broad idea is fruitfully deployed in this case, or correct in general, it's crucial to giving it at least a run for its money that one begin at the 'level' of language.

To set the record straight, then: I did not mean, in the Whitehead lectures, to side with Wittgenstein's view of these matters. But I did want to set things up in a way that allows his view to be heard. One can imagine a version of Snowdon's complaint being leveled against the early pioneers of expressivism about ethical discourse: "Why the preoccupation with the way we *talk* morally, why don't we just get on and study the nature of the moral facts and our cognitive relationship to them?" That response would simply render invisible the question that the ethical expressivists wanted to raise, namely whether the "propositional surface"[8] of ethical discourse did not in fact mislead as to the nature of the role and content of that discourse, and whether indeed the whole notion of the "ethical facts" did not incorporate a metaphysical mistake. In the present case, the possibility of mistake that is relevant would be not metaphysical but epistemological. But that possibility will simply not be in view if we start out locked into the assumption that the features of the discourse – the first–third person asymmetries – that strike us as surprising and in need of explanation are to be attributed to special cognitive advantages that selves enjoy in relation to their own mental states. I therefore reject Snowdon's suggestion that the preoccupation with avowals slants the discussion in Wittgenstein's favor. Rather, it merely puts us in position to appreciate what, rightly or wrongly, he may have been driving at.

---

[8] Simon Blackburn's (1993) nice phrase.

Before moving on, let me quickly address one objection Snowdon makes to the 'primitivist' view. Taken at the level of discourse, the three proposed marks of self-knowledge are expressed in terms of inappropriateness, incongruity, absurdity, and so on. Thus, it is inappropriate to request that someone gives her grounds for a self-ascription of pain; incongruous to challenge such a self-ascription in normal circumstances; and absurd that somebody might profess themselves ignorant of whether they had a severe headache or not. Yet these are not, Snowdon correctly observes, the types of parameter of appraisal that are in general characteristic where primitive and constitutive rules of practice are involved. It would not, for example, be somehow *absurd*, or *incongruous*, if the Bishop were to be empowered with different ranges of movement in chess. It would just be a different game. In general, the suggestion would be, when a rule is primitive and groundless, then there will be, just for that reason, no space for any kind of basis or support for it – so that the idea of dropping or modifying it in certain respects should not clash with anything important and thus should involve no attendant absurdity or sense of impropriety. There will be nothing to misrepresent, or compromise.

Although this thought would sustain a more extended discussion that I shall give it here, I very much doubt that there is a telling objection to Wittgenstein's primitivism to be developed along these lines. The objection overlooks that the "rules of grammar" that are part of the Wittgensteinian road map are rules that fix our concepts of what is possible, that determine what *makes sense* to us. It is, for example, or so I would suggest, a good candidate for a Wittgensteinian "rule of grammar" that "knows," at least as normally used, is factive. That factivity of knowledge is not something imposed on us from above, as it were. Factivity is something we built in to our notion of the highest cognitive accomplishment. No doubt there are reasons for that, but at the same time it is readily conceivable that there be communities whose notions of the ways a belief may be in good standing include none that actually requires factivity. Still, although the factivity of "knows" is in this sense a shallow fact, it's still the case that professions of knowledge of what is as a matter of fact false will strike us as absurd, rather than merely breaches of some groundless convention.

5

In Wright (2001) I wrote that

It seems safe to suppose that we must begin by distinguishing two broad classes of avowal. The first group – what I will call *phenomenal avowals* – comprise examples like "I have a headache", "My feet are sore", "I am tired", "I feel elated", "My vision is blurred", "My ears are ringing", "I feel sick" and so on.[9]

And of this group I wrote that

they are *strongly authoritative*. If somebody understands such a claim, and is supposed to make it sincerely about themselves, that's a guarantee of the truth of what they say. A doubt about such a claim has to be a doubt about the sincerity or the understanding of its author. Since we standardly credit any interlocutor, absent evidence to the contrary, with sincerity and understanding, it follows that a subject's actually making such a claim about themselves is a criterion for the correctness of the corresponding third-personal claim made by someone else: my avowal that I am in pain must be accepted by others, on pain of incompetence, as a ground for the belief that I am.[10]

I contrasted phenomenal avowals with *attitudinal avowals*, illustrated by examples like "I believe that term ends on the 27th," "I hope that noise stops soon," "I think that professional philosophers are some of the most fortunate people on earth," "I am frightened of that dog," "I am thinking of my mother," where the states of mind concerned are partially individuated by the propositional content, or intentional direction, which they contain. About this group I remarked, first, that their characteristic linguistic expressions may be, and quite often are, used not to make avowals, properly so regarded, but rather to affirm opinions about oneself arrived at by means broadly coincident with those that others also use to arrive at opinions about oneself – when, in other words, they express the products of exercises in self-interpretation; and second, that even when used as avowals, to express distinctively first-personal self-knowledge, they are at most, in contrast with phenomenal avowals, merely *weakly authoritative*, where weak authority involves that besides insincerity and failures of understanding, a small range of additional categories are open whereby falsehood may be explained, including paradigmatically self-deception, wishful thinking, and the like. My thought was that the presence of these additional categories nevertheless leaves space for a kind of authority, since there is again a standard presumption that subjects are not self-deceived, or thinking wishfully, and so on.

Although this division is no doubt crude, it does at least serve to make the important point that the details of privileged access may vary with the type of psychological state avowed. But Snowdon is – I think justifiably – dissatisfied with it on a number of counts. First, there are cases that do not seem to be comfortably allocated to either category. For example, what about first-person perceptual reports like, "It looks to me

---

[9] Wright 2001, p. 321.   [10] Ibid.

as if there is a ship on the horizon"? Here the avowed state is partially individuated by content, so by the terms of Wright (2001) its avowal should count as attitudinal; but the avowal also reports a characteristic kind of visual experience. So it seems to have a case for being placed both as phenomenal *and* as attitudinal. Then there are avowals of mood like, "I am depressed," or "I am calm," that convey no specific propositional content, or intentional direction, but nor are they comfortably viewed as reporting a distinctive kind of experience or feeling either. And what about avowals of action like, "I am heading home"? That too seems unhappily assimilated either to "My vision is blurred" or "I believe that term ends on the 27th," for it reports neither any distinctive experience or feeling nor a state with a characteristic content or direction upon an object.

It would be pointless to respond by proposing that all avowals should count as phenomenal which are not individuated by intentional content, reserving the remainder as attitudinal. That will classify "It looks to me as if there is a ship on the horizon" as attitudinal, unhappily as before, since it both reports an experience and expresses no particular attitude. And some of the cases that will thereby be classed as attitudinal on the grounds that they involve intentional direction – for instance "I am thinking of my mother" and "I am exasperated by that noise" – may well also express certain distinctive kinds of experience, whereas other attitudinals, like "I expect that noise will stop soon" and "I believe that term ends on the 27th," need not do so. And in any case it may seem theoretically uncomfortable in the first place to adopt a categorization that slides over the difference between content-involvement and object-direction.

Nor is it plausible in general that the avowals which get classified as attitudinal in the terms of Wright (2001) are one and all candidates for expressions of the conclusions of processes of self-interpretation or, relatedly, liable in certain contexts to defeasibility on grounds of self-deception. Perhaps "I am thinking of my mother" might, in some bizarre contexts, fit that bill. But surely not "It seems to me that there is a ship on the horizon" or "I am watching that snake." On the other hand, and conversely, some reports, like "I am ashamed" or "I am elated," which Wright (2001) would classify as phenomenal, might well be arrived at, as it were, third-personally, as conclusions to explain one's behavior ("I realized, with his skilful prompting, that the discomfort I was feeling was actually that of shame."), and may also give expression to self-deception ("You don't really feel any shame. You are merely uncomfortable at having been found out.").

So, although I don't think that in Wright (2001) I was under any illusion that there were important differences *within* examples of the two overarching categories that I there proposed, it is clear that the phenomenal-attitudinal taxonomy needs rethinking. Snowdon's view is that it is unlikely that any successful account of self-knowledge will be indifferent to the distinctions that he notes within the category I originally classified as "attitudinal." I am inclined to agree with that, although I would suggest that the contrast between what we might regard as limiting cases of the two original categories – pure expressions of attitude like, in a typical context, "I believe that water is wet," unmarked by any characteristic phenomenological colour or feeling, on the one hand, and pure expressions of personal experience, like "I have an intense headache" – remains crucial. But what should be made of the complications and cross-cuttings among kinds that Snowdon's discussion reminds us of?

Snowdon is cautious about suggesting any new overall taxonomy.[11] But, dispensing with the notion of avowals, he is happy to characterize as 'phenomenal' those *judgment*s that

concern the way experiences are, irrespective of what they indicate or seem to mean. Thus if you characterize how you feel as being 'as if my leg is bent' you characterize your experience in terms of what it indicates is the case (though without committing yourself to its being that way), whereas if you characterize what you feel as simply a pain or an itch that is not in terms of what the experience indicates or means. I take it therefore that descriptions of your after-images as, for example, blurry or red should count as phenomenal. (Wright's list does not mention such cases.)[12]

---

[11] He does make the tentative suggestion that one epistemologically important distinction is that between self-knowledge of what he calls *experience states* and self-knowledge that is not of such states – with the later encompassing but not exhausted by one's knowledge of one's propositional attitudes. And he suggests, "the reason that this twofold distinction seems significant is that self-knowledge of non-experience-states is not in any plausible way to be treated as grounded in or derived from what might be called inner observation or inner-scrutiny" (Snowdon 2012, p. 249). That seems right – and indeed close to the spirit of my original distinction – though it broadens the phenomenal wing to include avowals of experience states whether these are content bearing or intentionally directed or not.

One may well wonder of course what for these purposes is covered by Snowdon's notion of an "experience state." Some readers may feel that they understand well enough the kind of thing that he has in mind: an experience state is one with a distinctive phenomenology, a state such that "there is something that it is like" to be in it. I myself don't think that familiar paraphrastic slogan clarifies very much. (After all, there is something it is like to be a stone – it is to be smallish, grey maybe, composed of igneous material, etc.) But I certainly don't want to maintain that one should be skeptical about the distinction for which it gropes.

[12] Ibid., p. 248.

Snowdon selects this class of judgments as the primary focus of his subsequent critical examination of the alleged marks of privileged access, partly as he says for the not very interesting reason that much post-Wittgensteinian discussion of self-knowledge has inherited Wittgenstein's tendency to scrutiny of examples of this kind in the *Philosophical Investigations* discussion of privacy, but much more interestingly because it

> may further seem that this scrutiny can itself be justified. What has often seemed to be the case to philosophers is that such self knowledge (of the phenomenal) is, in some way, what one might call especially good knowledge. We are particularly well placed to get such knowledge. Now, it is hard not to think that if, on reflection, there is nothing, as one might put it, special at all about so called phenomenal self-knowledge (and belief), then there is going to be nothing special about psychological self-knowledge in general. If that conditional claim is plausible, [it is tempting] to see this sort of phenomenal self-knowledge is a crucial test case.[13]

Snowdon expresses, I think wisely, some caution about the conditional claim. But it remains that his goal appears to be to argue that there is, perhaps, "nothing special," or nothing obviously special, about phenomenal self knowledge (and belief) so characterized. I will turn shortly to the question how well his reflections tend to suport this deflationary tendency.

My own reaction to the complications and cross-cuttings is that an adequate taxonomy of the permissible subject matter of avowals will have to be much more complex than anything yet envisaged. We do seemingly have distinctive first-personal knowledge of what our current experiences are like – our "experience states"[14] – and of our propositional attitudes and their contents. But, as remarked at the start, we also seemingly have such knowledge of what we are currently doing, of how we feel (within parameters of mood and emotion), of what we seem to be perceiving, and of what our thoughts and emotions are intentionally directed upon. These aspects may be multiply present in a given state of mind. That is, any given state of mind may involve some or all of

> A distinctive phenomenology or "raw feel"
> A distinctive content (that P)
> A distinctive attitude (belief, desire, fear, hope . . .)
> A distinctive direction (of the state's being *of*, or *at* so-and-so)
> A distinctive emotional affect

[13] Ibid. [14] See footnote 11.

A sense of agency
A sense of perceptual, or memorial reception
A sense of mental causation

– and perhaps much more. One very striking aspect of the kind of self knowledge in which we are interested – the especially effortless, immediate, reliable, and comprehensive kind (however exactly these features should be characterized) – is that it not merely often embraces these aspects of our mental states but also (though care is needed with this) that it is normally seemingly closed over their adjunction in a single state. Thus I can properly avow, for example, something as complex as that "The intensity of my toothache and the realization how long I had neglected it made me especially apprehensive at the approach of the long unexperienced but nevertheless all too familiar high pitched whine of the drill ... " The prototypical raw feels and the phenomenologically colorless attitudes-cum-contents that motivated my original phenomenal–attitudinal contrast are just two simple, radically contrasted possibilities of combination among this larger range of parameters. The 'data' which a philosophical account of self knowledge is charged to explain are indeed much more complex than is suggested by my earlier discussion. But they are also more complex than is suggested by Snowdon's discussion. Were it indeed to prove that there is "nothing special" about phenomenal self-knowledge, it should be clear that it would still be an egregious *non sequitur* to conclude that there was nothing special about self-knowledge anywhere. A spreading variety of cases need to be reviewed individually and in detail.

So, a philosopher who wants to solve, or dissolve, "the problem of self-knowledge" confronts the following series of tasks. First, one of two cases must be argued for: *either* a case that it is simply an illusion that any of the aspects of our mental states listed above, or any other aspects of them, exhibit anything close to the trio of marks of privileged access distinguished; *or* a case in which all (or some) of the listed aspects of our mental states do indeed (characteristically, or often) fall within the purview of privileged access, perhaps characterized as I have suggested, or perhaps in somewhat other terms – although I do not think we will recognize the problem if it is presented in terms of a notion of privileged access that is too different from what I have proposed. In the latter case, the next task will be carefully to characterize all instances where there is privileged access, what if any local variations in its character are manifest (witness, for example, my own earlier somewhat obtuse contrast between strong and weak authority). And finally, when the 'data' are thus placed in clear view, the task will be *either* to debunk the project of a philosophical explanation of them *or* to offer philosophical insight into *why* privileged access, whether epistemically or linguistically characterized, holds sway over our own mental states but stops short of others': what it is about the subject matter of avowals, or our relationship to that subject matter, or their broad function in our rational economy, or their semantic or pragmatic function, or ... (and here I show that, to me at least, it is uncertain what are the admissible categories of distinctively *philosophical* explanation that one might invoke to serve this project) – what it is that, once brought to our attention, serves to make sense of privileged access without unacceptable additional philosophical costs.

I do not think that anything that philosophy has so far achieved comes anywhere near to a satisfactory accomplishment of this project.

6

Let us restrict our attention from this point forward to avowals of pure experiential phenomenology, as it were – those expressive of Snowdon's category of phenomenal judgment, typified by the self-ascription of pains, itches, after-images, and so on, and encompassing just characteristics of felt experience dissociated from any form of content or intentional direction[15] – and turn to Snowdon's detailed challenges to the broad, three-element account of privileged access that informed my earlier discussions. The three elements, once again, specialized to this class of avowals, were these:

> *Immediacy* I wrote that "The demand that somebody produces reasons or corroborating evidence for such a claim about themselves – 'How can you tell?' – is always inappropriate."[16]
> *Strong authority* "A doubt about such a claim has to be a doubt about the sincerity or the understanding of its author."[17]
> *Salience* "Where P is an avowal of the type concerned, there is typically something absurd about a profession of the form, 'I don't know whether P'."[18]

Snowdon charges that this class of avowals – I will continue with the terminology of "phenomenal avowals" – are not in fact characterized by these features. Before reviewing his reasons for that claim, let me quickly note a point about its significance.

---

[15] Of course, the claim that there are any such avowals is controversial, and contested for example by Michael Tye. See e.g. Tye 1995.
[16] Wright 2001, p. 321. [17] Ibid. [18] Ibid.

If one's aim is to get the data about self knowledge right, and then either to provide an explanation of them (or to argue convincingly that none is needed, or anyway is going to be forthcoming), then of course it's vital that the features proposed be indeed characteristic of the target phenomena. But there is a Wittgensteinian project nearby for which strict accuracy is not required. That is the project of *diagnosis* of the grip exerted on us by bad pictures of the mind and of our relationship to our mental states. For this diagnostic project, it is necessary in order to explain the attraction of such a bad picture only that avowals prove to have certain *apparent* similarities to statements of some other kind where a certain kind of model of the subject matter, and/or of our cognitive relationship to it, is appropriate enough. That will be enough to explain the attraction of a corresponding picture of the mental. Seduction by such a model does not require that there be an exact or even a close fit between the relevant aspects of the two discourses. It suffices that there be enough of an appearance of fit to lure in unsuspecting ordinary thought and cause it to erect a bad picture based on a spurious analogy. Of course there is a further step, in Wittgenstein's own approach, to the conclusion that no "theory," that is, picture or model of our cognitive relationship to the relevant subject matter, sufficing to explain the distinctive aspects of the discourse, should be sought, or indeed is to be had. Wittgenstein's quietism, however, is not the topic of this chapter.

In Snowdon's view, the three generalizations I suggested about our linguistic practice with phenomenal avowals are hasty and overgeneralized. Perhaps they are acceptable for severe pain and a few other central cases but, he argues, they are hardly assertible straight off without a detailed review of cases. And in fact, he suggests, each seems to be subject to counterexamples when we take a wider look round.

For the case of strong authority, consider the victim of a road accident who has previously taken a substantial quantity of amphetamines. He screams and claims he is in severe pain as the doctor examines him, although the doctor can find no sign of significant physical injury. We might want to say, surely, that his screaming and impression that he is in pain is a product of fear and confusion and intoxication, and in that case we might be inclined to discount what he says without regarding him either as insincere of as guilty of some linguistic misunderstanding. More qualifiedly, we might anyway be inclined to discount his avowals without thereby feeling committed to interpreting him as either insincere or as misunderstanding what he is saying, although venturing no clear alternative explanation, and feeling no need to do so.

As against salience, suppose you are having your eyes tested for the suitability of a new pair of glasses. The optometrist asks you, "Which of these lenses gives a better focus?" You may very possibly not find it easy to say, when basing your judgment just on the phenomenal appearances. Nevertheless there may be a fact of the matter that emerges when, for instance, you attempt to read print in different font sizes using the two lenses. Or consider "My ears are ringing." Is it absurd to express ignorance in the form of the remark, "I do not know whether my ears are ringing or not"? Not at all – perhaps what you are hearing is an effect of the circulation of coolant in the central heating system, or of distant machinery.

Finally on groundlessness/immediacy, Snowdon opines that my discussion confused the inappropriateness of asking for evidence with the inappropriateness of the question, "How do you know?" Indeed, he suggests, to the contrary, that the appropriateness of the latter must go with the very idea of knowledge in the first place. (I will come back to this later.)

7

These observations give pause. However, as noted, Snowdon is in any case unhappy about conducting the examination at the level of discourse about the mind rather than at the level of the mental subject matter itself. His countersuggestion is that insofar as there is any plausibility in ascribing the three listed features to avowals, it is grounded in that of certain conditionals which concern *the beliefs* that avowals express. Thus: if it is inappropriate to ask for the evidence upon which an avowal is based (groundlessness), that can only be because the belief (or knowledge) to which an avowal gives expression is not itself based on evidence. And if a doubt about an avowal must commit one to doubt about (either) the author's sincerity or his understanding of the language (strong authority), that, Snowdon suggests, can only be because when an avowal does give expression to a belief, that belief must be right. (Snowdon terms this *incorrigibility*.) Finally if, where P would express a pure phenomenal avowal, one cannot ever appropriately say "I do not know whether P or not," that can only be because its not possible for P to be the case and the subject not realize it. (Snowdon calls this *self-intimatingness.*)

Snowdon charges, however, that both incorrigibility and self-intimatingness fail even for the beliefs expressed by pure phenomenal avowals. So restricted, self-intimatingness may, as a first approximation, be expressed by the conditional:

> Necessarily, if any purely phenomenal condition C applies to S, then S knows that he/she is in C.

Snowdon quickly observes that this formulation is routinely counter-exemplified by animals, infants, and demented adults, all of whom, we conceive, may be in determinate phenomenal states without the attendance of any appropriate knowledge. He moves to the obvious modification:

> Necessarily, if phenomenal condition C applies to S, and S possesses the relevant concepts, then S will know that C applies to him/her.

But Snowdon finds two general problems even with this. First, he suggests, there are presumably some phenomenal properties whose detection requires implementation of some kind of procedure. Suppose the question is, for example, whether a particular after-image that I am experiencing has twelve spots on it or not. To find that out, I will need to attend to it over a period of time and count up. So surely I can sensibly say when the question is raised but before I count up, "Well, I do not know whether my after-image has twelve spots on it or not." That is an apparent counter-example to self-intimatingness as reformulated.

There is, though, a natural worry about this kind of apparent counter-example. It is that when the answer to a question about an after-image, or any phenomenal state, presents as verifiable only by a process of temporally extended attention, we have to presuppose that we can place independent trust in the *stability* of the image, or state, through the requisite process. What criterion do we have for such stability? If I do attend to the image and count up the spots, what reason can I give for thinking that their number has been invariant through the process of counting? By contrast, there are all kinds of ways one might get reason to think that an external object – say a piece of paper with some number of dots scattered on it – is relevantly stable. Suppose I count up the spots on the after-image twice, getting different results. On what might I justifiably base the conclusion that the image has changed, rather than that I have miscounted, or vice versa?

The point here is not a skeptical one – as if one or the other account might be correct beyond my ken, as it were. Rather, it is that the whole idea of attending to and investigating a phenomenal object over a period of time in effect treats it on the model of an external object presented to attention, akin to a kind of percept. And such a model demands that distinctions make sense which we are not empowered to draw. So while the model does indeed, as Snowdon in effect is observing, put the self-intimatingness of the phenomenal in jeopardy – at least as self-intimatingness is formulated above – it begs a large philosophical question about the nature of introspective awareness and its objects.

Snowdon's second objection to self-intimatingness is less tendentious. Suppose we make

the general naturalistic assumptions that the occurrence of the experience requires a physical realization, and that the occurrence of the extra uptake or recognition does so as well. Now, this second physical occurrence must presumably be causally related to the physical occurrences which constitute the experience itself. Finally, understood this way, the physical causal processes [*sic*] involved in the uptake is such that it need not occur of necessity. In principle, something could happen to stop it occurring. It seems to follow that the knowledge of the experience need not occur. Experiences are not self-intimating.[19]

This thought can seem compelling. But a friend of self-initmatingness might doubt it actually takes us beyond the point already made by the possibility of animal, infant, and demented adult experience. Granted, if self-knowledge, even in purely phenomenal cases, is a genuine cognitive achievement, then it must consist in something over and above the occurrence of the state known, and there will presumably be a causal connection between the occurrence of that state and the attendant knowledge. But we already moved to a complication of the original formulation of self-intimatingness to include the additional condition in the antecedent that the subject possesses the relevant concepts. So where is the sting? Well, what is true, presumably, is that possession of concepts is one thing and *their successful exercise on a particular occasion* is something further – there may be other conditions that frustrate their successful exercise which may obtain alongside the occurrence of the appropriate experiential state. Amphetamine-induced panic, for example, reverting to Snowdon's example, might be such a condition. Surely, indeed, there is a whole range of common-sense possibilities of ignorance here – a simple lack of attention owing to "panic, fear, drug-induced jitteriness," or "an inability to take the thing in accurately owing to being primed to expect something else ... "[20] Indeed, Snowdon suggests, even a case of severe pain need not be self-intimating. If S has a severe pain in his left foot and has the appropriate concepts, must he be aware that he has? What about cases of overload, where S has multiple injuries and complains in the first instance of pain elsewhere. The attendant medic asks him, with one eye on the bruising and swelling on his ankle, "What about your foot?" He replies "That's OK – no, wait, no it isn't OK; in fact its extremely painful." Isn't it natural to say in such a case that the pains felt elsewhere in his body have *distracted* the subject from his painful foot, at least temporarily?

---

[19] Snowdon 2012, p. 257.   [20] Ibid., p. 258.

Well, as before, there is a metaphysical issue here about the stability and persistence of the state. What objection would there be to saying that the effect of the other pains was as an at least partial *anaesthetic* and that the anaesthesia becomes less effective when the subject directs his attention to his foot? Again, there is a worrying indeterminacy.[21] However I think it clear that Snowdon's discussion does bring out that transparency, or in his terms self-intimatingness, formulated as above, is still at best a crude formulation, and stands in need of qualification. The single most important qualification that is suggested – one that perhaps, indeed, corrals all Snowdon's reservations about self-intimatingness – is that, irrespective of subject matter, and whatever difficulties there may be with the idea of a state of that subject matter persisting unchanged, there are certain intrinsic difficulties in the idea that the mere occurrence of a situation can provide a metaphysical guarantee of an appropriate judgment about it in any subject, however advantageously he or she may be placed. The point is obvious enough if we reflect on the situation of perceptual judgment made under unimprovable external conditions by a thinker whose sense organs are functioning impeccably. There must still be scope for the possibility that no such appropriate judgment is made, simply because some additional condition obstructs the exercise of the appropriate conceptual and judgmental capacities. Snowdon's catalogue of possibilities – distraction, panic, fear, drug-induced jitteriness, and so on – are all cases where such an interference with judgmental capacity operates. Surely this point must hold both for the perceptible *and* the phenomenal, so long as the latter is conceived as a potential object of genuine knowledgeable judgment at all.

How far away, though, from the idea that "there is something special" about phenomenal self-knowledge does the concession take us? Maybe it's impossible to circumscribe all such possibilities in a finite formulation and write it into a complication of the self-intimatingness conditional above in such a way as to ensure a conceptually necessary truth. But something like the following may yet be a schematic approximation to such a truth:

> Necessarily, if phenomenal condition C applies to S and S possesses the relevant concepts and is in no condition that would impair their exercise in judgment, then S will know that C applies to him/her.

---

[21] Snowdon (ibid.) brings another more theoretical doubt to bear: the suggestion that occurrences of a phenomenal state might, in a suitably (temporarily) impaired subject, fail to trigger any application of "the self concept" – so that he might not be moved by such an occurrence to make a judgment that he himself is in pain, even though possessed with the concept of himself and that of pain. (A classic fictional case is that of Mrs. Gradgrind in Charles Dickens's *Hard Times*.)

This formulation is, to be sure, bland and nonspecific. But it's not trivial. It is failed, for example, by all judgments of the obtaining of nonphenomenal conditions based on perception and memory. It is also failed by judgments of all kinds involving inferential processing and judgmental skills going well beyond those involved in normal possession of the relevant concepts. It is of interest to consider for what range of psychological conditions an analogue might hold good. But, at least for phenomenal states whose appraisal does not require extended attention, it impresses as true.

8

Snowdon formulates *incorrigibility* like this:

Necessarily, if S believes that he/she is in C, then S is in C.

Some of the objections that he runs against this principle are in effect reapplications of points made in connection with self-intimatingness. But there are some differences too. Snowdon observes that if enough is at stake, we may want to revisit certain self-ascriptions of sensation. A good example is given by C. B. Martin's medical diagnosis case:

> Imagine you are having troubling pains in your stomach. The doctor after an examination says, "It is one of two complaints. There is a test to determine which. I shall apply pressure to a region and it will cause pain in two areas – one left and one right – and which ever hurts most tells us what the problem is." He then applies the pressure and you judge that the left area hurts most. The doctor then says, "Oh dear, that means that you have a very serious condition, requiring drastic treatment. If it had been the right side then it would have been minor." Confronted with this, do you say, "Since my judgement is incorrigible go ahead with the drastic treatment." Or might you say, "Do you mind if we repeat the test? Maybe I was a little bit hasty – I would like to make sure and check things." The final claim is that we would indeed opt for the second response, and not the first. We would not view anyone doing so as overlooking some basic principle that we cannot make mistakes in these sorts of judgements.[22]

Actually the last claim is doubtful in full generality. Suppose we change the example slightly and make the question at issue not which of two concurrent sensations is the more painful but whether, for example, a single sensation is experienced on the left of the abdomen rather than on the right. You *might* still want to run the test again, but you would probably do so with a sense of irrationality and a sinking feeling, in tension with the idea that you would merely be checking whether the original

---

[22] Ibid., p. 259.

judgment might simply have been mistaken. So the crucial feature implicitly claimed for the original example – that it would not be irrational to run the test again – is trading on a tacit understanding that the relevant description of the sensation may be one whose application might *anyway* occasion some difficulty, even in less emotionally fraught circumstances. But neither incorrigibility nor self-intimatingness precludes the possibility that the phenomenal should allow for vagueness and 'hard cases'. And there is in any case a question whether, if the patient does run the test a second time, and wishes to return a different verdict, that is necessarily evidence that the first assessment was mistaken. Would not such a test anyway be likely to be formulated in terms of a dependable *regularity* of judgment?

Snowdon repeats, under the heading of incorrigibility, his points about cases where some extended investigative procedure is required, and about the range of common-sense possibilities – panic, influence by drugs, and so on – that disrupt judgment. "Suppose," he writes, "that someone is extremely frightened and nervous at the prospect of torture by having acid dropped on their skin, and to the accompaniment of misleading noises, etc., is very suddenly doused in water. It is highly likely they will be under the impression initially that the acid torture had started, and along with it the horrible pain." Well, yes indeed. But the point this makes is only, as before, that a robust formulation of incorrigibility, if such a thing is possible, would have to exclude conditions where the subjects capacity for judgment is, for whatever reason, seriously impaired.

Snowdon also brings up the experiments at Harvard where people thought they were experiencing visual images when in fact they were seeing patterns projected on to a wall. The example stands comparison with the ringing-in-the-ears case mentioned earlier. But I think it is fair to say that these cases should be dismissed as irrelevant. A genuinely phenomenal judgment should not be interpreted so as to exclude a real external percept; it should be neutral on that. The interpretation of "My ears are ringing" so as to be defeasible by the discovery that actually one is hearing an external sound violates that principle.

So the moral, I suggest, is much as it was for the discussion of self-intimatingness. Snowdon's formulations of both principles are indeed put in difficulty by the considerations that he advances. But the right conclusion is not that the incorrigibility and self-intimatingness of phenomenal judgment are quite misguided contentions, but that they have been too crudely formulated. The conditions for success for phenomenal judgment, like the conditions for judgment in general, have to incorporate provisos to ensure that the subject is not in some way temporarily disabled from exercising his judgmental competences. All the states of the subject, and types of external circumstance that Snowdon marshals to make trouble for his formulations of the two principles, are such that their obtaining would pose obstacles to a subject's exercise of *any* judgmental competence, about any subject matter.

It may be replied that that is the whole point: that Snowdon is after all trying to support the contention that there is nothing special about self knowledge – no special security, either in the direction of self-intimatingness or in the direction of incorrigibility applies. But to establish that of course requires more: it requires argument that there are no *other* conditions which, while their obtaining may impair judgments about other subject matters, exert no deleterious impact on judgments concerning the phenomenal states of oneself. And that isn't so, not even if we restrict attention to *noninferential* judgments of other kinds. No counterpart of the refined thesis of self-intimatingness, nor of a corresponding refinement of incorrigibility, is remotely plausible when the subject matter of the judgment concerned is taken to be not the subject's phenomenal states but for example states in the past within his memory, or the states of his local perceptible environment.

The explanation of that has to do with the proper understanding of the notion of the immediacy of phenomenal judgment, to which I now turn.

9

There is quite a bit of tidying up to do here, for Snowdon is, I think, quite right that what I have said in earlier work about groundlessness (immediacy) encourages (and betrays) confusion. There are a number of relevant but distinct notions. In Wright (2001), I primarily intended a point of analogy with observational judgments, so that "groundless" did not mean made without support, or "out of the blue," but rather: lacking articulatable, independently appreciable reasons. In this sense, observational judgments are groundless too. It is true that, if charged to supply grounds for my thinking that my screen saver just clicked on, I may reply, "I saw it do so." But that is not to offer grounds for my judgment so much as to explain why, as I think, I do not need to. To claim perceptual awareness that P is not to give one's reasons for believing P. That I take myself to be perceptually aware that P is not the reason why I believe it. Rather, that my experience is shaped as of P's being so leads me both to believe that P and to believe that I am perceptually aware that P.

Still, though both may be groundless in this sense, there is a crucial difference between the phenomenal and perceptual cases. When P is a

Self-knowledge: the reality of privileged access 71

perceptual judgment, I could normally have had, and may actually have, *other* types of ground – indirect evidence, testimony, memory, and so on – for the same judgment. And in a case where I am perceptually unaware that P, I might *only* have such indirect grounds. But if P is a phenomenal judgment, there seems to be no sense in the idea of being in a position where I could rely only on such auxiliary grounds – if I were in such a position, they would be auxiliary grounds for something false. There is nothing for them to do if the very basis in awareness for the truth of P itself, viz., the relevant phenomenal state, is missing.

Thus, while it would be a perfectly respectable terminological proposal to identify the 'immediacy' (or 'groundlessness') of a judgment with its noninferentiality, or (not exactly the same thing) with its not being based on reasons – so that observational judgments, and phenomenal judgments, would be alike immediate (at least if we take it that the basis for observational judgment is not inferential) – there is a deeper difference, and a perhaps more worthwhile sense of 'immediate', to distinguish the two kinds of judgment. The reason why the idea of reliance purely upon indirect grounds – of the sort on which others have to rely – for one's being in a certain phenomenal state is absurd, is because there is, crudely, no faculty of apprehension that mediates one's awareness of one's phenomenal states as sense perception mediates one's awareness of the disposition of objects around one, or memory mediates one's awareness of one's own past. There is no mode of awareness that gives one *access* to one's phenomenal states as sense perception, and memory, give one to access to the disposition of material objects and one's past. Rather phenomenal states *are* states of awareness.

This contrasts in turn with a third possible sense of 'immediate', in accordance with which a mental state would count as immediately available to a subject only when lacking in any distinctive phenomenology, any distinctive "what it is like to be in it." In this sense, one's awareness of an occurrent belief might be unmediated by any distinctive state of consciousness and in this respect would contrast with one's awareness of a headache, or a ringing in one's ears. But I will not further pursue this third notion here.

How do any of these distinctions impact on the propriety of my earlier gloss on immediacy, rejected by Snowdon, that "the question, how do you know, makes no sense"? In Snowdon's view, if there really is such a thing as knowledgeable phenomenal judgment, then there has to be such a thing as *the way one knows*. Naturalistically viewed, knowledge always comes to one somehow, so there must be an answer to the "how" question. And he is surely right that there is no commitment to thinking that just because there is an answer to this question, a subject who possesses the knowledge must be in a position to provide the answer. Still, if knowledge does indeed require that there be a correct answer to the question "How do you know?", then there is an issue whether someone who has no inkling of what that answer might be is after all in position to *claim* knowledge in the appropriate circumstances. And surely we are, when in pain, in position to claim to know that we are. So we have a puzzle.

What is available by way of a plausible answer to the question, how someone might know that they are in pain? Snowdon himself rejects two bad-seeming answers. The first is that "You know you are in pain by feeling the pain." That seems bad because being in pain *is* feeling the pain and "You know you are in pain by being in pain" doesn't seem terribly good; after all, we wanted to clarify *the connection* – we wanted to explain how the subject, as it were, keeps track of the pain. Snowdon's second rejected answer is "You know you are in pain by introspection." For what is *introspection*? The etymology suggests some conception of an "inner eye." But, as Snowdon observes, if a creature has pains, it doesn't need any additional quasiperceptual mechanism, if that is what introspection is, to be aware of them.

I think the right answer is the first: that if Snowdon's principle, that where there is knowledge, there must be a "how," is accepted, then the proper answer to the question, "How do you know that you have a headache?", is indeed: by having the headache (and exercising routine judgmental competences). This seems bad only because the corresponding answer in the case of perceptual knowledge – an answer that just cites the (perceptible) fact that P – is obviously bad. In the perceptual case, an account of the "how" needs to say something about the sensory mechanisms that enable one to detect the fact that P. But if the states that provide the objects of phenomenal judgment are already states of awareness, then there is no need for detection. And all that remains to do is to articulate one's states of awareness in judgment.

Immediacy, then, in the second sense canvassed above, whereby noninferential observational judgments still count as mediated rather than immediate, is not at odds with the significance of the question, "How do you know?". I was wrong to suggest that there is any useful sense of groundlessness, or immediacy, associated with the senseless of that question. Rather, what immediacy, so understood, is at odds with is any kind of answer to it that makes a comparison with ordinary inferential or noninferential judgment. When I am in pain, I am able to know that I am precisely because I am in pain and pain states are immediately accessible states.

10

Let me venture some tentative conclusions. First, Snowdon's examples serve as an effective reminder that all judgment draws on certain capacities – of focus, attention, and general cognitive lucidity – that are not assured simply by the possession of relevant concepts, and hence that any satisfactory elucidation of the dependencies that the ideas of authority and salience gesture at will have to incorporate provisos that recognize this. This point does not, however, have any tendency to establish that "there is nothing special about self-knowledge." What is special is that a whole range of *other* factors that, in the case of other kinds of knowledge, and in particular other kinds of noninferential knowledge, can lead to mistakes and ignorance, are inoperative where phenomenal self-knowledge is concerned – and indeed, one might suggest, where any kind of self-knowledge is concerned which may properly generate an avowal. Suitably qualified, and *pace* Snowdon, immediacy, authority, and salience remain as useful headings in terms of which to try to plot the distinctiveness of psychological self-knowledge, and so properly to articulate the problem which it poses.

Second, one prime source of such "other factors" is located in *cognitive interaction* – in the causality involved in perception and memory, for instance, between the state of affairs known about and the knowing subject. Where knowledge depends on such interaction, the needed interactive process may be variously impaired, or even nonexistent. But the immediacy of phenomenal states, their essence as states of awareness, closes out all space for such interaction and, with that, pre-empts all scope for the operation of the kind of other factor that, in cases where cognitive interaction is involved, may be responsible for mismatches between opinion and fact.

Third, that reflection indicates that in the case of phenomenal judgment, authority and salience are *sourced* in immediacy. It is because a subject's awareness of her own phenomenal states is unmediated by any interactive cognitive capacity that her impressions of them stop short of absolute authority only modulo conceptual shortcomings and the other kinds of judgmental failings whose possibility Snowdon emphasizes. And it is for the same reason that although not absolutely salient – not such as to guarantee knowledge whenever they occur – the possibilities for a relevantly conceptually competent subject's phenomenal states to elude her recognition are narrow and strained, and involve factors that tend to call into (temporary) question her fitness for judgment generally.

Others of our mental states and attributes that fall within the scope of avowal, however, are not immediate in the relevant sense: there need be nothing in my consciousness, in the sense in which toothaches, and tickles, and tinnitus, are elements of consciousness, that constitutes the occurrence of an intentional state, or mood, for example. So it follows, fourth, that insofar as authority and salience, or close relatives of them, apply in cases of nonphenomenal self-knowledge, their explanation will not prioritize immediacy as it applies to the phenomenal but will have to proceed along other lines. This observation belongs with what I suspect may be the more general insight that there are very likely to be important local variations among psychological states and attributes in the exact forms in which immediacy, authority, and salience are instantiated, and corresponding variations in their explanation (should they allow of explanation at all).

Finally, for anyone inclined to take the 'linguistic turn' – inclined to suppose that the most illuminating approach to the problem of self-knowledge will indeed involve concentration first and foremost on the language game of self- and other-ascription of psychological properties – we have found no serious cause in Snowdon's discussion for loss of confidence. And the same goes for sympathizers with Wittgenstein's anti-explanatory deflationism. The feasibility of the explanatory project, and the correctness of Wittgenstein's defeatist assessment of it, both remain live possibilities.

4 Contrastive self-knowledge and the McKinsey paradox

Sarah Sawyer

Introduction

According to the traditional account of knowledge, knowledge is a two-place, categorical relation between a subject and a proposition known: Ksp (S knows that p). According to a contrastive account of knowledge, knowledge is a three-place, contrastive relation holding between a subject, a proposition, and a contrast class: Kspq (S knows that p rather than that q). There is reason to believe that knowledge is contrastive.[1] Self-knowledge is a kind of knowledge. This means that there is reason to believe that self-knowledge is contrastive.[2] In this chapter I will argue that understanding self-knowledge as contrastive provides the means to overcome a perceived tension between two otherwise plausible theses: the thesis that we have privileged access to the contents of our own psychological states; and the thesis that our psychological states are anti-individualistically individuated – that they are individuated with essential reference to our environment. The apparent tension arises, in brief, because privileged access to the contents of one's anti-individualistically individuated psychological states appears to provide broadly a priori knowledge of the environmental conditions which serve in part to individuate those states. This strikes most as wildly implausible – how could we have broadly a priori knowledge of our environment? It also seems to provide an implausibly quick response to the external world skeptic. This is the core of the so-called "McKinsey paradox." I will argue that a contrastive account of self-knowledge shows how we can have privileged access to our anti-individualistically individuated psychological states

---

This chapter was written in connection with Project FFI2012-38908-C02-02, "Self-Knowledge, Expression and Transparency," funded by MINECO, a branch of the Spanish government.

[1] See for example Karjalainen and Morton (2003), Schaffer (2004, 2005, 2007, and 2008), Morton and Karjalainen (2008), and Schaffer and Knobe (2012).
[2] See Sawyer (2014) for a defense of the view.

without the unwanted implication that we thereby have broadly a priori knowledge of our environment. Consequently, the perceived tension between privileged access and anti-individualism disappears. Moreover, a contrastive account of self-knowledge clarifies the extent to which we can have privileged access to our anti-individualistically individuated psychological states, and shows why such privileged access cannot provide an easy answer to the external world skeptic.

The structure of the chapter is as follows. In the next section I provide a brief characterization of the thesis of anti-individualism. In the third section I provide a brief characterization of the thesis of privileged access. In the fourth section I explain the apparent tension between the two theses as illustrated by the McKinsey paradox. In the fifth section I set the stage for a contrastive solution to the McKinsey paradox and introduce a contrastive account of self-knowledge. In the final section I show how a contrastive account of self-knowledge can solve the McKinsey paradox. This then provides an understanding of how – and the extent to which – we can have privileged access to our anti-individualistically individuated psychological states, and shows why such privileged access cannot be used to refute external world skepticism.

Anti-individualism

Anti-individualism is the thesis that certain of an individual's nonrepresentational, causal relations to objective properties in her environment are constitutive of her representational mental kinds, and hence of what she can represent in thought. Anti-individualism implies that two individuals who are intrinsic physical duplicates may well instantiate different representational mental kinds – may well have different thoughts – in virtue of being related to different objective properties in their respective environments. This contrasts with individualism, according to which intrinsic physical duplicates necessarily instantiate the very same representational mental kinds – necessarily have the same thoughts – because, according to individualism, the thoughts an individual has are constitutively what they are independently of any relations she has to her particular environment.[3]

Anti-individualism is notoriously supported by Twin Earth thought experiments.[4] These invite reflection on counterfactual scenarios in

---

[3] The dispute between individualists and anti-individualists turns on the question of whether relations to objective properties in one's environment play a constitutive role in determining one's representational mental kinds. It is consistent with both positions that relations to such properties play a causal role.

[4] See Putnam (1973) for the original "Twin Earth" thought experiment as applied to linguistic meaning. See also Kripke (1972/1980). See Burge (1979, 1982, and 1986) for

which an individual's intrinsic physical make-up is hypothesized to remain constant while the wider environment in which she is embedded is hypothesized to differ. According to the anti-individualist, the hypothesized differences in the individual's wider environment would result in corresponding differences in the individual's thoughts. Take the following example. Suppose a subject, Alex, is related in the right kind of nonrepresentational way to silver – she has a silver bracelet, her mother has a silver tray and a silver tankard, and so on. As such, she acquires the concept *silver*, and comes to believe that silver must be polished to prevent it from tarnishing. Now consider a counterfactual scenario in which there is no silver; a counterfactual scenario in which Alex's bracelet and her mother's tray and tankard are not made of silver, but are instead made of a hypothetical lookalike metal which Alex would be unable to distinguish either practically or theoretically from silver. Let's call the lookalike metal in the counterfactual scenario 'twilver'. In the counterfactual scenario, Alex is by hypothesis related in the right kind of nonrepresentational way not to silver, but to twilver – she has a twilver bracelet, her mother has a twilver tray and twilver tankard, and so on. This makes it plausible to think that whereas Alex acquires the concept *silver* and comes to believe that silver must be polished to prevent it from tarnishing, counterfactual Alex acquires the concept *twilver*, and comes to believe that twilver must be polished to prevent it from tarnishing. The difference in representational content between the belief Alex has and the belief Alex would have lies in relations to her wider environment – nonrepresentational relations to silver and twilver respectively.

The example of Alex illustrates the fact that an individual's thoughts can depend constitutively on her relations to natural kind properties in her environment. Other Twin Earth thought experiments illustrate the fact that an individual's thoughts can also depend constitutively on her relations to certain sociolinguistic properties, such as how words are standardly used by members of her linguistic community. I will leave the details of these other Twin Earth thought experiments to one side here for the sake of simplicity.[5] This is because Twin Earth thought experiments of all varieties demonstrate a constitutive dependence of one's thoughts on objective properties in one's environment, and this fact alone suffices both to capture the crucial insight of anti-individualism, and to generate the McKinsey paradox, which is the primary focus of the chapter.

---

three different applications to mental kinds. Putnam (1996) accepts the application to mental kinds.

[5] For a recent taxonomy of different kinds of anti-individualism, see Sawyer (2011). See also note 4.

The Twin Earth thought experiment most often cited in the literature comes from Putnam (1973). In that paper we are introduced to Oscar, an inhabitant of Earth, and his intrinsic physical duplicate, Toscar, who inhabits a planet, Twin Earth, which is exactly the same as Earth except for the fact that the liquid on Twin Earth that occupies the functional role that water does on Earth is not water (H_2O), but a lookalike with a different molecular structure (XYZ). For reasons that parallel the example of Alex, we are invited to conclude that while Oscar possesses the concept *water*, and believes that water is good for quenching thirst, Toscar possesses the concept *twater* and believes that twater is good for quenching thirst. I will draw on this example throughout the chapter simply because of its central role in the literature.[6]

Privileged access

The thesis of privileged access is the thesis that an individual's epistemic access to the contents of her psychological states is privileged relative to the access others have to the contents of those states. In basic terms: an individual knows what she is thinking in a way in which others do not. To illustrate, suppose Jo believes that the bus is late and is worried that she might miss the start of her lecture. To find out what Jo is thinking, others will have to rely on empirical means. They will have to watch her agitated behavior, to notice the frequent glances at her watch and her intent focus on the bend in the road around which the bus ought to be coming, to listen to her quiet mumbling about being late for yet another lecture, and so on. For Jo, in contrast, this kind of dependence on empirical means is unnecessary. Jo already knows, before she glances at her watch and hears her worried voice, that she believes what she does and fears the perceived consequence. Jo knows her own thoughts not empirically, as others do, but nonempirically – or, as I shall say, broadly a priori.[7]

---

[6] As is now widely recognized, the example is problematic because Oscar and Toscar could not be intrinsic physical duplicates if Oscar's body is made up partly of water, while Toscar's body is made up partly of twater. Since the Twin Earth thought experiments are general in their application, this problem is not systemic, and hence I will treat it as inconsequential for the purposes of the chapter.

[7] It is standard in the literature on anti-individualism – as opposed to in the literature on self-knowledge – to classify privileged access as a form of a priori knowledge. It is also standard in the literature on anti-individualism to acknowledge that this classification is not unproblematic. There are clear differences between mathematical and logical knowledge, which provide paradigms of a priori knowledge, and self-knowledge. In addition, some models of self-knowledge specifically liken self-knowledge to a form of empirical knowledge but directed inward rather than outward toward the wider environment. I leave these issues to one side here, since they do not affect the force of my argument. By "broadly a priori"

The claim that we have privileged access to the contents of our psychological states is consistent both with our sometimes being wrong about what we think, and with the claim that sometimes others are better placed than we are to determine what we think. The core of the thesis is simply that in many cases, an individual knows what she is thinking in a broadly a priori way.

The McKinsey paradox

There is good reason to think, first, that our psychological states are anti-individualistically individuated, and second, that we have privileged access to their contents. However, it has been argued that if an individual's psychological states were to depend constitutively on relations to objective properties in her environment, this would preclude the very possibility of her having privileged access to the contents of those states. The apparent inconsistency between anti-individualism and privileged access comes out in two ways, which Martin Davies has called 'the achievement problem' and 'the consequence problem' respectively.[8] According to the achievement problem, if anti-individualism were true, then we could not achieve the kind of privileged access to the contents of our psychological states that we think we have. According to the consequence problem, the hypothesis that we do have privileged access to the contents of our anti-individualistically individuated psychological states apparently has the prima facie absurd consequence that we can have broadly a priori knowledge of the environmental conditions which serve in part to individuate those states. In what follows I will set aside the achievement problem[9] and concentrate exclusively on the consequence problem – also known as the McKinsey paradox, after the introduction of the perceived problem into the literature by Michael McKinsey.[10]

The McKinsey paradox brings to the fore an apparent inconsistency between three theses, each of which appears to be true. These theses are as follows:

I simply mean "without recourse to empirical investigation of the individual's environment."

[8] See Davies (1998).
[9] My reasons for setting aside the achievement problem here are twofold: first, not doing so would take us beyond the scope of the chapter; and second, I think the achievement problem has been adequately resolved. See for example Burge (1988) and Heil (1988). See also Sawyer (2002). Of course, an understanding of self-knowledge as contrastive might provide a somewhat different perspective on the resolution, but I don't think it would alter the general spirit of it.
[10] See McKinsey (1991).

(T1) An individual has privileged access to, and hence broadly a priori knowledge of, the contents of her own psychological states.
(T2) The contents of an individual's psychological states depend essentially on relations between her and objective properties in her environment.
(T3) An individual cannot have broadly a priori knowledge of objective properties in her environment.

The apparent inconsistency between these theses can be illustrated by means of an example. Suppose I reflect both on my thoughts and also on the thesis of anti-individualism, then I can reason as follows:

(W1) I am thinking that water quenches thirst.
(W2) If I am thinking that water quenches thirst, then I am related to water (either directly or indirectly).[11]

Therefore:

(W3) I am related to water (either directly or indirectly).

I can know (W1) broadly a priori because this is an unproblematic case in which I have privileged access to the content of my thought. This is an implication of (T1). I can know (W2) broadly a priori because the fact that psychological states depend for their individuation on objective properties in one's environment is a philosophical thesis. This is an implication of the broadly a priori status of T2. But (W3) follows directly from (W1) and (W2). Consequently, it appears that I can have broadly a priori knowledge of (W3), and hence broadly a priori knowledge of an objective property in my environment. This contradicts (T3).

The McKinsey paradox has generated a significant body of literature. For present purposes I set aside responses which reject either (T1), the thesis of privileged access, or (T2), the thesis of anti-individualism.[12] Since the primary aim here is to show how we can have privileged access to our anti-individualistically individuated psychological states, responses that reject either (T1) or (T2) are not to the point. But the primary aim of the chapter is not merely to show how we can have

---

[11] I would be related to it directly if I had interacted with it myself; I would be related to it indirectly if I had not interacted with it myself but there was a chain of communication connecting me to someone who had interacted with it directly.
[12] I do not know of anyone who explicitly rejects (T1). Segal (2000) provides a clear rejection of (T2), partly, although by no means entirely, on the grounds that it is inconsistent with (T1).

privileged access to our anti-individualistically individuated psychological states, but to do so without the unwanted implication that we thereby have broadly a priori knowledge of our environment. Given this, I also set aside responses which reject (T3).[13]

My focus, then, will be on responses that aim to preserve the truth of all three theses – (T1), (T2), and (T3). Such responses fall into three broad camps. According to the first, knowledge is not closed under known logical entailment, and hence, applying this in the context of the McKinsey paradox, broadly a priori knowledge of (W1) and (W2) does not imply broadly a priori knowledge of (W3). According to the second, although knowledge is closed under known logical entailment, the warrant for (W1) and (W2) fails to transmit to (W3), which means that (W3) cannot be known broadly a priori *on the basis of* broadly a priori knowledge of (W1) and (W2). According to the third, broadly a priori knowledge of (W2) is unavailable either because (W2) is false, or because, if true, it cannot be known broadly a priori. Let me offer a few brief remarks about each response in turn.

The first response begins with the claim that knowledge is not closed under known logical entailment.[14] Fred Dretske provides a number of examples which, he maintains, demonstrate the failure of the closure principle. According to Dretske, then: (Zebra) I might know on the basis of my visual experience that there's a zebra in front of me, know that if it's a zebra it's not a cleverly disguised mule, but not know that it's not a cleverly disguised mule; (Wall) I might know on the basis of my visual experience that the wall in front of me is red, know that if it's red then it's not white and cleverly illuminated by red lighting, but not know that it's not white and cleverly illuminated by red lighting; (Hands) I might know on the basis of my visual experience that I have hands, know that if I have hands I'm not a brain-in-a-vat, but not know that I'm not a brain-in-a vat[15]; and so on. If Dretske were right, and the application to the McKinsey paradox were legitimate, then it would follow that broadly a priori knowledge of (W1) and (W2) would not imply broadly a priori knowledge of (W3). This would resolve the McKinsey paradox in such a way as to preserve all of (T1), (T2), and (T3).

There are, however, two concerns with the response. First, it is not clear that the examples really do support the claim that knowledge is not closed under known entailment. Few philosophers have been willing to

---

[13] See Sawyer (1998, 2001 and 2006). See also Warfield (1998).
[14] Dretske rejects the closure principle in his 1970, but see also his 2004. See also Nozick (1981). So far as I know, no one has endorsed the denial of closure specifically as a response to the McKinsey paradox.
[15] The reference in (Hands) is to Moore's proof of an external world. See Moore (1939).

accept the view, and there are other interpretations of the examples which undermine it.[16] Second, the application to the McKinsey paradox is in any case problematic because it involves a shift in application from perceptual knowledge to broadly a priori knowledge. This is problematic because the intuitive appeal behind the original examples trades on the fact that the visual experience that supports the initial claim in each case is inadequate to support the claim which is known to be entailed by it; but because (W1) is known broadly a priori, there is no evidence to cite which might plausibly support (W1) but not (W3). This leaves us with no general explanation for why closure should fail in such a case.[17]

The second response starts from the claim that restricting knowledge by inference does not require us to reject the closure principle. Accordingly, it upholds the closure principle but maintains nonetheless that the warrant for (W1) and (W2) fails to transmit to (W3).[18] The core idea behind transmission failure is that an argument can be valid, and have both warranted premises and a warranted conclusion, and yet the warrant for the conclusion be such that it is not *derived from* the warrant for the premises – which is to say that the premises provide no *first time* warrant for the conclusion. Transmission, then, is a matter of the structural relations between warrants rather than a matter of their availability. The examples that Dretske takes to demonstrate the failure of the closure principle, Martin Davies and Crispin Wright think are best understood in terms of transmission failure. If this were right, and the application to the McKinsey paradox were legitimate, it would follow that (W1) and (W2) would not provide a *first-time* warrant for (W3), and hence that (W3) could not be known broadly a priori *on the basis of* broadly a priori knowledge of (W1) and (W2).

But, again, there are problems.[19] First, the claim that the arguments underlying (Zebra), (Wall), and (Hands) suffer from transmission failure

---

[16] For reasons not to reject closure, see for example Hawthorne (2004).
[17] Two questions arise. First, there is the question of how privileged access to one's own psychological states could yield knowledge if it is not based on evidence. I will not address this question here. Second, there is the question of whether closure might fail not because the evidence that supports a premise is insufficient to support a known consequence of it, but because the known consequence must itself be presupposed in order for the evidence to count as evidence. This way of understanding the issue might provide the basis for an extension from the original, empirical examples to the current, a priori example. The presuppositional status of the conclusion (W3) is addressed in the context of the warrant transmission failure response which I consider next.
[18] See for example Davies (1998, 2000, 2003b, and 2004) and Wright (2000, 2003, and 2011). 'Warrant' is a term of art and different philosophers understand it differently. For my own view, warrant is a positive epistemic property that subsumes both justifications and entitlements. See Burge (1993).
[19] I have argued against the transmission failure response in more depth in Sawyer (2006).

depends upon a controversial assumption about the epistemic relation between perceptual experience and perceptual belief. According to the transmission failure response: in (Zebra), my perceptual experience as of a zebra warrants my belief that there's a zebra in front of me only if I am already warranted in believing it's not a cleverly disguised mule; in (Wall), my perceptual experience as of a red wall warrants my belief that the wall is red only if I am already warranted in believing it's not white and cleverly illuminated by red lighting; in (Hands), my perceptual experience as of hands warrants my belief that I have hands only if I am already warranted in believing I'm not a brain-in-a-vat, and so on. We can agree that perceptual experience warrants perceptual beliefs only if certain background conditions obtain.[20] But the claim that perceptual experience warrants perceptual beliefs only if we are warranted in believing that those background conditions obtain is a much stronger claim, and many philosophers rightly reject it.[21] We can also agree that the warrant that perceptual experience confers on one's perceptual beliefs may be undermined by, for instance, doubts about the honesty of the zoo, doubts about the lighting conditions, doubts about the external world, and so on; but in the absence of such doubts, no prior positive warrant is needed for one's perceptual experience to warrant one's perceptual beliefs. It may be that the beliefs which must be warranted in order for perceptual experience to warrant perceptual beliefs are more general in character than the examples just given suggest – that in (Zebra) one must already be warranted in believing that you're not subject to an elaborate hoax, that in (Wall) one must already be warranted in believing that the lighting conditions are normal, and that in (Hands) one must already be warranted in believing that there is an external world. But the basic worry remains. If this is right, then the examples cannot be understood in terms of transmission failure. The second problem with the transmission failure response is that it is committed to the closure principle and hence committed to the claim that if (W1) and (W2) are known a priori, then so is (W3). Of course, (W3) is known a priori not on the basis of a priori knowledge of (W1) and (W2), but antecedently; but it is still hard to see how this constitutes a *solution* to the McKinsey paradox. The claim that (W3) is known a priori constitutes a rejection of (T3).

The third response maintains that broadly a priori knowledge of (W2) is unavailable either because (W2) is false, or because, if true, it cannot be

---

[20] Exactly what those background conditions are, of course, is a further question.
[21] See for example Pryor (2000) and Burge (2003).

known broadly a priori.[22] There is an element of truth in this response – there is indeed no straightforward connection between possession of a concept and the existence of entities that fall within its extension. According to the anti-individualist, representation in thought depends on nonrepresentational relations to objective properties in one's wider reality. However, it is clearly possible to possess a concept in the absence of entities to which that concept applies.[23] This is consistent with an anti-individualist understanding of the nature of representation. The anti-individualist claim is simply that there could be no representation in thought without *some* relations to objective properties in one's environment. This line of thought is sometimes backed by the example of the chemist who possesses the concept *water* despite living in a world with no water. If her world contained hydrogen and oxygen, and she possessed concepts of each of these elements, it is suggested, she could come to possess the concept *water* in virtue of theorizing about hydrogen and oxygen combining in the appropriate ratio. The example appears originally in Burge (1982), and has been cited prolifically since, with almost universal assent. But the example is problematic. To my mind, such a theorizer might come to possess the concept H_2O, which represents water, but could not come to possess the concept *water*. The example errs in treating *water* as a reducible concept, which it is not. Water may be identical to H_2O, but *water* is not identical to H_2O. While compound concepts, such as H_2O, can be possessed in the absence of their instances, irreducible concepts cannot. Understood correctly, the example does provide support for the claim that a concept can be possessed by an individual who has had no contact with its instances – either direct or indirect – since the chemist in the example could come to possess the concept H_2O, which is a natural kind concept but one that lacks application in her world. Possession of a fundamental, irreducible concept, in contrast, depends essentially on causal relations to its instances. This means that which statements of relations between an individual's concepts and objective properties in her environment are true will depend on which concepts are the fundamental, irreducible ones – and this is plausibly not something that we could know a priori. I propose to leave this third response to one side for now, and this is for three reasons. First, a contrastive account of self-knowledge provides the means to overcome the McKinsey paradox even if (W2) is knowable broadly a priori. Second, a contrastive account of self-knowledge provides a diagnosis of the

---

[22] See for instance Goldberg (2003), although his reasoning differs slightly from the reasoning offered here.
[23] For further discussion of an anti-individualist treatment of empty concepts, see Sawyer (2003 and 2004).

McKinsey paradox as a part of a general diagnosis that also explains (Zebra), (Wall), and (Hands). Third, the fact that it is possible to possess a concept in the absence of entities to which that concept applies in fact serves to strengthen the contrastivist solution to the McKinsey paradox.

Contrastive self-knowledge

According to the traditional account of knowledge, knowledge is a two-place, categorical relation holding between a subject and a proposition known: Ksp – S knows that p. According to the contrastive account of knowledge, knowledge is a three-place, contrastive relation holding between a subject, a proposition and a contrast class: Kspq – S knows that p rather than that q.[24] It is important to note that the contrast class denoted by 'q' is a set of propositions rather than a single proposition; that the contrast class will typically contain some but not all propositions that contrast with p; and that the set of propositions in the contrast class will therefore typically not be equivalent to ~p.[25]

The contrastive account of knowledge was foreshadowed by Dretske when he wrote: "To know that x is A is to know that x is A within a framework of relevant alternatives, B, C, and D. This set of contrasts, together with the fact that x is A, serves to define what it is that is known when one knows that x is A" (Dretske 1970, p. 1022).[26] This forms part of Dretske's development of the relevant alternatives theory of knowledge. Since the framework of relevant alternatives which, according to Dretske, partly defines what is known will vary depending on the content of what is known, the theory provides a general principle for rejecting closure, and a general understanding of (Zebra), (Wall), and (Hands). According to the relevant alternatives theory, in each case, the framework of relevant alternatives within which the first claim is known is a framework of relevant alternatives within which the claim which is known to be entailed is not known. For example, in (Zebra), the framework of relevant alternatives within which I know that there's a zebra in front of me includes alternatives such as there being an elephant in front of me, there being a giraffe in front of me, there being a pantomime horse

---

[24] For proponents of the view, see note 1.
[25] There will be exceptions. It may be that I know that I exist rather than that I don't. Here, the contrast class relative to which I know the proposition that I exist is identical to the negation of the proposition I know. This is a limiting case: the knowledge is infallible, and hence the proposition known is known in contrast to every other proposition with which it is incompatible.
[26] In fact, much of what Dretske says in his 1970 can be understood as supporting a contrastive account of knowledge. Contrastivism also draws on insights that have been thought to favor a contextualist approach to knowledge. For details, see Schaffer (2004).

in front of me, and so on. Broadly speaking, this is because I can discriminate zebras from elephants, giraffes, pantomime horses, and the like. But, crucially, the framework of relevant alternatives within which I know that there's a zebra in front of me is not one within which I can know that there's not a cleverly disguised mule in front of me, since, again broadly speaking, I cannot discriminate zebras from cleverly disguised mules (at least not on the basis of vision). The theory entails the rejection of the closure principle – from my knowledge that it's a zebra, I can come to know the negation of any of the relevant alternatives which provide the framework for my knowledge – but I cannot come to know any claim that lies outside that framework, even one that I know is entailed by what I know. In Dretske's terms, the epistemic operator 'S knows that' does not penetrate to the contrast consequences of what S knows (Dretske 1970, p. 1017).

But there are reasons to retain closure, and the contrastive account can do so while at the same time accommodating Dretske's crucial insight that knowledge essentially makes reference to sets of contrasts. The difference lies in the role that the sets of contrasts play in the two different theories of knowledge. The relevant alternatives account sees a contrast set as providing a framework against which a single proposition is known – thus retaining the traditional binary account of knowledge. But the contrastive account sees a contrast set not as providing a framework against which a single proposition is known, but as a very part of what is known, thereby replacing the traditional binary account of knowledge with an account of knowledge as a ternary, contrastive relation. The contrastive account of knowledge, then, maintains that each of the statements in (Zebra), (Wall), and (Hands), while true, is elliptical – what look to be statements of a binary relation between a subject and a proposition known, are really elliptical statements of a ternary relation between a subject, a proposition, and a contrast class. Here, then, is the contrastivist understanding of the statements in (Zebra):

(Z1) I know that it's a zebra rather than that it's an elephant, that it's a giraffe, that it's a pantomime horse ...

(Z2) If I know that it's a zebra rather than that it's a cleverly disguised mule, then I know that it's not a cleverly disguised mule rather than that it is one.[27]

---

[27] There is a complication in the formulation here. The original linking statement is a statement of knowledge of a conditional, whereas (Z2) is a statement of a conditional between states of knowledge. Nonetheless, (Z2) states a closure principle as understood in contrastive terms. Similarly, we have (Z2)*. If I know that it's a zebra rather than that it's an elephant, then I know that it's not an elephant rather than that it is one.

(Z3) I don't know that it's not a cleverly disguised mule rather than that it is one.

This allows us to make sense of Dretske's claim that I can know that it's a zebra, know that if it's a zebra then it's not a cleverly disguised mule, and yet not know that it's not a cleverly disguised mule. But it does so without having to give up on closure. This is because what Dretske understands as a failure of the epistemic operator 'S knows that' to penetrate to the contrast consequences of what S knows, the contrastivist accommodates explicitly by the fact that the conditional (Z2), while true, does not connect in the right way to the initial knowledge claim (Z1). To connect in such a way as to allow an inference to be drawn, (Z2) would have to have (Z1) as its antecedent, which, now the proper structure of the sentences has been exposed, we can see clearly not to be the case. An inference from 'I know that it's a zebra rather than that it's an elephant' and 'if I know that it's a zebra rather than that it's a cleverly disguised mule, then I know that it's not a cleverly disguised mule rather than that it is one' to 'I know that it's not a cleverly disguised mule rather than that it is one' is a plainly invalid inference. The examples Dretske takes to illustrate the failure of the closure principle, then, the contrastivist understands simply as invalid inferences which, misled by the surface-level grammatical structure of the statements, we mistakenly think are valid.[28]

The question is whether the same contrastivist strategy can provide a solution to the McKinsey paradox. One clear difference between the cases is this: a correct understanding of (Zebra), (Wall), and (Hands) depends on a contrastive understanding of perceptual knowledge, but the McKinsey paradox arises from considerations not of perceptual knowledge but of broadly a priori knowledge – specifically, it arises from the claim that we have privileged access to the contents of our anti-individualistically individuated psychological states. This means that in order to solve the McKinsey paradox in contrastive terms, what we need is a contrastive account of *self*-knowledge. There is independent reason to think self-knowledge is contrastive, although I will not defend the view explicitly here.[29] Rather, I will outline the view, and then, in the next section, argue that it can indeed be used to solve the McKinsey paradox.

---

[28] Similarly, what Dretske thinks of as consequences to which the epistemic operator 'S knows that' *does* penetrate will be understood as valid inferences by the contrastivist. This preserves the crucial point of closure, namely that knowledge can be extended by known entailment.

[29] See Sawyer (2014), where I also argue for the contrastivity of the propositional attitudes.

The claim that self-knowledge is contrastive entails that the form of self-knowledge is correctly represented as: S knows that she ψs that p rather than that S⋆ Øs that q. Here, S⋆ marks out a contrast in the subject of the first-order attitude, Ø marks out a contrast in the attitude S takes toward the proposition that provides the content of her first-order psychological state, and q marks out a contrast in the proposition to which S takes that attitude. It is important to note that the contrastivity of self-knowledge is properly located not in the *content* of the self-knowledge (which may or may not be contrastive), but in the subject's *state* of self-knowledge. Thus the content of S's state of self-knowledge when she knows that she ψs that p rather than that S⋆ Øs that q is simply: I ψ that p. But when S knows she ψs that p rather than that S⋆ Øs that q, she will be in a state of knowledge that places her in relation not only to the proposition that she ψs that p (the proposition that provides the content of her self-knowledge) but also to a set of contrasting propositions which differ from it along any or all of the three specified dimensions. Since the McKinsey paradox arises as a result of the constitutive relation between the *content* of a subject's psychological state and relations to her environment, in what follows I will focus exclusively on the contrast class marked out by q – the contrast class that concerns the content of a subject's first-order psychological state when she is in a state of self-knowledge. The contrastive account of self-knowledge proposed is, of course, just a specific instance of the more general contrastive account of knowledge: S knows that p rather than that q.

Solving the paradox

We are now in a position to see how a contrastive account of self-knowledge can be used to solve the McKinsey paradox. In order to solve the McKinsey paradox, it will be remembered, we need an explanation of how (T1), (T2), and (T3) are compatible. And the reason this stands in need of explanation is that there are broadly a priori arguments that appear to show that (T1) and (T2) imply the negation of (T3). Let us state such an argument explicitly in terms of knowledge attributions and refer to it as (Water):

(Water1) I know broadly a priori that I am thinking that water quenches thirst.
(Water2) I know broadly a priori that if I am thinking that water quenches thirst, then I am related to water.[30]

---

[30] For ease of exposition, I have dropped the qualifying expression 'either directly or indirectly'.

Therefore:

(Water3) I know broadly a priori that I am related to water.

What is the contrastivist to say? Just as with (Zebra), (Wall), and (Hands), the contrastive account of knowledge maintains that each of the statements in (Water) is elliptical – what look to be statements of a binary relation between a subject and a proposition known, are really elliptical statements of a ternary relation between a subject, a proposition, and a contrast class. The hope, then, is that by understanding self-knowledge as contrastive, and by providing an explicit statement of the contrasts that are typically left implicit, (Water) will be revealed to be an invalid argument with true premises and a false conclusion. We would then have no reason to think (T1), (T2), and (T3) incompatible.

But there is a question as to the correct specification of the relevant contrasts. In (Zebra), (Wall), and (Hands), the relevant contrasts were marked out by what the subject could and could not distinguish. The natural assumption, then, is that the relevant contrasts in (Water) will also be marked out by what the subject can and cannot distinguish. But it is not the subject's ability to distinguish amongst *objects* that needs to be considered here, but her ability to distinguish amongst *concepts*. How might this be understood? Reflection on the Twin Earth thought experiment involving Oscar and Toscar provides us with the following suggestion: perhaps I am able to distinguish the concept *water* from concepts such as *coffee, alcohol, crackers, silver,* and so on, but am unable to distinguish the concept *water* from the concept *twater*. After all, the Twin Earth thought experiment appears to illustrate the possibility of distinct concepts which are phenomenologically indistinguishable – things would seem the same to me whether I had grown up on Earth and possessed the concept *water* or grown up on Twin Earth and possessed the concept *twater*. Perhaps, then, the following argument, which I will henceforth refer to as (Twater), provides an explicit statement of the contrastivist understanding of (Water):[31]

> (Twater1) I know broadly a priori that I am thinking that water quenches thirst rather than that I'm thinking that alcohol quenches thirst, that I'm thinking that coffee quenches thirst, that I'm thinking that crackers quench thirst...

---

[31] For ease of exposition, I will limit the possible contrasts to variations in the 'water'-place, since this is the relevant anti-individualistically individuated concept, but the contrasts would, of course, be much more varied than this simplified account accommodates.

(Twater2) If I know broadly a priori that I am thinking that water quenches thirst rather than that I'm thinking that twater quenches thirst, then I know broadly a priori that I am related to water rather than that I am related to twater.

Therefore:

(Twater3) I know broadly a priori that I am related to water rather than that I'm related to twater.

If (Twater) provides an explicit statement of the contrastivist understanding of (Water), then we have revealed (Water) to be an invalid argument. However, this is insufficient by itself to solve the McKinsey paradox. In order to solve the McKinsey paradox (Water) must be revealed to be an invalid argument with true premises and a false conclusion. And here we see that (Twater) fails to deliver the right result: while (Twater) is invalid, its conclusion is nonetheless true. Here's why.

It may be true that things would seem the same to me whether I had grown up on Earth and possessed the concept *water* or grown up on Twin Earth and possessed the concept *twater* – it may be true, that is, that there are possible concepts which are phenomenologically indistinguishable from my own. But it doesn't follow from this that I cannot in fact distinguish the concept *water* from the concept *twater*. To think so would be to conflate two different perspectives: that of the *subject* of the Twin Earth thought experiment and that of the *theorist*. From the perspective of the subject of the Twin Earth thought experiment, the concept *water* and the concept *twater* are plausibly indistinguishable. But adopting the perspective of the theorist not only makes it possible for me to distinguish the concepts – it depends on my ability to do so. And, crucially, the McKinsey paradox requires me to adopt the perspective of the theorist, because it requires that I understand the Twin Earth thought experiment – it requires that I know that there are constitutive connections between my psychological states and objective properties in my environment. It follows that the McKinsey paradox depends on my ability to distinguish the concept *water* from the concept *twater*, and hence that it cannot be solved by understanding (Water) as (Twater).

The contrastivist needs to identify a concept which I cannot distinguish from the concept *water* even from the perspective of the theorist. Only such a concept could serve as the relevant contrast in the conclusion of (Water), since only such a contrast could make the conclusion of (Water) false. But what could that concept be? In order to answer this question, we need to look not to Twin Earth, but to Dry Earth.[32] Dry Earth is a planet which is exactly the same as Earth except for the fact that there is no liquid that occupies the functional role that water does on Earth – rather, the inhabitants of Dry Earth suffer from a pervasive and collective hallucination as of a watery substance. Just as on Earth I would possess the concept *water*, and on Twin Earth I would possess the concept *twater*, let us say that on Dry Earth I would possess the concept *dwater*.[33] All three concepts are indistinguishable from the perspective of the subject. But, as we have seen, adopting the perspective of the theorist in the Twin Earth thought experiment requires that I be able to distinguish the concept *water* from the concept *twater*. This prevents the contrastivist from using the concept *twater* as the relevant contrast in the conclusion of (Water). It might be thought that Twin Earth and Dry Earth are relevantly analogous, and hence that if the concept *twater* is one that the theorist must be able to distinguish from the concept *water*, then the concept *dwater* must also be one that the theorist must be able to distinguish from the concept *water*. In fact, however, adopting the perspective of the theorist in the Dry Earth thought experiment does *not* require that I be able to distinguish the concept *water* from the concept *dwater* – indeed, distinguishing the concepts remains impossible. As such, the concept *dwater* is exactly the concept the contrastivist needs to identify as providing the contrast in the conclusion of (Water).

Why is there this difference? Despite their superficial similarity, the Twin Earth thought experiment and the Dry Earth thought experiment are fundamentally different. The expressions 'Twin Earth', 'twater', and 'the concept *twater*' should be treated with care. Take the expression 'the concept *twater*', for example. It is not an expression that refers to a single concept – by hypothesis it is an expression that aims to refer to a concept that we do not possess. As such, the expression 'the concept *twater*' functions like a variable expression that ranges over all the concepts that are concepts of kinds that are indistinguishable from the kind that we assume our concept *water* refers to. This is the sense in which the expression has an indexical component. And it is this indexical component that ensures that we can distinguish between our own concept and standard twin concepts from the theorist's perspective. The expressions

---

[32] The example is introduced by Boghossian (1997).
[33] What I say here is consistent both with the claim that inhabitants of Dry Earth would fail to express a concept by their use of the term 'water', and with the claim that inhabitants of Dry Earth would possess a concept that fails to refer. For arguments that favor the second option, see Sawyer (2003 and 2004).

'Twin Earth', 'twater', and 'the concept *twater*' shift reference depending on the context of utterance. This means that I can know a priori that I am not on Twin Earth, *no matter what planet I am actually on*. This is analogous to knowing a priori that I am here and not there, no matter where I actually am. Similarly, I can know a priori that I am not related to twater, *no matter what substance I am actually related to*; and I can know a priori that my term 'water' does not express the concept *twater, no matter what concept my term expresses*.

The Dry Earth thought experiment, in contrast, presents a situation where things seem the same to me even though my term fails to refer to an objective property in my environment. This can be understood, in contrast to the Twin Earth thought experiment, as a standard skeptical scenario. This means that for all I know, I am on Dry Earth; for all I know, my term 'water' does not refer to an objective property in my environment; and for all I know, my term 'water' expresses the concept *dwater* – the concept *water* and the concept *dwater* may well be the very same concept. I cannot distinguish the concept *water* from the concept *dwater* on the basis of perception, because it is consistent with my perceptual experience that any one of my concepts that I take to refer in fact fails to do so, and hence consistent with my perceptual experience that my term 'water' expresses the concept *dwater*. And I cannot distinguish the concepts a priori, because anti-individualism maintains merely that there could be no representation in thought without *some* relations to objective properties in one's environment, and hence doesn't guarantee that any one of my concepts that I take to refer to an objective property in my environment in fact does so.

I propose, then, that the following argument, which I will henceforth refer to as (Dwater), provides an explicit statement of the contrastivist understanding of (Water):

(Dwater1) I know broadly a priori that I am thinking that water quenches thirst rather than that I'm thinking that alcohol quenches thirst, that I'm thinking that coffee quenches thirst, that I'm thinking that crackers quench thirst, that I'm thinking that twater quenches thirst . . .

(Dwater2) I know broadly a priori that if I am thinking that water quenches thirst rather than that I'm thinking that dwater quenches thirst, then I know broadly a priori that I am related to water rather than that my concept fails to refer to an objective property in my environment.

Therefore:

(Dwater3) I know broadly a priori that I am related to water rather than that my concept fails to refer to an objective property in my environment.

(Dwater) is an invalid argument with true premises and a false conclusion, which is exactly what was needed. Since (Dwater) states explicitly the contrastivist understanding of (Water), (Water) is also, according to this contrastivist proposal, an invalid argument with true premises and a false conclusion. Consequently, (Water) cannot be used to show that (T1), (T2), and (T3) are inconsistent. This solves the McKinsey paradox.

An understanding of self-knowledge as contrastive, then, shows how we can have privileged access to our anti-individualistically individuated psychological states without the unwanted implication that we thereby have broadly a priori knowledge of our environment. As such, it provides a solution to the McKinsey paradox. It also clarifies the extent to which we can have privileged access to our anti-individualistically individuated psychological states, and shows why such privileged access cannot be used to refute external world skepticism.[34]

---

[34] The contrastivist solution to the McKinsey paradox presented in this chapter has more in common with the solution I proposed in my 1998, 2002 and 2006 than might at first appear. Particularly in the last of those papers, I stressed that privileged access to one's anti-individualistically individuated psychological states could yield a certain amount of a priori knowledge of one's environment, but that the knowledge would not suffice to defeat the external world skeptic.

Part 2

Content Transparency

5 Further thoughts on the transparency of mental content

Paul Boghossian

Introduction

In this chapter I want to look further at the question of whether thoughts should be held to obey a principle of transparency: roughly, whether it ought to be a constraint on an adequate theory of concepts, the constituents of thoughts, that a thinker is always able to tell introspectively whether her thoughts exercise the same or distinct concepts (this thesis will be formulated with more care in a moment).[1]

I am spurred to this further examination by a recent book by Mark Sainsbury and Michael Tye (hereafter S&T), *Seven Puzzles of Thought* (2012). In that book, the authors present a novel and intriguing picture of concepts according to which concepts are individuated by their *origins*.

As S&T realize, their theory is committed to denying the transparency thesis. However, unlike most theorists who are similarly committed, they don't merely note this consequence; they try to mitigate its seemingly unpalatable consequences. Their discussion provides us with a valuable opportunity for re-examining the topic of transparency and for reassessing the prospects for doing without it.

The transparency thesis

S&T formulate the transparency thesis as follows:

I am grateful to Mark Sainsbury and Michael Tye for very productive and enjoyable exchanges on these topics, and to Gregory Bochner and Kit Fine for helpful comments on an earlier draft of this chapter. Some of the material was presented at a three-part lecture series at the École Normale Supérieure (Institut Jean Nicod), Paris, in May 2012, and then at an Author Meets Critics session at the Pacific APA in March 2013. I am grateful to the members of those audiences and especially to Michael Murez, Laura Schroeter, and Francois Recanati for helpful feedback.

[1] For my previous discussions of this issue, see Boghossian 1992a, 1994, 2011.

(IKCC) When our faculty of introspection is working normally, we can know a priori via introspection with respect to any two present, occurrent thoughts whether they exercise the same or different concepts. (Transparency)[2]

I will accept this formulation for present purposes. IKCC can be broken up into two distinct and independent theses:

(IKCCS) If S's faculty of introspection is working normally, then if S occurrently thinks two thoughts that exercise the *same* concepts, he will be able to know that fact introspectively. (Transparency of Sameness)

(IKCCD) If S's faculty of introspection is working normally, then if S occurrently thinks two thoughts that exercise *distinct* concepts, he will be able to know that fact introspectively. (Transparency of Difference)

What are some theories under which IKCCS is violated?

Millianism offers one well-known example. According to Millianism (at least as I shall understand it for present purposes), the meaning of (or concept expressed by) a proper name just is its reference. On such a view, it is very easy for there to be cases in which a speaker has two names which mean the same but where that fact is introspectively inaccessible to him. Kripke (1979) describes a now famous example. Peter hears the Polish pianist Ignace Paderewski and comes to believe:

(1) Paderewski is a great pianist.

He also goes to a political rally featuring the Polish prime minister Paderewski. Since he believes that no politician could also be a great musician, he believes of the prime minister

(2) Paderewski is not a great pianist.

The two occurrences of 'Paderewski' have the same reference, but clearly Peter is unable, merely introspectively, to know that. On a Millian view, Peter has two occurrent thoughts that exercise the same concept, but is unable to tell purely introspectively that they do.

As Loar (1988) has shown, IKCCS will also be violated by Fregean views of concepts, if those concepts are individuated in the way advocated by externalist views. Take, for example, the sort of social externalism defended by Burge (1979). On such a view, a thinker may be credited

---

[2] Some object to using 'a priori' for knowledge gained introspectively. This issue plays no role in the discussion to follow.

with a concept, even though he radically misunderstands that concept, provided he is disposed to defer to the norms adopted by his community. Paul, having been brought up in a sheltered way by his French nanny, learns the French word for cat, namely, 'chat', but without observing the animals themselves. He learns to assent to

(3) All chats have tails.

Because he defers in his use of 'chat' to the community of competent French speakers, by the terms of social externalism, his use of 'chat' expresses the concept *cat*. Later he visits his English cousins, who have a Manx cat, and so he learns to assent to

(4) Not all cats have tails.

Once again, externalist views of concept individuation have it that a thinker is exercising the same concept twice over but is unable to tell introspectively that he is.

As these cases illustrate, if a thinker were to violate the transparency of sameness,

> (CT) He would be disposed to affirm contradictory thoughts; and he won't be able to recover from this condition on a purely introspective basis.
> (RVI) He would be disposed to refuse to perform inferences that are in fact perfectly valid from a logical point of view, on the grounds that they are logically invalid; and he won't be able to recover from this condition on a purely introspective basis.

What are some theories under which IKCCD is violated?

In his 1988, Burge described the case of a subject, call him "Switched Peter," who has been stealthily switched between Earth and Twin Earth, each time staying long enough to acquire the concepts characteristic of each place – *water* on Earth and *twater* on Twin Earth.

In my 1994, I argued that for a subject like Switched Peter, a thesis of *Cohabitation* will be true: earthly and twearthly concepts will commingle in Peter's psychology, without his being aware of that fact. Peter will have both the *water* concept and the *twater* concept, but he will be unaware that he has two 'water' concepts instead of one. Assuming him to be on Twin Earth, and to put it simplistically for present purposes, the *water* concept will get activated when he is recalling 'water' experiences had while on Earth, whereas the *twater* concept will get activated when he is thinking about his current environment. In such a scenario, Switched Peter would clearly violate the Transparency of Difference.

Cohabitation is by no means uncontroversial. In his interesting 1998, Michael Tye denied that switching would lead to cohabitation of twinned concepts. By contrast, Burge (1998) insists that Cohabitation is true. Both Burge and I have presented arguments in favor of Cohabitation, on externalist assumptions. For present purposes, I will simply assume that Cohabitation is correct.[3]

As these cases illustrate, if a thinker were to violate the transparency of difference:

> (WCT) She would be disposed to think that certain pairs of thoughts are contradictories when they are not; and she would be unable to recover from this condition on a purely introspective basis.
>
> (PII) She would be disposed to perform logically invalid inferences, thinking that they are perfectly valid; and she would be unable to recover from this condition on a purely introspective basis.

For example, Switched Peter might perform an inference that he would express in public language like this:

(Pavarotti)
(1) Whoever floats on water, gets wet
(2) Pavarotti once floated on water
(3) Therefore, Pavarotti once got wet

According to the cohabitationist, though, the actual contents of his inference may well be this:

(Pavarotti)
(1) Whoever floats on twater, gets wet
(2) Pavarotti once floated on water
(3) Therefore, Pavarotti once got wet

However, Peter will not be able to tell introspectively that he is committing a fallacy of equivocation.

Externalist theories of concepts, then, are highly likely to violate both the Transparency of Sameness and the Transparency of Difference. So what? Why is it in any way problematic for a view of concepts that it allows for such violations?

---

[3] It would be a mistake to think that cohabitation of twinned concepts would arise only as a result of extreme science fiction scenarios involving stealthy removal to far-off planets. If a Burge-style social externalism is true, according to which we possess the concepts that are expressed by the experts in our community, regardless of whether the conceptual roles that we associate with our concepts matches theirs, then cohabitation would arise all the time, as we drift back and forth between different communities subscribing to different linguistic norms, without our realizing that we have done so.

The paradox

The problem can be expressed in the form of a paradox: we are simultaneously attracted to three propositions that form an inconsistent triad.

(Logical Rationality, LR) If S is rational, S is able, purely introspectively, to avoid simple contradictions and simple fallacious inferences.

(Illogical Peter, IP) Peter is unable to avoid, purely introspectively, simple contradictions or fallacious inferences in his thinking.

(Rational Peter, RP) Peter is a fully rational agent.

Externalist theories thus face a challenge. They appear to allow cases in which the conjunction of (IP) and (RP) are true. But these are not consistent with (LR). Something has to give, the only question being what. There is no question of living with all three propositions.

I will focus mostly on the case of Switched Peter, referring to (Unswitched) Peter as needed.

Rejecting illogical Peter or rational Peter

As I mentioned above, Tye (1998) argued against a cohabitationist construal of Switched Peter. He maintained that earthly and twearthly concepts won't cohabit in Peter's psychology. With each slow switch, one set of concepts will completely displace the other.

Burge (1998) also argued against (Illogical Peter). Burge did it not by denying Cohabitation but by arguing that the phenomenon of preservative memory, as it operates in reasoning, will ensure that Peter's inferences are free of undetectable equivocations, despite Cohabitation's being true.

Sorensen (1998) and Faria (2009) have suggested that it is (Rational Peter) that has to go. Being rational, they say, just like being moral, can be a matter of luck. And Peter is unlucky.

Rejecting logical rationality – I

The main line defended by S&T, however, is neither of these, but consists rather in arguing that the thesis of (Logical Rationality) is false: avoidance of simple contradictions, and of simple fallacies of equivocation, is not required for rationality. A thinker can be perfectly rational even while holding occurrent contradictory thoughts or while being inclined to engage in occurrent invalid inferences, provided certain conditions are met.

Before looking at S&T's alternative to (LR), let me briefly describe why (LR) has traditionally seemed attractive. Let us start with the question: What are we after when we hanker after a theory of rationality?

One guiding thought has been that we want to distinguish sharply between two different sorts of cognitive failure that someone may suffer from: between merely *lack*ing empirical information about the world, versus *mishandling* the information that one has.

We reserve the word 'irrational' for the second failing; we do not apply it to the first. We want to say that the recently and surreptitiously envatted brain, who is suddenly confronted with a steep loss of accurate information about his actual surroundings, can remain perfectly rational in continuing to believe what he believed previously. Indeed, it would be *ir*rational for this unfortunate person to suddenly come to believe that he is envatted, even if so believing meant that he would now have a much higher proportion of true beliefs. The surreptitiously envatted person who continues believing that he is in a normal environment is handling the information at his disposal in a rational way, correctly from the standpoint of the norms governing the handling of evidence, even though this way of handling the information results, in the circumstances, in a high number of false beliefs.

All of this is intuitive. However, now we may want to know: What, exactly, is it to handle information correctly?

Clearly, we may handle the information at our disposal correctly and yet believe something false. Indeed, it looks as though we could be handling the information at our disposal correctly and yet believe two propositions that are inconsistent with one another, that could not be true together in any possible world. But, then, what is it to handle information correctly? What is the substantive content of that idea?

An important part of a traditionally influential answer is that while a rational person cannot be counted upon to avoid falsehoods or even inconsistencies, she can be counted upon to avoid (occurrent, henceforth I will omit this qualification) thoughts that *logically contradict one another,* and inferences that are *logically invalid.*

For this to make any sense, though, there had better be a sharp distinction between a mere inconsistency and a contradiction. What's the difference supposed to be?[4]

A common description of the distinction is this: Two thoughts are *inconsistent* with one another iff it is metaphysically impossible for

---

[4] Similar remarks apply to the distinction between arguments in which the premises guarantee the conclusion's truth and those that are logically *valid.*

them to be true together. By contrast, two thoughts *contradict* one another if and only if they are inconsistent with one another *and* one consists of *the very same thought* as the other embedded in a concept for negation.

It would be intuitive to illustrate these distinctions with the following examples: (5) and (6) express thoughts that are merely inconsistent with one another:

(5) Water boils at 100 degrees.
(6) H_2O does not boil at 100 degrees.

However, the thoughts expressed by (5) and (7) *contradict* one another:

(7) Water does not boil at 100 degrees.

It's consistent with a thinker's being rational that she believe (5) and (6) together, but not that she believe (5) and (7) together. But this clarification pushes our question further back. Why should the difference between an inconsistency and a contradiction, as so outlined, *matter* from the standpoint of the theory of rationality?

S&T provide the beginnings of an answer when they say (p. 134): "Being contradictory is supposed to be a specially manifest way of being inconsistent." But this understates the point, which is that, if the traditional way of fleshing out the theory of the rational handling of information is to make sense, contradictions have to be not just especially manifest, but *introspectible*, knowable to obtain by mere reflection, without the benefit of further information about the external world. Otherwise, we will need empirical information to discover that our thoughts contradict one another, which would jeopardize the distinction we are after.[5]

So, if we give the traditional account of what distinguishes a mere inconsistency from a logical contradiction, it had better be that the relation of being the 'same thought as' is introspectively accessible.

This was, of course, guaranteed by Frege's theory: Thoughts are individuated not by their references, but by their *senses*, where two senses a and b are the same iff there are no circumstances under which a rational person would accept both

---

[5] Of course, some contradictions may involve such syntactically complicated pairs of propositions that the fact that they contradict each other may not be immediately manifest to an ordinary mind, equipped with the usual capacities for memory and computation. But the idea is that they would be introspectively manifest in principle, given enough time, memory, and computational power. In any case, we can restrict our attention here to syntactically simple cases.

Fa

and

−Fb.

Frege's theory is designed, in other words, to allow us to take a certain special kind of inconsistency – contradiction – as *constitutive* of someone's irrationality. If we know of a rational person that she is treating two of her thoughts as consistent with one another, then we know to individuate her thoughts in such a way that they don't contradict one another. Conversely, if we know how to individuate her thoughts, we know how to assess her rationality (at least in this basic respect).[6]

However, if we operated with a conception of sameness of thought that is not transparent in this Fregean way, we would have to give up on the idea that conforming to the basic principles of logic is partially constitutive of rationality. For it would then possible to describe completely rational thinkers who nevertheless fail to conform to the basic principles of logic in even the simplest of cases.

Rejecting logical rationality – II

Well, if conformity in simple cases to the basic principles of logic is not what rationality (partly) amounts to, what does it amount to?

S&T have an alternative picture in mind. Here, for example, is what they say about the rationality of Peter's (Pavarotti) inference:

> ... Paul is in no position to recognize the invalidity of the inference he has drawn, but ... this does not make him irrational. Paul, we may suppose, is like the person who upon hearing the following argument takes it to be valid.
>
> > All reindeer have four legs
> > Rudolph is a reindeer
> > So, Rudolph has four legs
>
> In reality, the argument is invalid since "Rudolph" in the second premise is used to refer to a reindeer, whereas "Rudolph" in the conclusion is used to refer to a human being. One who hears the argument and assumes that it is valid is not behaving irrationally. Indeed, if the false assumption that the name "Rudolph" is unambiguous is rationally based, rationality *requires* the hearer to draw the conclusion that Rudolph has four legs.

---

[6] For a discussion of the relation between Frege's cognitive significance test and the Transparency thesis, see Goldberg 2008c.

Paul is a bit like the person deliberating about what to do. An agent, given his knowledge of the situation he finds himself in, may come to a conclusion about the right course of action – a conclusion that is fully warranted by the information available to him – even though in the circumstances it was the wrong thing to do. Evaluating this person from the moral point of view, we may find no fault with his internal reflections, notwithstanding the fact that there was a bad upshot.

Correspondingly, evaluating Paul as a rational subject, we may find no reason for criticism, even though in the circumstances he holds bad beliefs and produces bad arguments.

S&T take a similar view of the 'Paderewski' case:

> Rational subjects are not always in a position to know whether they are exercising a fresh concept, or the same concept again. Peter thinks at the rally that he has learned a new concept PADEREWSKI different from the PADEREWSKI concept he had earlier acquired at the concert. He is wrong. But if this is a *reasonable* mistake, it is one that makes it reasonable for him to believe that his thoughts are not contradictory. (*2012, p. 134*)

How should we understand S&T's view? Their idea seems to be that the (LR) account of the rationality of first-order beliefs that we have been working with is too simplistic. Peter is not necessarily guilty of irrationality just because he is disposed to perform a simple fallacious inference or to embrace a contradiction. Rather, the correct account is disjunctive:

(STR) Peter is rational either if he is disposed to avoid fallacious first-order inferences or contradictions, or by having a rational second-order belief to the effect that his first-order beliefs do not harbor contradictions and his inferences are not fallacious.

S&T want to allow that a thinker can have rational first-order beliefs and inferences without the benefit of any second-order, meta-attitudinal beliefs. So, they don't want to rest the rationality of first-order attitudes and movements of thought merely on the rationality of second-order beliefs. As a result, their account has the disjunctive character that is captured in (STR).

The question is whether we can make sense of (STR).

Rejecting logical rationality with first-order resources

An experienced eye would hesitate both over the disjunctive and the second-order characters of the account. Trouble looms. Why did S&T go in this direction? Why didn't they look for an account that tried to solve the problem using only first-order resources? In the Switched Peter case, for example, why not say that Peter is rational in performing the (Pavarotti) inference because he is tacitly assuming that

(Identity) Twater is water.

To see why, let me begin with the observation that even if we were to grant that Peter is capable of judging (Identity), he would only be able to do so by accident. He wouldn't be able to judge (Identity) *intentionally*.

To be clear, what's at issue for the moment is not Peter's ability to intentionally think second-order thoughts of the type:

(SO-Identity) The concept expressed by the first token of 'water' in (Pavarotti) is the same as the concept expressed by the second token of 'water' in (Pavarotti).

What's at issue is his ability to judge (Identity) with the concepts *water* and *twater* occurring in the thought directly, and not merely under some description that picks them out.[7] Once that's made clear, it requires little argument to show that Peter would not be able to judge (Identity) intentionally. He doesn't know that he has two 'water' concepts; he thinks he has only one such concept.[8]

Now, if this is right, then the limitation in question is extremely interesting. For, by hypothesis, Peter has both the concept *water* and the concept *twater*. By hypothesis, both concepts figure in at least some of his first-order thoughts.

However, on our usual way of thinking about such matters, when we credit someone with possession of two concepts, A and B, we assume that he would be able to intentionally deploy those concepts in all the thought types that he is competent with. For example, since I have both the concept *coriander* and the concept *diamond*, I am able to ask myself:

Is coriander diamond?

however silly the question may be. But this is not true of Peter's ability to deploy the concepts *water* and *twater*.

Does this show that we were wrong to think that full deployment follows automatically from possession? Or does it show that transparency is an important part of the way in which we think about concept possession in the first place, so that there is a question about whether we were right to assume that Peter possesses both concepts? The question demands much more investigation.

---

[7] Nor is it at issue that he could have a thought of the form "This is that" where the first demonstrative refers to water and the second refers to twater.
[8] I am inclined to think that he Peter may not be able to judge (Identity) at all, whether intentionally or not, but won't argue for the stronger claim here.

Not only is Peter unable to think (Identity) intentionally, even if he were to think it by accident he wouldn't *realize* that he had thought it. He would believe that he had thought (Identity-Trivial).

(Identity-Trivial) Water is water.

As a result, it's clear that his thinking (Identity) would not help vindicate his rationality in performing the Pavarotti inference.

Second, given the *way* in which the two occurrences of 'water' will present themselves to Peter, it will seem absurd to him to think anything like the (Identity) thought. As Schroeter (2007) says of a related case:

You think "Bush smirks" and "Bush swaggers." You then draw the conclusion that "Someone both smirks and swaggers." ... the sameness of the man in question won't strike you as up for dispute: your thoughts simply present themselves to you as co-referential. (598)

In other words, the two occurrences of 'water' in the Pavarotti argument will seem *indisputably* co-referential to Peter. Given that appearance, it will seem absurd to Peter to guard against their possible failure to co-refer by interpolating anything like the (Identity) thought.

Finally, even if we could make sense of all this in the Switched Peter case, it's hard to see how it could be of any use in the Unswitched Peter's 'Paderewski' case.

For all these reasons, then, it looks as though S&T were right to avoid trying to solve our problem using only first-order resources.

Rejecting logical rationality with second-order resources

Let's turn then to a solution, like S&T's, that invokes second-order resources. Peter is to be counted as rational provided he has a rational second-order belief to the effect that his first-order beliefs and inferences are all right.

About any such solution, we need to ask three questions:

(A) Can we count on there being the appropriate second-order belief?
(B) What would it be for this second-order belief to be rational?
(C) Can the putative rationality of such a second-order belief help explain the rationality of Peter's first-order beliefs?

What is the second-order belief to be? How is Peter going to think a substantive identity belief linking his *water* and *twater* concepts when, by hypothesis, he doesn't know that he has two concepts and believes, indeed, that he has only one?

What Peter needs to do is to be able to refer to the occurrences of the concepts without exploiting their particular identities. The most plausible way for him to do that would be *metalinguistically*:

> (Water-SO) The concept in the first premise that I would express with the word 'water' is the same as the concept in the second premise that I would also express with the word 'water'.
>
> (Paderewski-SO) The concept expressed by the first occurrence of 'Paderewski' is distinct from the concept expressed by the second occurrence of 'Paderewski'.

But this implies that any second-order solution to our problem is constitutively limited to creatures that are capable of expressing their thoughts through a public language. (Merely assuming that the creatures have a language of thought won't do, since we don't have access to the words of a language of thought in the way that we do to the words of a public language.)

Furthermore, such meta-attitudinal, metaconceptual beliefs are very sophisticated: few thinkers will have them as a matter of course. Having such second-order thoughts requires having the concept CONCEPT, and some view about when concepts are identical and when they are distinct. Yet many thinkers for whom such thoughts will be out of reach may find themselves in Peter's situation. What account will we be able to give of their rationality on S&T's view?

Let's turn next to question (B). What would make beliefs like (Water-SO) and (Paderewski-SO) rational?

Peter's 'Paderewski' belief will clearly have been arrived at by inference. Since we have given up on (LR), we cannot say that his belief (Paderewski-SO) will be rational only if it has been arrived at on the basis of inferences that are not fallacious. Rather, it looks as though we are going to have to offer the following disjunctive condition:

> (Paderewski-SO) is rational *either* if it was arrived at on the basis of inferences that conform to logic, *or* Peter has a rational *third-order* belief to the effect that his inferences so conform.

And so on up the hierarchy.

It's not clear that we understand this notion of rational belief. It seems unhappily impredicative.

This seems like a strong reason for thinking that any satisfactory account of a first-order belief's rationality must consist in that belief's conforming to some norm all by itself, and cannot be handed off to the rationality of some higher-order belief.

Finally, in being *thoughts*, such second-order beliefs will themselves involve the exercise of concepts. That means that questions about the sameness and difference of the concepts involved in those second-order beliefs will also arise. How are those questions to be settled?

On pain of vicious regress, they cannot be settled via yet higher-order thoughts. But if they are not settled, then the ability of such second-order thoughts to secure the rationality of Peter's first-order thoughts is highly questionable.

For all these reasons, then, I don't see that S&T's alternative to (LR), (STR), as presented in the body of their book, has much prospect of succeeding.

S&T's further thoughts: rational "treatings"

S&T have responded to these arguments in a postscript to the paperback edition of their book. In that postscript, they concede that an adequate solution to our problem cannot be secured either through a first-order or through a second-order belief strategy.

They maintain, however, that the denial of transparency can be rescued through what is essentially a modification of the second-order belief strategy. They say:

> There are two crucial points: one is that a subject may be rational in *not* believing something; the other is that a subject may rationally *treat* concept-uses as uses of the same concept, or uses of a different concept, without having meta-conceptual beliefs. Not believing something does not require the exercise of concepts; and treating uses as uses of the same concept does not require believing that the uses are uses of the same concept (such a belief would require possession of the concept CONCEPT). (*2012, p. 184*)

In this section I will consider and assess these further thoughts of S&T. I should say that this discussion will of necessity have to be very preliminary since S&T's presentation of their new line of thinking is understandably cursory and the issues at this point are very complex.

I should also point out that those familiar with some of my work on the nature of inference – Boghossian (2012) – will know that I am sympathetic to the idea that person-level inferences involve something like the subject's "taking it" that the premises support the conclusion. In the case of a deductive argument, this will involve "taking it" that the relevant concept uses are uses of the same concept.[9] This is not very far from

---

[9] I discussed this point in the lectures I gave at the École Normale Supérieure, in Paris, in May 2012.

S&T's talk of "treating" concept uses as the same. So, I am somewhat sympathetic to the idea that they briefly outline. However, I myself don't see my way clear through the various difficulties that this proposal faces. In this section, I will emphasize those difficulties in the hope that this will help us get clear on the way forward.

Let me start with the question: What does this "treating as the same" or "treating as different" consist in, if it is not to consist in a belief? S&T are quite clear that it cannot be belief:

> Boghossian is right that it cannot consist in some further belief which attempts to express sameness or difference of concepts. A belief is a structure of concepts and we still need to know what it is for a subject of the belief to treat the concept-occurrences in that structure as occurrences of the same or different ones. (2012, p. 185)

Of course, it's not just beliefs that would cause a problem. Any construal of "treating" that took it to be a *propositional* attitude would raise similar issues.

So the question is: What sort of *nonpropositional* thing could "treating as the same" or "treating as different" be?

S&T say:

> We think that "treating as the same" is revealed in such cognitive behavior as forming the false belief about the validity of the Pavarotti argument. If this were all that could be said, its explanatory value would be small. But a wide variety of behavior can manifest "treating as the same". For example, we and Peter would not only rationally count as valid the following version of the Pavarotti argument, but would also be rational if we judged the rewording to make no substantive difference:
>
> > Whoever floats on water gets wet
> > Pavarotti once floated on it
> > So Pavarotti got wet
>
> The reworded argument is valid (though, as stated by Peter, unsound, assuming Pavarotti never encountered twater). It is as rational for Peter as for anyone else to believe that it is valid. Like us, he treats it as equivalent to the original argument, and has no beliefs that would make it rational for him to make any distinction between the validity or soundness of the one and the validity or soundness of the other. It is as rational for Peter as for us to believe that both arguments are valid. (2012, p. 185)

This is somewhat puzzlingly formulated since the idea was to supply a *nonpropositional* notion of "treating as the same" but the wording suggests that "treating as the same" is to be identified with various dispositions to form such-and-so *belief* or such-and-such *judgment*.

S&T probably meant to say that "treating as the same" should be identified not with the disposition to form the belief that the Pavarotti argument is valid, but with the disposition to behave *as if* one believed that the argument is valid.[10] Let's grant that this way of understanding the proposal manages to avoid being propositional. Can it help us with our problem?

Our problem, recall, is that we want to vindicate the claim that Peter is rational in performing the Pavarotti inference, despite that inference's suffering from equivocation.

We assume that not *everyone* who is disposed to behave as if his inference is valid, is *justified* in so behaving. Some subjects may be sloppy and careless and simply do not pay enough attention to whether they are being inconsistent. Jon Stewart, on his *Daily Show* news satire program, had an amusing example of this. A right-wing pundit who wanted to decry what he saw as America's "culture of dependence," and to praise personal self-reliance, was shown confidently saying: "I used to be on welfare and food stamps and no one helped me." A little reflection might have revealed to him that he was contradicting himself. I take it that pundit was not justified in behaving as though he wasn't contradicting himself.[11]

So, when is a subject *justified* in behaving as though his thoughts are not contradictory, or his reasoning valid, and when not?

S&T seem to think that their first observation – that we can be rational in *not* believing certain things – will help with this question. They say:

> Just as it is rational for you not to believe that the book you are holding in your hands will explode in ten seconds time, it is rational for us not to believe we are subject to switching. Suppose the very idea of switching has never entered our heads ... Without addition to our stock of concepts, we cannot form beliefs about switching, and so our rationality cannot depend on our having rational beliefs about it ... The argument strikes us as valid and we rationally lack defeaters for that opinion. Hence we are rational in believing it to be valid. (*2012, p. 184*)

There are two possible ways of reading the view here.

On the first, more minimal reading, if a subject is disposed to make an inference, then she is *ipso facto* justified in making that inference as a matter of default, provided there are no defeaters.

But the case of the right-wing pundit shows that principle to be false.

A different and richer view is suggested in the final sentence of the passage quoted above: if a subject is disposed to make an inference and,

---

[10] Mark Sainsbury and Michael Tye, in personal correspondence.
[11] It's true that this case involves a bit of conceptual unpacking – namely, that being on welfare is being helped (by the state) – but not in ways that affect the point.

after reflection on the inference, it continues to strike her as valid, and she lacks a defeater for the opinion that striking generates, then she is justified in making the inference.

Here there are two problems. First, the right-wing pundit continues to be a potential counterexample. Second, this way of putting it clearly relies on the subject's tokening *conceptual structures* – the structures involved in the argument's *striking* her as valid, and her subsequently justified *opinion* that it is valid – and, as we have seen, that is not on the cards.

One is tempted to say: Well, the contradiction in the pundit's case is *manifest* and so is something that he can be held responsible for. But the contradiction (or equivocation, or what have you) in the case of Peter is not manifest, being the result of switching, and so is not something that he can be held responsible for.

But the very question before us is whether we can make sense of the sameness and difference of concepts not being introspectively manifest. We can't simply *assume* that it does make sense.

S&T's further idea, which follows in the footsteps of Campbell (1987), is that we can make sense of a subject's rationally treating two concept uses of his as the same without this involving the tokening of some conceptual structure on his part. But it is not yet clear whether we have been able to make sense of this.

6 Counting concepts: response to Paul Boghossian

Mark Sainsbury and Michael Tye

Introduction

Paul Boghossian has mounted a sustained attack (dating back at least to 1994) on externalist semantic theories, on the grounds that they are inconsistent with transparency, understood along these lines:

Introspective knowledge of comparative content (IKCC) When our faculty of introspection is working normally, we can know apriori via introspection with respect to any two present, occurrent thoughts whether they exercise the same or different concepts.

The originalist theory we proposed in *Seven Puzzles of Thought* accepts externalist principles, and thus rejects IKCC. It must therefore address Boghossian's arguments. We did this in the first edition of our book, and we returned to the fray, benefiting from a further version of Boghossian's criticisms,[1] in the second (paperback) edition. Here the dialog continues: in the chapter to which this is a response,[2] Boghossian presents a new version of his criticisms. They are characteristically insightful and penetrating, and present a challenge to originalists: if transparency is abandoned, how can we understand rationality?

The challenge is brought out by examples, especially the cases of Paderewski-Peter and Switched-Peter, where both Peters are assumed to be entirely rational. Peter in the Paderewski case hears Paderewski at a concert, and forms the belief that he has musical talent. Later, Peter encounters Paderewski making a political speech at a rally. Peter has been told on good authority that no politicians have musical talent, and so rationally believes that he has now encountered a different Paderewski, one lacking musical talent. According to originalism, there is just one

---
[1] Presented at an Author Meets Critics session at the Pacific APA, in March 2013.
[2] Chapter 5 above. This is related to, but not identical with, his contribution to the Author Meets Critics session.

public concept PADEREWSKI, which Peter exercises both when he forms the belief that Paderewski has musical talent, and when he forms the belief that Paderewski lacks musical talent. In the originalist framework, Peter has contradictory beliefs: apart from negation, the beliefs are made up of just the same concepts in the same position. The challenge is to explain how Peter can, nonetheless, be rational. If a rational thinker can believe contradictions, do we not lose all grip on what makes a thinker rational?

Switched–Peter has been moved without his knowledge from Earth to Twin Earth. For the sake of the argument, we accept that he will retain his earthly concept WATER, but will after a time acquire the Twin Earth concept TWATER.[3] His word 'water' becomes equivocal, sometimes expressing the concept WATER and sometimes the concept TWATER. Boghossian suggests that, in the simplest case, Switched–Peter will activate the concept WATER when recalling experiences involving water on Earth, but will activate the concept TWATER when thinking about the waterlike liquid in his current environment. He will remain unaware of the fact that he is activating different concepts in these different contexts. Accordingly, he will be disposed to regard the following argument as valid, even though, as we imagine it issuing from his mouth, it is not, since it equivocates with respect to 'water':

(1) Whoever floats on water, gets wet
(2) Pavarotti once floated on water
(3) Therefore, Pavarotti once got wet

Peter's "regarding the argument as valid" need not amount to the explicit belief that it is valid, and so it is a state he can be in even if he lacks the concept VALID. He was in that state if he happily made the transition from premises to conclusion and was disposed to justify belief in the conclusion by pointing to those premises.

We have assumed that Peter is rational, yet he regards an argument as valid which is not. He has failed to appreciate that the word 'water' expresses different concepts on its two occurrences (first, the concept WATER, then the concept TWATER). If a rational thinker can make a mistake of this kind, do we not lose all grip on what makes a thinker rational?

---

[3] Both we and Boghossian regard the relevant description of the switched case as ultimately inappropriate. Boghossian thinks switching is impossible (as externalistically described), because it is inconsistent with transparency (IKCC), though the least bad version is the one in which the concepts WATER and TWATER cohabit in the mind of Switched-Peter. We think switching is possible, though we do not think that the concepts WATER and TWATER would cohabit: instead, Peter's concept TWATER would come to displace his concept WATER. These issues do not bear on the present discussion.

In thus describing the data offered by the examples of the two Peters, we have been careful not to ascribe to them any metaconceptual beliefs, for they might be in the relevant states even if they lacked the concept CONCEPT, and so could not even formulate any metaconceptual beliefs. As Boghossian stresses, we need to be equally careful in giving the originalist redescriptions of the cases in the light of which both Peters are shown to be rational.

For Paderewski–Peter, it's as if he believes he has two concepts PADEREWSKI when in fact he has one. For Switched–Peter, it's as if he believes that his word 'water' expresses just one concept when in fact it expresses two. We say "it's as if" in both cases, since, for the reason given in the previous paragraph, we cannot count on Paderewski–Peter to believe he has two concepts PADEREWSKI, or on Switched–Peter to believe he expresses different concepts on different occasions when using the word 'water'.

If it's as if Paderewski-Peter believes he has two concepts, his dispositions to form first-order thoughts expressible with the word 'Paderewski' coincide with the dispositions of a thinker as similar to him as possible except believing that the word is equivocal, expressing now one, now another, of two concepts. If it's as if Switched-Peter believes that his word 'water' is not equivocal, he is disposed to make invalid inferences from premises expressible with the word 'water'. More generally, his belief-forming dispositions are those of someone who explicitly believes that the word is not equivocal.

Both being contradictory and being valid essentially depend on how many concepts are involved. We agree with Boghossian that thinkers' thought-forming dispositions are normally appropriate to the number of concepts they are using.[4] This normally enables them to avoid certain simple contradictions, and to make correct assessments of the validity-value of simple arguments. We disagree with Boghossian that rational thinkers cannot have thought-forming dispositions that are out of line with the number of concepts they are in fact exercising. We regard the Peter cases as demonstrating that point: Paderewski-Peter has thought-forming dispositions appropriate to his having two concepts PADEREWSKI when in fact he has just one. Switched-Peter has dispositions appropriate to there being just one concept expressible by 'water' when in fact there are two.

---

[4] We agree that Boghossian's pundit is irrational if he believes he has been on welfare but has never been helped. This is not strictly contradictory, but entails a contradiction in the presence of obvious further facts, e.g. that welfare is a form of help. The pundit has no excuse for not believing these facts or for failing to see that they ensure that he is committed to a contradiction.

This brings us to the heart of Boghossian's challenge: How in that case can we say what it is for a thinker to be rational? We will show that the Peter cases pose no problem for a theory of rationality set within an originalist framework.

Originalists allow that there are circumstances, however rare, in which thinkers behave as if they were mistaken about how many concepts their thoughts involve; or about whether a pair of thoughts is contradictory; or about whether an argument fails to be valid through equivocation. Moreover, originalists hold that sometimes it can be *rational* so to behave. When this occurs, a *rational* thinker may believe a contradiction, or make an incorrect estimate of whether or not an argument is valid. It is not that the thinker identifies the thought as a contradiction, and then rationally believes it. Rather, the thinker rationally fails to detect the contradictory character of the thought, or rationally believes that it is not contradictory.

Boghossian challenges us to provide a theory of rationality according to which this could be so. We meet that challenge as follows:

> R: Thinkers who believe contradictions, or who incorrectly assess the validity status of simple arguments, or who make fallacious inferences from simple arguments, are irrational, unless they have an excuse.

The two Peter examples on which Boghossian draws serve to illustrate kinds of excuse that may make it not merely not irrational, but positively rational, for a thinker to believe a contradiction, or to incorrectly evaluate an argument's validity status. We show that in the two examples on which Boghossian's challenge primarily turns, it is not hard to see what excuses the thinkers had. Paderewski–Peter rationally believes that there are two Paderewskis, and this blinds him to the contradictory character of a pair of his thoughts. Switched–Peter is rational *not* to believe that he expresses more than one concept by his word 'water', and this blinds him to an argument's equivocal nature.

Paderewski–Peter

Peter was told on good authority that no politicians have musical talent. It was rational for him to believe this, even though it is false, and, given the story, an immediate consequence is that there are two Paderewskis: Paderewski the pianist and Paderewski the politician. Peter believes this and it is rational for him to do so.[5] According to originalism, concepts are

---

[5] We are unclear on which side of Boghossian's division this falls: is it lacking empirical information (that there is just one Paderewski) or is it mishandling information (not appreciating how the informational elements are related)?

identical if and only if they have the same historical origin. So, *if* there are two Paderewskis, it follows that there are two concepts, one for Paderewski the pianist, and one for Paderewski the politician. So, Peter believes something (that there are two Paderewskis) that, given originalism, entails the falsehood that there are two concepts PADEREWSKI, and hence entails that there are noncontradictory beliefs to the effect that Paderewski has musical talent and that Paderewski lacks musical talent. Peter's rational beliefs entail that he can believe these things without believing a contradiction. This is his "excuse" in the sense of R. Our attribution to Peter of a single concept PADEREWSKI, and the consequences of this attribution, do not entail that Peter is irrational, and are inevitable, given originalism, once it is allowed that he is rational in believing that there are two Paderewskis.

Switched-Peter

Paderewski-Peter has rational beliefs that entail he has more concepts than he actually has. By contrast, Switched-Peter rationally fails to have beliefs that would entail that he has two 'water' concepts, and so rationally behaves as if he had just one.

One option would be to iterate the structure appropriate to the Paderewski case. Then we would say that Switched-Peter has the rational belief that he has not been switched, and this entails that he has just one concept WATER. We could then appeal to the previous idea, that if a thinker's rational beliefs entail facts about how many concepts she has, she is rational to form beliefs which, *on that supposition*, would not be contradictory, even though they are *in reality* contradictory.

But, as Boghossian points out, this may be too demanding. Perhaps Switched-Peter has never envisaged or heard of Twin Earth, and so is in no position to form any belief or supposition about his relation to it. That's why we stressed, when responding to Boghossian in the second edition of *Seven Puzzles*, that a rational lack of belief can do the same kind of work as the presence of a rational belief. Switched-Peter is rational not to believe he has been switched; it would be crazy for him to believe he has been, just as crazy as it would be for you or us to believe such a thing. If he has not been switched, he has just the concept WATER, and not the concept TWATER. It would be irrational of him to believe his situation to be one in which he has two concepts expressible by 'water'. So in treating, as he does, all occurrences of 'water' in his mouth as he would if he had the explicit belief that they express the same concept, he is avoiding the irrationality of treating these occurrences as the equivocal things they really are. This is his 'excuse', in the sense of R. He is rational to lack a belief that, if he possessed it, would unlock a correct assessment of the validity status of the Pavarotti argument. So he is rational not to believe that the Pavarotti argument is invalid through equivocation. Moreover, the argument strikes him as valid; he is rational to lack any belief that would undermine the claim that it is valid; hence he is rational to believe it is valid, and rational to use the premises as a basis for believing the conclusion. This is the position that all ordinary (unswitched) people are in when they confront the argument. The argument strikes them as valid. Knowing nothing of Twin Earth, it's rational for them not to believe any Twin-Earth-related defeater for this belief. Hence it is rational for them to hold it. Given his ignorance of the switch, Switched-Peter's rationality in regarding the argument as valid is exactly like that of ordinary people.

Conclusion

The Paderewski-Peter case relies on the idea that a false belief can be rationally held, if one is presented with misleading evidence. The Switched-Peter case relies on the idea that there can be truths that it is rational for one not to believe, for one may have no shred of evidence for them. We take it that these ideas are platitudes common to every discussion of rationality, yet they are the only ones on which we have drawn in illustrating the kinds of excuses relevant to R. Hence we do not believe that our originalist defense of the rationality of both Paderewski-Peter and Switched–Peter calls for any startling novel doctrines about rationality. We agree with Boghossian that there are deep and difficult issues in this area. But we also believe that the specific attributions of rationality to the two Peters are resolved within an originalist framework by rather simple considerations.

7 Internalism, externalism, and accessibilism

Brie Gertler

Feldman and Conee (2001) observed that the term 'internalism', as used in epistemology, is ambiguous. It sometimes denotes the view that justification supervenes on factors within the thinker, whereas at other times it refers to the view that justification is accessible to the thinker. Feldman and Conee labeled these views 'mentalism' and 'accessibilism', respectively.

As used in the debate about mental content, 'internalism' corresponds to mentalism. Content internalism is the thesis that thought content supervenes on factors internal to the thinker; content externalism is the denial of this thesis.[1] Strikingly, however, it is the question of *accessibilism* that is the target of many internalist and externalist arguments. Internalists allege that externalism is incompatible with our privileged introspective access to our thoughts. Externalists charge that internalism overestimates such access, by implying that we can explicate our thoughts (i.e., uncover their truth conditions) through mere reflection.

In this chapter I argue that the focus on thinkers' access to their thoughts is misplaced, even in that aspect of the debate about content that concerns cognitive value. Claims about introspective or explicatory knowledge of thought contents, which concern (higher-order) thoughts *about* thoughts, will not settle the debate between externalism and internalism about cognitive value. That debate instead hinges on the significance of external factors for rational relations between

---

I would like to thank Sanford Goldberg, who provided extremely valuable comments on an earlier draft of this chapter. I am also grateful to Alan Sidelle for discussions about these issues.

[1] I argue elsewhere that 'content internalism' and 'content externalism' are irremediably ambiguous, in that no way of specifying the boundary of the thinker – and thereby cashing out the crucial idea of what is *internal to the thinker* – will fit with the standard ways of classifying particular views as externalist and internalist, and standard views about the commitments of externalism and internalism (Gertler 2012). But I put that reservation aside for present purposes.

first-order thoughts. The shift away from issues of accessibility neutralizes both the 'incompatibility' objection to externalism and the charge that internalism overestimates first-person access. But this shift is not entirely neutral between these views. The revised understanding of the debate, as concerning the significance of external factors for rational relations between first-order thoughts, supports a broadly Fregean approach to individuating cognitive values. I develop a version of this approach and defend it from a prominent externalist objection. Since this approach individuates cognitive values narrowly, my argument ultimately supports internalism.

My exclusive concern is with externalism and internalism about cognitive value, that aspect of content that figures in rational explanations of deliberation, inference, and behavior. Internalists generally allow that some kinds or aspects of content, such as *de re* contents, are wide; content internalism is standardly internalism about cognitive value. And at least one leading externalist, Burge, explicitly characterizes his externalism as a claim about cognitive value. My topic here is the debate over the question whether thought contents *individuated by cognitive value* supervene on features internal to the thinker.

The chapter is divided into two parts. Part 1 argues that familiar arguments about the accessibility of thought contents are misplaced. Externalism is compatible with the idea that we can access our own thoughts using a uniquely first-personal, especially reliable method. And while externalism may be incompatible with the claim that thinkers are generally in a position to explicate their thoughts – that is, to identify their thoughts' truth conditions – this incompatibility does not threaten externalism. For this claim about explicatory abilities is dubious – or so I will argue. What will decide the dispute between internalism and externalism is not the question of higher-order access but, rather, the question whether external factors bear directly on rational relations between *first-order* thoughts.

The second part of the chapter addresses this question. I argue against externalism by developing and applying a qualified version of Frege's "differential dubitability" test for sameness and difference of cognitive value. The leading externalist response to this kind of Fregean argument interprets it as resting on the claim that thinkers can always explicate their thoughts. I show that this interpretation confuses differential dubitability, which concerns relations between first-order thoughts, with explicatory access, which involves relations between first-order and higher-order thoughts. The Fregean argument for internalism exclusively concerns relations between *first-order* states, and does not rest on an accessibility thesis. For this reason, internalism is neutral about whether thinkers can explicate their thoughts.[2]

Part 1 Externalism and access

Externalism's alleged incompatibility with introspective access

There is now a large literature discussing the alleged incompatibility between externalism and introspective access. The initial worry is that externalism is incompatible with the fact that we have privileged access to our thoughts, in that we can know what we're thinking through introspection, a uniquely first-personal and especially reliable method. The externalist can, of course, deny that we have introspective access to our thoughts. But he need not do so, since externalism can accommodate this claim about introspective access. (Wikforss (2008a) makes this case in an especially persuasive and illuminating way.) The claim about introspective access pertains to *how we know* our thoughts or attitudes: how higher-order judgments like "I am now thinking that p" or "I believe that q" relate to the lower-order thoughts they concern. The outlook on that issue is not constrained by the supposition that some thought contents are individuated by reference to external factors. Perhaps most significantly, the externalist can simply maintain that higher-order judgments *inherit* their contents from the lower-order thoughts they concern (Burge 1988, Gibbons 1996). This inheritance of content may occur through a uniquely first-personal process of introspection; and if higher-order judgments (such as *I'm now thinking that* p) inherit contents from the lower-order thoughts they concern (such as the thought that p), those judgments may be especially likely to be true.[3] So externalism is compatible with the claim that the thinker has access to her own thoughts that is distinctively first-personal and especially reliable – access that is in this sense *privileged*. Externalists can thus defuse this initial incompatibility worry.

---

[2] Wikforss argues for a similar conclusion: in her words, "the real challenge posed to externalism concerns not self-knowledge, but understanding or concept grasp" (Wikforss 2008a, p. 416). I encountered her argument as I was completing this paper. While our arguments are similar in spirit, they differ in some details and, especially, in how we develop the case for internalism. The addition of my arguments strengthens her already strong case for our shared conclusion: that the debate over content will not be decided by questions of access, and the shift away from questions of access favors internalism.
[3] The inheritance of content might occur through the kind of *containment* relation posited by Burge (1988), or it may occur some other way: e.g., through an appropriate causal connection between lower-order and higher-order thoughts. So the content inheritance strategy can be used in conjunction with a variety of epistemic views about self-knowledge.

Some philosophers have pressed a related, more nuanced incompatibility worry. This worry is motivated by the idea that our privileged access to our own thoughts doesn't simply consist in the ability to reliably track them through a uniquely first-personal method. For possessing that ability does not ensure that the thinker truly *understands* her current thoughts. As Goldberg says, "one can count as knowing *that* one is thinking that *p* without knowing *what* one is thinking in (knowing that one is) thinking that *p*" (Goldberg 2003c, p. 254). The more nuanced incompatibility worry is that externalism is incompatible with the fact that thinkers can truly grasp – that is, genuinely *comprehend* – what it is they're thinking.

Specifically, the worry is that externalism cannot accommodate the fact that, through introspective reflection, rational thinkers can achieve a meaningful grasp of the contents of their thoughts – a grasp that enables them not just to think thoughts that inherit those contents but to *explicate* their lower-order thoughts, that is, to identify (substantive) truth conditions for them. Following Burge, I will use the term 'explicatory knowledge' to refer to knowledge of the truth conditions of one's thoughts (and/or of the criteria for satisfying concepts exercised therein). The worry, then, is that externalism is incompatible with what I'll call the 'Explicatory Access' thesis.

> EXPLICATORY ACCESS thesis: No thought can contribute (by virtue of its content) to a rational thought process unless the thinker could, in principle, explicate the thought – correctly identify its truth conditions and the criteria for satisfying concepts exercised in thinking it – purely through reflection, and without investigating the physical or social environment.

The tension between externalism and the Explicatory Access thesis is illustrated by variations on two influential arguments against externalism, the McKinsey argument (McKinsey 1991) and the 'slow-switching' argument (Boghossian 1989). I begin with a version of the McKinsey argument. Given content externalism, the criterial truths about *water* are tied to certain facts in the environment (roughly, the presence of a molecular kind like H_2O or a community that has interacted with such a kind). Given Explicatory Access, one could grasp these criterial truths about *water* through introspective reflection. Introspection would then license an inference to the conclusion that certain external things (H_2O or a community that has interacted with H_2O or ...) exist.

I now turn to a version of the 'slow-switching' argument. Given content externalism, a move from Earth to Twin Earth would (eventually) result in a change in the truth conditions of thoughts expressible by "water quenches thirst," from those associated with *water quenches thirst* to those associated with *twin water quenches thirst*. Given Explicatory Access, the thinker who was moved to Twin Earth and remembered her Earthian thoughts could grasp this difference in the truth conditions of her thoughts through introspection. So one who was switched from Earth to Twin Earth without her knowledge could come to realize that she had switched environments, simply by relying on introspection and memory.

There have been numerous responses to these kinds of arguments. Some of these question the arguments' background assumptions – e.g., whether warrant 'transmits' from introspective beliefs to beliefs about the external world, in the way required for licensing the conclusion about the external world (Davies 1998); and whether previous concepts survive the switch to a new environment (Heal 1998, Ludlow 1995, Tye 1998).[4] But most responses involve acknowledging that externalism is incompatible with *some* kind of access to our own thought contents, and denying that we have that kind of access.

Most importantly for our purposes, many externalists – including Burge – respond to 'slow-switching'-style arguments by rejecting the idea expressed in the Explicatory Access thesis. The cases Burge uses to support externalism involve subjects who, as Burge describes them, are ignorant or mistaken about the truth conditions of their thoughts. His famous subject, Bert, purportedly exhibits basic ignorance about the criteria for *arthritis* and, hence, that the thought he expresses by saying "I have arthritis in my thigh" may be true. Burge contends that such explicatory ignorance or misunderstanding is no impediment to rational thought.

> Thus, I can know that I have arthritis, and know I think I have arthritis, even though I do not have a proper criterion for what arthritis is. It is a truism that to think one's thoughts ... one must understand what one is thinking well enough to think it. But it does not follow that such understanding carries with it an ability to explicate correctly one's thoughts or concepts via other thoughts and concepts; nor does it carry an immunity to failures of explication. So one can know what one's thoughts are even while one understands one's thoughts only partially, in the sense that one gives incomplete or mistaken explications of one's thoughts or concepts. (*Burge 1988, p. 662*)

Moreover, Burge thinks that Bert can learn of his mistaken understanding of *arthritis* only through interaction with others. No amount of introspective reflection will accomplish this. So on Burge's interpretation

---

[4] Goldberg (2003c, p. 254) tentatively suggests that the McKinsey argument can be blocked by acknowledging that we don't know *what* we are thinking, in the relevant sense – at least, that we don't qualify as having that knowledge in the skeptical context, where the standards for knowledge may be especially high.

of the case, Bert is not only mistaken about *arthritis*; he lacks reflective access to the proper explication of his *arthritis* thoughts. This case is thus a counterexample to the Explicatory Access thesis.

Many externalists, including Burge, grant that externalism is incompatible with the Explicatory Access thesis but regard this as unproblematic because they reject that thesis. In fact, at times Burge appears to regard the Explicatory Access thesis as a defining commitment of internalism. (I return to that issue in Part 2.)

Explicatory knowledge and rationality

I won't attempt to determine whether the Explicatory Access thesis is true. In light of its incompatibility with externalism, what matters is whether the externalist can reasonably reject it.

Why might one think that rational thought requires explicatory access? Here is one simple argument. Consider a thinker who infers that q from (i) "p or q" and (ii) "not-p." If this thought process is truly *rational* (rather than brute), then the thinker qualifies as rational for engaging in it. A thinker cannot be credited with rationality in virtue of a particular thought process unless she can understand what makes the process a rational one. What makes a thought process *rational* is the relations among the contents of the thoughts involved: for example, the relations between the truth conditions of (i) and (ii) and her conclusion. So to understand what makes a thought process *rational*, a thinker must have explicatory knowledge. And since such an understanding must be available, in order for the thought process to be rational, rational thought depends on the thinker's ability to achieve explicatory knowledge.

Rational thought does seem to require a genuine grasp of what it is that one is thinking. After all, one cannot employ the belief *alligators are dangerous* in deliberation if one has no clue (or is radically mistaken) about what kind of worldly conditions would make this thought true or false.

The idea that rational thought involves understanding – that it isn't "brute" – is compelling. But we can accommodate this idea without appealing to anything as strong as the Explicatory Access thesis. The simple argument presented above presumes that a thinker qualifies as rational, in virtue of engaging in a rational thought process, only if she understands what makes that process rational. But a less demanding alternative is to say that a thinker qualifies as rational simply in virtue of engaging in a rational process (in the right way): for example, in virtue of arriving at a given conclusion *because* it follows from premises she believes.

The following passage from Shoemaker will be useful in elucidating this less demanding picture of rationality.

> [I]t is essential to being a rational being that one be sensitive to the contents of one's belief-desire system in such a way as to enable its contents to be revised and updated in the light of new experience, and enable inconsistencies and incoherences in its content to be eliminated. (*Shoemaker 1994, p. 285*)

The sensitivity to the contents of one's attitudes described here – sensitivity manifested in revisions sparked by new experiences or (looming) inconsistencies – may consist purely in relations among first-order states (thoughts, experiences, and attitudes). It need not involve thinking *about* one's thoughts or attitudes, or being able to explicate them.[5]

Consider the following example. Rita loves to swim in the ocean, but only on sunny days. When she hears the weather forecaster say "tomorrow will be sunny and clear," she plans a trip to a nearby beach for the following day. As she prepares to embark the next morning, she observes a dark, threatening sky. The contents of her "belief-desire system" are appropriately "revised and updated in the light of [this] experience": she abandons her plan to go to the beach, because she no longer believes that it will be sunny. Crucially, these revisions may take place entirely at the first-order level. Rita may abandon her previous plan upon seeing the dark clouds, without thinking *about* her belief that dark clouds indicate rain, or *about* her aversion to being at the beach when it's raining (etc.). And for all I have said, Rita may be unable to explicate her belief *dark clouds indicate rain*, or to articulate how it contributes to rationalizing the change in plans. These revisions nonetheless seem *rational* in precisely the sense that Shoemaker suggests: they manifest (or partly constitute) the appropriate sensitivity to new experiences and to potential inconsistencies between attitudes.

The plausible idea that rational thought requires a grasp of what one is thinking – or, to make the first-order aspect of content explicit, that it requires thinking comprehendingly – can be accommodated without invoking the Explicatory Access thesis. Rita's belief *dark clouds indicate rain* rationally contributes to her thought process by virtue of its cognitive value. This value is manifested in (or perhaps consists in) its role in her cognitive economy: in this case, in its contribution to her

---

[5] Shoemaker separately proposes that this sensitivity suffices for knowledge of one's own attitudes. This is his *constitutivism* about self-knowledge, according to which "believing that one believes that P can be just believing that P plus having a certain level of rationality, intelligence, and so on" (Shoemaker 1994, p. 289). However, the knowledge he has in mind seems not to involve the kind of higher-order reflection at issue here. For some worries about Shoemaker's use of this argument, see Gertler 2011a, ch. 5.

transition from seeing dark clouds to abandoning her prior belief that the day would be sunny.

We do sometimes reflect on, and attempt to explicate, our own attitudes. But rational revisions of our attitudes typically occur without any reflection *about* our attitudes or their contents. And if one can exhibit rationality without even attempting to achieve explicatory knowledge, it's not clear why rationality should require the in-principle availability of such knowledge. In any case, the externalist can claim that thinking and reasoning comprehendingly is a matter of relations among *first-order* thoughts, attitudes, and experiences. He can therefore reject the Explicatory Access thesis.

In the simple argument for the Explicatory Access thesis sketched above, it was claimed that the thinker couldn't be credited with rationality unless she had explicatory access. The current suggestion that the patterns of relations constituting rationality need not involve higher-order reflection raises an interesting question. Does the presence of the appropriate patterns among a thinker's first-order states justify crediting *the thinker* with rationality? This is a complex question, and one that I cannot adequately address here. But there is some reason to favor an affirmative answer. Simply put, a thinker may be constituted by her thoughts, attitudes, and experiences, and the patterns of relations among them. To identify the thinker with these states and relations is not to adopt a bundle theory of the thinker, since these states and relations include dispositions. Beliefs, intentions, and other attitudes are largely dispositional; and the thinker's cognitive and emotional dispositions will be manifested in the patterns of relations amongst her thoughts, attitudes, and experiences. Now it might be objected that rationality partly consists in acknowledging the presence of first-order thoughts, and responding appropriately: for example, acknowledging that one sees dark clouds gathering, and that one should therefore abandon the belief that it will be sunny. This picture of rationality is reminiscent of "hierarchical" accounts of agency, which identify the locus of agency or "real self" with higher-order attitudes. But this picture of the rational thinker faces a familiar worry for those accounts of agency. It is not clear how the move to higher orders of the same kinds of attitude (in the case of agency, the relevant attitude is usually thought to be a pro-attitude such as desire or endorsement) could effect the envisioned qualitative shift to genuine or full-blooded intentional agency. Similarly, it is not clear how the move from first-order to higher-order attitudes could effect the envisioned shift from "brute" or nonrational processing to rational thought.

In any case, we can remain neutral on whether these relations among first-order attitudes – for example, the expectation that *it will be sunny today* being appropriately sensitive to the experience of dark clouds combined with the background belief that dark clouds indicate rain – justify crediting *Rita herself* with rationality. The important point is that this kind of sensitivity qualifies the *process*, which ends in the revision of that expectation, as rational. (For convenience, I will sometimes express the occurrence of a rational process as an instance of the thinker's rationality; and I will sometimes describe an attitude's being suitably sensitive to other attitudes as the thinker's sensitivity. In every case, the descriptions in question can be translated to statements purely involving states and their interrelations.)

Rationality does seem to require a certain kind of sensitivity to thought contents, a kind of sensitivity that constitutes thinking with comprehension. (It may even consist in such sensitivity.) But the externalist can reasonably claim that relations among first-order states suffice for the requisite kind of sensitivity. So the externalist can make sense of the requirement that rational thinkers comprehend what they're thinking – or just: think comprehendingly – without claiming that they are always in a position to achieve explicatory knowledge of their thoughts.

Explicatory access and "transparency"

Contributors to the debate between internalism and externalism often discuss whether externalism is compatible with (what they call) the "transparency" of sameness or difference of thought content. I have avoided this term because I find it less than pellucid. But because of its prominence in the literature, it's worth getting clear on how transparency relates to my central distinction between first-order reasoning – thinking *with* comprehension – and higher-order, explicatory access to thoughts.

The "transparency" of content is sometimes construed as a matter of first-order relations: that is, as the sameness or difference of thought contents *making* a difference to first-order reasoning. At other times, it is construed as a matter of higher-order (introspective) availability: that is, as a thinker's ability to *determine whether* any two of his thoughts share a content or differ in content, by introspective reflection alone.

Authors often shift between the first-order and the higher-order construals. For example, Boghossian argues that externalism is incompatible with a thesis he calls "epistemic transparency": "for any two expressions in a person's repertoire, it must be possible for that person to come to know whether or not they mean the same ... purely *introspectively*, without the benefit of further empirical investigation" (Boghossian 1994, p. 33). He further characterizes epistemic transparency as "the intuitive idea that we can know the contents of our thoughts in the sense that we can introspectively *discriminate* between them" (ibid., p. 36). In these passages, Boghossian seems to have the higher-order notion in mind. But his main arguments concern first-order relations: for example, first-order inferences to which "twin Pavarotti swam" makes the same contribution to first-order reasoning as "Pavarotti swam."

Brown similarly shifts between first-order and higher-order construals. In cashing out the notion of transparency, she says:

[T]he relevant notion of a rational agent could be made more precise by saying that, with respect to simultaneously held thoughts, a rational subject should avoid simple contradictions in belief, make simple valid inferences, and avoid making simple invalid inferences. Correspondingly this chapter will focus on whether a subject can grasp a priori relations of sameness and difference of content between simultaneously held thoughts. (*Brown 2004a, p. 159*)

Now it may be that these authors do not see this shift, between transparency as a relation among thought contents at the first-order and transparency as a matter of higher-order access to those contents, *as* a shift. They may understand notions like "introspectively discriminable" and "a priori" in a very weak way, so it is trivial that whatever "makes a difference to rational processes" falls into these categories.

My purpose in mentioning the talk of transparency is only to clarify where this falls in my discussion. As a first-order phenomenon, the sameness of content is transparent insofar as two thoughts with the same contents would, in the relevant circumstances, make the same contribution to rational processes like deliberation and inference; the difference of content is transparent insofar as two thoughts with different contents would make different contributions to rational processes. As thus understood, one lesson of the previous subsection is that rationality does seem to require first-order transparency.

Whether rationality requires higher-order transparency is a separate issue. And this issue is, strictly speaking, orthogonal to the question dividing internalism and externalism, namely, whether capturing cognitive values sometimes requires individuating thought contents narrowly. What defines a thought's cognitive value is its contribution to rational processes. It is a further question whether a thinker who *reasons with* certain thoughts – who thinks them comprehendingly – must be in a position to grasp *that* the thoughts share a content or differ in content. To put this point another way: the commitment to do justice to cognitive value, which is shared between the versions of internalism and externalism under consideration, does not automatically commit one on the question whether rational relations must be accessible to higher-order reflection.

Summing up: externalism and access

Neither version of the charge that externalism is incompatible with privileged access succeeds. Externalism is compatible with the claim that thinkers have access to their own thoughts through a uniquely first-personal, especially reliable method. For the externalist can invoke the idea that higher-order judgments inherit the contents of lower-order thoughts. Externalism may be unable to accommodate the more robust kind of access, expressed in the Explicatory Access thesis. But the externalist can argue that the case of Rita suggests that the apparent plausibility of the Explicatory Access thesis stems from the genuine plausibility of a subtly different thesis, namely, that thinking a thought comprehendingly requires rational sensitivity to its content. And this sensitivity may be exclusively a matter of relations among first-order states (thoughts, attitudes, and experiences). So the externalist can preserve the intuition that rational thought requires a meaningful grasp of what one is thinking – and, hence, that capturing a thought's contribution to rational processes requires individuating it by cognitive value – while denying the Explicatory Access thesis.

One might argue that the capacity for explicatory reflection is necessary for being rational and, hence, a prerequisite for rational thought. But the Explicatory Access thesis imposes significantly more strenuous demands on rational thought, in requiring that a rational thinker must be capable of explicating each thought she employs in reasoning. The externalist is on a firm footing in rejecting that stronger claim. So externalism is not threatened by its apparent incompatibility with the Explicatory Access thesis.

The issue of whether externalism is compatible with introspective or explicatory access to their thoughts is a red herring. The debate between internalists and externalists about cognitive value hinges on a different question: whether external factors directly affect rational relations among *first-order* thoughts and attitudes. Part 2 takes up this question.

Part 2 Differential dubitability

The question dividing externalists and internalists is whether external factors directly affect a thought's cognitive value: that feature by virtue of which it stands in rational relations to other thoughts. The lesson of Part 1 is that, to evaluate this question, we should direct our attention to the primary locus of rationality, the relations between *first-order* mental states.

I will approach this question by using a famous Fregean thesis about cognitive value. According to Frege, the thought that p and the thought that q differ in cognitive value if a rational thinker can believe that p while doubting that q.[6] In other words, *differential dubitability* implies a difference in cognitive value. Significantly, this Fregean thesis does not entail that a rational thinker will be able to explicate her thoughts through reflection. It directly involves only the first-order sensitivity described in the previous section. It is because rational thinkers are sensitive to the cognitive values of their thoughts – regardless of whether they could accurately explicate them – that a rational thinker could not differentially doubt two thoughts that shared a cognitive value. To put this another way: a system of thought would not be *rational* if the belief that p wasn't appropriately sensitive to the doubt that p (where "p" expresses a single cognitive value).

Frege drew on this thesis to explain how a rational thinker could doubt that Hesperus is Phosphorus while believing that Hesperus is Hesperus, despite the fact that "Hesperus" and "Phosphorus" are co-referential. That these thoughts differ in cognitive value demonstrates that cognitive value can vary independently of actual reference, and of the (*de re*) truth conditions associated with actual reference.

The Fregean thesis that differentially dubitable thoughts differ in cognitive value may appear to conflict with externalism. Consider an example given by Loar (1988). A child named Paul says "chats have tails," expressing a belief he formed on the basis of what his French nanny tells him about the cats around him. On the rare occasions that Paul sees his parents, cats are never present; yet they tell him about animals called "cats" and, in particular, that "cats have tails." Because Paul doesn't realize that "chat" and "cat" are co-referential, the beliefs he expresses with "chats have tails" and "cats have tails" are differentially dubitable (for him). So, according to the Fregean thesis, they differ in cognitive value. But the external factors that purportedly contribute to the cognitive value of his *chat* thoughts – roughly, that the term associated with it refers to felines – are precisely those that contribute to the cognitive value of his *cat* thoughts. So one might conclude that externalism will imply that these two beliefs *share* a cognitive value.

---

[6] In my use, p and q represent propositional contents of thought, contents which can be entertained at different times and by different thinkers. I remain neutral as to whether such contents are best understood as abstract propositions, modes of presentation of propositions, sentences in a language of thought, etc.

But externalism is not directly threatened by this Fregean thesis. The externalist does not claim that it is *only* external factors that individuate contents; externalism is compatible with the claim that a difference in *internal* factors can suffice for a difference in contents. So the externalist can attribute the differential dubitability of the thoughts Paul expresses with "chats have tails" and "cats have tails" to a difference in cognitive value between these, a difference anchored in factors internal to Paul. And it is plausible that these thoughts do differ internally, given the disparate etiologies of Paul's "chat" and "cat" concepts. More generally, since externalism does not claim that cognitive value is individuated by external factors *alone*, it is not directly threatened by cases in which cognitive value varies independently of external factors. So the Fregean thesis mentioned above, that differential dubitability implies a difference in cognitive value, poses no direct threat to externalism.

This point does not resolve the main worry about externalism, that the cognitive values of our thoughts seem independent of external factors. It merely reveals the proper expression of that worry. The problem for externalism is not that differential dubitability is *sufficient* for a difference in content, but rather that it is *necessary* for a difference in content.[7] (For valuable discussion of this point, see Brown 2004a, pp. 161–66.) Wikforss puts this succinctly:

The content externalist holds that thought content is individuated by the individual's environment in such a way that two individuals may be internally identical and yet have different thoughts. This thesis implies that there may be a *difference* in content that cannot be discerned from the first person point of view, but it does not imply that there may be *sameness* of content that is not discernible from a first person point of view. (*Wikforss 2006, pp. 164–65, notes elided*)

What I have described as the main worry about externalism is best pursued by focusing on the implication that, in Wikforss's terms, "there may be a *difference* in content that cannot be discerned from the first person point of view." As I will put this, it is that there may be a difference in content to which rational thinkers cannot be sensitive (in the sense discussed above): that is, a difference that is not appropriately reflected in the relations among first-order attitudes, including the relation of differential dubitability. Developing an objection to externalism along these lines requires supplementing the Fregean thesis about cognitive value.

---

[7] The terms 'sufficient' and 'necessary' are used, as is standard, to express purely logical relationships. So the thesis that differential dubitability suffices for a difference in cognitive value is neutral as to whether differential dubitability *reflects* or *constitutes* (etc.) this difference.

The differential dubitability thesis

Cognitive value is that aspect of a thought that bears on rational assessments of a thinker's psychological profile (her thoughts, attitudes, and experiences, and relations among these) – or, perhaps equivalently, of the thinker herself. A way of individuating thoughts by their cognitive values must therefore meet two conditions. It must be fine-grained enough to capture differences between cognitive values to which a rational thinker could be sensitive. This requirement is reflected in Frege's thesis that differential dubitability – which reflects first-order sensitivity – *suffices* for a difference in cognitive value. But it must also be coarse-grained enough to ignore distinctions beyond those to which a rational thinker could be sensitive. This second condition implies that, for a restricted range of thoughts, differential dubitability is also *necessary* for a difference in cognitive value. It is this latter requirement that most directly challenges externalism.

The idea that differential dubitability is necessary for a difference in cognitive value faces immediate obstacles. One problem is that there may be some thoughts that a rational thinker cannot doubt, and others that a rational thinker cannot believe. Unless we are willing to say that there is a single cognitive value shared by all indubitable thoughts (such as, perhaps, 2 + 3 = 5 and *I exist*), and another shared by all unbelievable thoughts (e.g., 2 + 3 = 7 and *I do not exist*), the requirement of differential dubitability must be restricted in its scope.

I propose that, for any pair of thought contents (*p*, *q*) meeting the following three restrictions, the differential dubitability of the thought that *p* and the thought that *q* is not only sufficient but also necessary for a difference in cognitive value.

(i) *p* and *q* are each rationally dubitable and rationally believable; and neither *p* nor *q* are conjunctions that include an indubitable or unbelievable conjunct.[8]

(ii) Neither *p* nor *q* concerns one's occurrent thoughts.[9]

---

[8] The latter clause excludes contents like (a) *no bachelors are married and snow is white* and (b) *2 + 3 = 5 and snow is white*. Each of these is believable; each is dubitable; it may be impossible to believe that (a) while doubting that (b), or vice versa; yet (a) and (b) plausibly differ in cognitive value.

[9] The problem with thoughts about thoughts stems from the possibility that thoughts are self-intimating, a possibility on which I remain neutral. If thoughts are self-intimating, then it will be impossible to differentially doubt *I am having exactly one occurrent thought right now* and *I am having exactly one occurrent thought right now and snow is white*. For if thoughts are self-intimating, it is not possible to have both occurrent thoughts while believing that one has only a single occurrent thought. (I am grateful to Alan Sidelle for bringing this point to my attention.)

(iii) 'p iff q' is not knowable a priori.[10]

These restrictions may introduce a worry of triviality: it may seem obvious that all distinct contents meeting these conditions will be differentially dubitable. (Condition (iii) appears especially worrisome in this regard.) But the cases to which I apply this test are precisely cases that, according to the externalist, meet conditions (i)–(iii), but are not differentially dubitable.

I remain neutral as to whether each of these restrictions is needed. My aim is not to defend a general Fregeanism, but only to develop and apply a broadly Fregean strategy for differentiating cognitive value within the realm in which it is least problematic: viz., among pairs of contents that meet the restrictions just outlined. My proposal is as follows.

DIFFERENTIAL DUBITABILITY thesis: For any pair of thought contents (p, q) that meet conditions (i)–(iii):

p and q differ in cognitive value IFF a rational thinker (capable of entertaining each p and q) can believe that p while doubting that q OR believe that q while doubting that p.

The Differential Dubitability thesis extends the Fregean thesis discussed earlier, and shares its motivating idea: that differences in cognitive value are precisely those to which rational thinkers can be sensitive, where this means those that are manifested in (or consist in) relations among first-order states.

As Burge recognizes, the Differential Dubitability thesis is at odds with externalism about cognitive value. Consider Bert, who is stipulated to be rational and has a belief he expresses by saying "I have arthritis in my thigh." Burge says that, while this belief is false, Bert would have a *true* belief in a counterfactual situation in which he retains all of the same (nonintentionally specified) internal properties and history, but in which "physicians, lexicographers, and informed laymen apply 'arthritis' not only to arthritis but to various other rheumatoid ailments" (Burge 1979, p. 105). Given that Bert would have a true belief in that situation, it seems that in the actual situation he cannot differentially doubt *I have arthritis in my thigh* and *I have a rheumatoid ailment (of the relevant, more inclusive kind) in my thigh*. (To avoid worries about whether the subject could entertain the latter thought, we can suppose

---

[10] Consider the case where p = "this figure is a right triangle," and q = "the square of the length of this figure's hypotenuse is equal to the sum of the squares of the length of its other sides." Since it is a priori that p iff q, a rational thinker may not be able to believe that p while doubting that q (or vice versa). Some may claim that p and q share a cognitive value, but I wish to remain neutral on that issue.

that he has been switched, without his knowledge, from an environment that fits the counterfactual situation Burge describes.) And as Burge construes these thoughts, they meet conditions (i)–(iii). So according to the Differential Dubitability thesis, these share a cognitive value. But the principal thesis of Burge's externalism is precisely that these thoughts differ in cognitive value. So Burge's externalism conflicts with the Differential Dubitability thesis.[11]

Burge's proposed modification to the Differential Dubitability thesis

While Burge recognizes this conflict, he is concerned to preserve a measure of Fregeanism, perhaps because he regards cognitive value as closely tied to differential dubitability. In an effort to reconcile externalism with Fregeanism, he proposes that a modified version of differential dubitability can serve as a rough test for sameness or difference of cognitive value. "Frege's test for differential dubitability, *when accompanied with requirements that doubt be supportable by publicly recognized methods*, is a defeasible but profoundly valuable tool in individuating cognitive values" (Burge 1986, p. 717; my emphasis).

Burge's proposal, that doubt must be publicly supportable, seems to target the claim that differential dubitability by an individual suffices (on its own) for a difference in cognitive value. But as we saw above, the conflict with externalism derives not from this claim but, rather, from the claim that differential dubitability is *necessary* for a difference in cognitive value. To avoid this conflict, the externalist must allow that two thoughts may differ in cognitive value even if a rational thinker is unable to differentially doubt them. Burge's proposed modification supports this position if it is also applied, as seems reasonable, to the claim that differential dubitability is necessary for a difference in cognitive value. When thus modified, Burge's proposal is that p and q differ in cognitive value iff adherence to relevant social norms would enable a thinker to believe that p while doubting that q (or vice versa).

---

[11] Goldberg (2008c) sketches a bold strategy, on behalf of the externalist, to neutralize examples of differential dubitability phenomena that challenge externalism. He recommends that the externalist use, as a premise, the claim that, in the cases at issue, cognitive values are individuated widely. In that case, a subject who differentially doubts two thoughts that share cognitive values (individuated externalistically), or who finds herself unable to differentially doubt two thoughts that differ in cognitive value (individuated externalistically), thereby shows herself to be irrational. But since differential dubitability is a guide to cognitive value only on the assumption of rationality, these cases don't challenge externalism after all. The assumption of externalism is unobjectionable in a purely defensive strategy. But since I aim to consider the differential dubitability phenomena on their own, that assumption is not legitimate here.

Unsurprisingly, Burge's modification individuates cognitive value externalistically. For example, the differential dubitability of *I have arthritis in my thigh* and *I have a rheumatoid ailment in my thigh* is clearly "supportable by publicly recognized methods" of discriminating arthritis from other rheumatoid ailments. So these differ in cognitive value, according to Burge's proposed "tool" for individuating cognitive values. Similarly, *chats have tails* and *cats have tails* are differentially dubitable, for Paul, only insofar as he fails to adhere to social norms (which dictate that "chat" and "cat" refer to a single kind of creature). So these would count as sharing a cognitive value, according to Burge's modified criterion.

Burge's proposal introduces an external factor into the test for sameness and difference of cognitive value. If this is needed to ensure the (rough) accuracy of the Differential Dubitability thesis, as Burge in effect suggests, then external factors can directly affect cognitive value. Given the close tie between cognitive value and differential dubitability, the debate between internalism and externalism might well be decided by the question whether there are genuine counterexamples to the original Differential Dubitability thesis and, if so, whether Burge's proposed modification better captures the link between differential dubitability and cognitive value.

What reason might there be to think that there are counterexamples to the Differential Dubitability thesis?

Externalist suspicions about the Differential Dubitability thesis appear to stem from the perception that it overestimates thinkers' access to their own thought contents. After all, differential dubitability is most obviously a guide to cognitive value when the contents of two thoughts, or the relations between them, are easily accessible. For instance, a rational thinker will be able to differentially doubt *some Spaniards play tennis* and *some Spaniards are 8 feet tall*; this is an easy case because those with the requisite concepts generally have enough explicatory knowledge to recognize that "all and only tennis players are 8 feet tall" does not express a criterial truth.

As I argued above, externalism seems to imply that we don't always have explicatory knowledge of our thoughts and, hence, that we may not be in a position to grasp the criterial truths that contribute to the cognitive values of our thoughts. Burge explicitly denies that we have such explicatory access (e.g., in the passage quoted in the first section of Part 1 above). His view seems to be that it is precisely our *lack* of explicatory information, or access thereto, that prevents differential dubitability from tracking differences in cognitive values. To adapt one of his examples (Burge 1986): it appears that a rational person may be unable to differentially doubt *I'm seated on a chair* and *I'm seated on a piece of furniture with legs, intended for sitting (by a single person)*. But these thoughts do differ in truth conditions: if I were seated on a ski-lift chair, the former would be true while the latter was false. The implication is that what one can differentially doubt is influenced by criterial beliefs (e.g. the mistaken criterial beliefs that chairs must have legs), whereas cognitive value has to do with the actual criteria for *chair*. Burge thus seems to think that the influence of mistaken criterial beliefs – one dimension of explicatory ignorance – is enough to undermine the Differential Dubitability thesis.

The Differential Dubitability thesis conflicts with externalism. Burge objects to that thesis, on the grounds that mistaken criterial beliefs can prevent differential dubitability from tracking difference of cognitive value. His proposed modification is intended to avoid the conflict while preserving a measure of Fregeanism.

Defending the Differential Dubitability thesis

The phenomenon of mistaken criterial beliefs does not, I think, undermine the Differential Dubitability thesis. I will draw on another example of Burge's to show that even the possibility of radically misguided criterial beliefs does not threaten the Differential Dubitability thesis. The externalist construal of such cases, as counterexamples to the Differential Dubitability thesis, rests on a confusion between the differential dubitability phenomena and explicatory knowledge of thoughts. In effect, it mistakenly takes the Differential Dubitability thesis to depend, for its truth, on the Explicatory Access thesis.

The example I have in mind is Burge's subject A, who thinks that sofas are religious objects.[12] A believes that what makes something a sofa is that it is a religious artifact of a certain sort. A recognizes that others regard *sofas are intended for sitting* as a criterial truth, but he thinks that they are mistaken. Clearly, A has inaccurate criterial beliefs about *sofa*.[13] And in failing to believe that sofas are intended for sitting, he is ignorant of a key criterial truth about *sofa*.

Consider A's position relative to these two thoughts.

---

[12] Burge uses the case of A for a different purpose; I discuss his use of it below.

[13] Burge describes A's views as "nonstandard theory." But they are clearly (also) criterial beliefs, as they are beliefs about what *makes* something a sofa. "*A* doubts the truisms and hypothesizes that sofas function not as furnishings to be sat on, but as works of art or religious artifacts ... *A* admits that some sofas have been sat upon, but thinks that most sofas would collapse under any considerable weight and denies that sitting is what sofas are pre-eminently *for*" (Burge 1986, p. 707).

(r) *The green item in the corner is a certain sort of religious artifact.*
(s) *The green item in the corner is a sofa.*

Recall that the objection to the Differential Dubitability thesis is that mistaken criterial beliefs can affect what is differentially dubitable for an individual. According to that line of reasoning, A's religious theory of sofas will prevent him from believing (s) while doubting (r). Further supposing that A takes sofas to be the only religious artifacts of the relevant sort, A will be similarly unable to believe that (r) while doubting (s).

The challenge to the Differential Dubitability thesis is clear. Thoughts (r) and (s) seem plainly to differ in cognitive value, yet they are not differentially dubitable for A (who is stipulated to be rational). This appears to be a counterexample to the component of the Differential Dubitability thesis that threatens externalism, namely, the claim that rational thinkers will be able to differentially doubt any two thoughts that differ in cognitive value. Moreover, Burge's proposed modification resolves this problem. Since the differential dubitability of (r) and (s) is clearly "supportable by publicly recognized methods," as reflected in the ordinary views about sofas that A regards as mistaken, these differ in cognitive value, according to Burge's modification.

However, this challenge to the Differential Dubitability thesis fails, and does so in an illuminating way. The case of A is a counterexample to the Differential Dubitability thesis only on an unsustainable interpretation of that case. A cannot entertain s unless he has the concept *sofa*. And given his unorthodox views about the things he calls "sofas," it is not obvious that he has that concept. In an attempt to silence this worry, Burge stipulates that A is willing to submit his religious theory to empirical testing, and to relinquish that theory if it is disproven according to communal norms of evidence. "We may imagine that if we were to carry out [A's] proposed experiments [meant to establish that sofas are religious artifacts], A would come to admit that his theory is mistaken" (Burge 1986, p. 263). So although A does not defer to others' criterial beliefs about *sofa*, he does defer to communal epistemic norms about how to determine what makes something a sofa.

The stipulation that A is willing to relinquish his religious theory, under those conditions, may justify crediting him with the concept *sofa*. At least, we can grant that it does. But this does not allow the case to threaten the Differential Dubitability thesis. In fact, this stipulation *defuses* the challenge to that thesis. A's willingness to relinquish his religious theory, under those conditions, ensures that A *can* differentially doubt (r) and (s) after all. A can believe that (s) while doubting that

(r) precisely by imagining that his proposed experiments have disproven his religious theory of sofas. (Alternatively, we could bring him to believe this by actually conducting the experiments or duping him into believing that we have.)

This defense of the Differential Dubitability thesis cannot be blocked simply by revoking the stipulation that A is willing to abandon his religious theory under certain conditions. Suppose that A's adherence to the belief that sofas are religious artifacts were unshakeable. If A were disposed to maintain his religious theory come what may, then what A expressed with "sofa" would not be *sofa* but, rather an idiosyncratic concept that he mistakenly associates with "sofa." (The actual extension of this idiosyncratic concept would presumably be empty.) Lacking the concept *sofa*, A could not entertain (s) at all. So A's willingness to abandon his religious theory is both necessary for his possessing the concept *sofa* and, assuming that he has the other concepts required to entertain (r) and (s), sufficient for him to differentially doubt (r) and (s).

I have focused on A's radically mistaken criterial beliefs. Burge uses this case for a different purpose: to show that the argument for externalism does not rest on factors present in his earlier arguments, viz., "incomplete linguistic understanding and ignorance of expert knowledge" (Burge 1986, p. 708). But the argument involving A shares a central characteristic of those earlier arguments. All of these arguments involve a thinker who lacks (some) explicatory knowledge about a concept he uses, and *defers* to an external (usually social) factor about that concept. A is unusual in that he does not defer directly to the beliefs of his community, or experts therein, about what makes something a sofa. He defers to the results of his proposed experiments and/or communal epistemic norms about *how to determine* what makes something a sofa. It is this deference which constitutes his willingness to relinquish his religious theory and thereby allows him to be credited with the concept *sofa*.

Burge's externalist arguments involve rational thinkers who are purported to exercise concepts in thought while harboring mistaken criterial beliefs about those concepts (or exhibiting other sorts of explicatory errors or ignorance).[14] These thinkers cannot correct their errors or cure their ignorance through introspective reflection: they can be corrected only by external factors (communal usage, local experts, the outcome of

---

[14] This is not to say that external factors are irrelevant in cases where the individual knows the salient criterial truths. Since external factors contribute to fixing criterial truths, according to externalism, the truth of the subject's criterial beliefs depend, in part, on external factors.

empirical testing, etc.). These cases thus appear to be counterexamples to the Explicatory Access thesis.

But these cases do not directly threaten either the Differential Dubitability thesis or internalism. They do not threaten the Differential Dubitability thesis because explicatory beliefs, including criterial beliefs, are beliefs *about* one's own thoughts and concepts, whereas differential dubitability is a matter of first-order sensitivity: how one *reasons with* a thought, and how *employs* the concepts exercised therein. The Differential Dubitability thesis is neutral on the question whether rational thinkers can achieve reflective, explicatory knowledge *about* their thoughts; it is thus neutral about whether they can *recognize that* two of their thoughts differ in (or share a) cognitive value.

Burge's cases do not threaten internalism because internalism is not accessibilism: it is neutral about whether thinkers have explicatory access to their thoughts. Internalism holds that the cognitive values of thoughts are fixed by factors internal to the thinker. In other words, internal factors fix the rational role of a thought that p – the conditions under which one is disposed to believe that p, this thought's rational relations to other thoughts, the kind of inferences into which it enters, etc.[15] This role is (at least primarily) a matter of relations between first-order states. Internalism is neutral as to whether any relations to higher-order states are implicated in rationality. Internalism is true so long as the cognitive value of thoughts supervenes on factors within the thinker, regardless of whether the thinker has reflective access to the proper explication of those thoughts. (This is not to deny that most internalists believe that we do have such access, of course.) Cognitive value is largely a matter of dispositions, including dispositions that constitute *deference* to external factors.

Deference and indexicality

Burge's externalist arguments highlight a central dimension of our dispositions to apply certain concepts: *deference*. (It shares this feature with the anti-descriptivist arguments of Putnam (1975) and Kripke (1980).) The objects of deference can be social or physical; what is important to

---

[15] The idea that the cognitive value of a thought is fixed by the individual's dispositions, including dispositions that constitute deference to communal norms, is a familiar one. This idea forms the basis of semantic two-dimensionalism, which is internalist about the cognitive value of thoughts (what Chalmers calls their *primary intension*) while allowing that other kinds of content (including Chalmers's *secondary intensions*) depend on external factors (Chalmers 2006).

Burge's externalist arguments is that we routinely defer to factors external to ourselves.

Internalism can accommodate the phenomenon of deference by construing deferential concepts as *indexed to* the social or physical factors to which the thinker defers. Burge criticizes this strategy at numerous places; here are two representative passages.

> 'Sofa' in our attributions to *A* is not indexical ... One could perhaps modify the italicized phrase to *thing of a kind relevant to understanding what I (or we) usually refer to when I have this sort of experience (or, alternatively, when I use 'sofa')*. But now it is clear that no one but a philosopher would think of sofas in that complex, meta-level way. A complex analysis or theory of reference should not be conflated with the way *A* thinks of sofas. (*Burge 1986, note 12*)

> Sometimes *arthritis* is called a 'deferential concept'. This phrase seems to me very misleading. Nearly any concept can be employed in such a way that the employer depends on others for the range of the concept's application, and even for instruction on explicational principles and other norms governing the concept. Our reliance on others places us under standards and norms that we may not have fully mastered. Moreover, we cannot in general tell by simple reflection whether and how we depend on others. The dependence commonly is buried in the history of one's usage and in dispositions not all of which are open to reflective recognition. The main issue has to do with what objective reality we are connected to and what standards for full understanding apply to those aspects of our usage that rely on such connection. (*Burge 2006, p. 173*)

These passages are illuminating. Burge appears to regard the claim that *sofa* or *arthritis* are indexical concepts, as implying that this fact is readily available to introspective reflection. But internalists generally regard explication as a complex process, one that involves carefully considering various possible scenarios (including possible discoveries). We have already seen one example of this: *A*'s considering the scenario in which certain experiments are run and yield results he finds surprising (results that suggest that sofas are not religious artifacts). In any case, the internalist can remain neutral on the Explicatory Access thesis. She can maintain that my *arthritis* concept is indexed to social factors to which I defer, without committing herself to the claim that I can *recognize* that it is deferential. Thought contents may supervene on internal factors even if thinkers cannot always explicate them, through introspective reflection; and even if a rational thinker was unable to recognize the correct "complex, meta-level" analysis of her *arthritis* concept. Internalism is not – and does not imply – accessibilism.

Why would Burge (or anyone) think that these are linked? The answer might lie in an implicit conception of what is "internal to the thinker." I have recently argued that there is no univocal reading of this phrase, and hence no single boundary of the thinker, operative in the current debate over content (Gertler 2012). Burge's criticisms of the idea that concepts like *arthritis* are narrow, indexical concepts, would be justified if "thoughts and concepts supervene on factors internal to the thinker" implied "thoughts and concepts are explicable by the thinker." So although Burge's explicit characterizations of what makes a factor internal or external are not epistemic, his criticisms of the internalist construal of deferential concepts may rest on an implicit conception of what is "internal to the thinker" as what she can explicate. That is, these criticisms seem implicitly to construe internalism as accessibilism.[16]

While Burge rightly emphasizes the difference between having a particular thought and being able to explicate that thought, he neglects some of the possibilities this difference opens up. For his discussion implies that we face a stark choice: either allow that cognitive value constitutively depends on factors external to the thinker, or claim that rational thought requires access, through reflection, to the proper explication of one's thoughts. But there is a third option. The cognitive value of a thought is fixed, in part, by the subject's implicit dispositions – to employ the thought in inferences, to revise other attitudes in certain ways, in light of the thought (etc.). The cognitive value of a concept – what it contributes to the rational role of thoughts – is fixed, in part, by the thinker's implicit dispositions to apply the concept to certain things and to defer to certain authorities. Internalism is true so long as the factors determining cognitive value are within the thinker. These may be dispositions (and the bases thereof). They needn't consist in explications of content.

A crucial component in Burge's case for externalism (and, relatedly, against the Differential Dubitability thesis) are arguments intended to show that thinking doesn't require reflective access to truth conditions or criterial truths. These arguments target the Explicatory Access thesis. But the internalist need not be committed to that thesis. So even if these arguments succeed, they pose no direct challenge to internalism.

---

[16] Farkas (2003) supports a related construal of internalism; I express some worries in Gertler 2012.

8 The insignificance of transparency

Åsa Wikforss

The question of whether semantic externalism is compatible with a plausible account of self-knowledge has been much debated over the last couple of decades, and by now the positions are well established. There are the two well-known incompatibilist lines of argument: the switching argument (according to which externalism implies that there can be changes in content which are not discernible a priori) and the reductio argument (according to which compatibilism has the absurd consequence that we can know facts about the external environment a priori).[1] And there are the two well-known lines of response, a switching response (SR) and a reductio response (RR):

> (SR) We must distinguish between *introspective knowledge of an occurrent thought* (as in "I am thinking with this thought that water is wet") and *knowledge of comparative content* (being able to tell WATER thoughts from TWATER thoughts).[2] Self-knowledge merely requires the former, not the latter, and content externalism does not threaten the former, since basic self-ascriptions of occurrent thoughts are self-verifying. Even if the subject is in a switching scenario, her self-ascriptions will be correct.[3]
> (RR) Knowing that one is thinking that water is wet does not require knowing anything about how the content of this thought is

---

Thanks to Kathrin Glüer, Peter Pagin, and Francois Recanati for illuminating discussions on the topic of transparency and for comments on earlier drafts, and to Sanford Goldberg for helpful comments on the penultimate draft. Thanks also to the audience at the City University of New York Graduate Centre Colloquium, where a version of the paper was presented on 24 October 2012.

[1] For the switching argument, see for instance Boghossian 1989 and 1994. For the reductio argument see McKinsey 1991 and Boghossian 1996.
[2] For this distinction, see for instance Brown 2004a, pp. 37–59, and Falvey and Owens 1994, pp. 109–10.
[3] The classic statements of this compatibilist argument can be found in Burge 1988 and Davidson 1987.

determined or whether it is dependent on the external environment. For instance, I may know that I am thinking that water is wet, without knowing whether WATER is a natural kind concept, and it is only if WATER is a natural kind concept (actually picking out a natural kind) that it depends on the external environment.[4]

It should be clear that there is a connection between the two lines of defense. In both cases it is argued that basic self-knowledge, knowledge of an occurrent thought, should be distinguished from a more demanding type of knowledge involving detailed knowledge of the *content* of the thought: in (SR), knowledge of comparative content; in (RR), knowledge of the semantics of the content (in particular, its metasemantics).[5] The strategy, therefore, is to clearly separate the issue of self-knowledge from issues concerning knowledge of content.[6] Prima facie, this is a reasonable proposal: knowledge of content, in both sense (SR) and (RR), is a meta-level knowledge, and as such it is cognitively demanding. Knowledge of an occurrent thought, by contrast, is something (intuitively) that can be achieved by a small child (once she has acquired the concepts of the relevant mental states). Consequently, we should be skeptical of an account of self-knowledge that requires this type of meta-level knowledge of contents and semantics. To the extent that the incompatibilist relies on this requirement, compatibilism seems to be in good shape.

However, the incompatibilist has another line of attack, one that has drawn much attention recently and which is derived from considerations of reasoning and rationality, according to which the issue of 'knowledge of content' cannot be so easily dismissed. Externalist theories of mental content, it is argued, undermine 'the transparency of mental content', the thesis that subjects can tell a priori, on the basis of introspection, whether two thoughts have the same content. A standard formulation of the thesis is the following:

---

[4] See for instance McLaughlin and Tye 1998b and Brown 2004a.
[5] It could be asked whether knowledge of the metasemantics of 'water' would really make a difference to the reductio argument. For instance, I might know that if I am on Earth and the watery stuff is H_2O then 'water' expresses WATER, whereas if I am on Twin Earth and the water stuff is XYZ, then 'water' expresses TWATER, etc., but this does not suffice for the reductio to go through. It would lead too far to discuss this conditional proposal here, but it should be noted that it too presupposes separating the two types of knowledge: the suggestion is that one can have knowledge of one's occurrent 'water' thoughts without knowing anything about the actual determination of the content (indeed, one would not even know whether the determination is internalist or externalist). For a discussion, see Häggqvist and Wikforss 2007.
[6] For a very clear statement of this strategy, see Goldberg 2003c.

(TrC) For any two thoughts, or thought constituents, that S entertains at time t, S can realize a priori, at t, whether they have the same contents.[7]

That externalism poses a threat to transparency is illustrated already by the switching argument. However, according to this new line of attack, the real worry does not concern self-knowledge but that the transparency of content is presupposed by the role played by content in assessments of rationality and the explanation of action. For instance, Paul Boghossian has argued that the claim that content is transparent is a "semantically significant thesis," one that plays an important role in our ordinary conception of mental content (Boghossian 1994, p. 45).[8] Even if the compatibilist is right to suggest that there is a basic type of self-knowledge that is not threatened by content externalism, therefore, the question remains whether the fact that content externalism undermines transparency is compatible with an acceptable account of *reasoning*.

This sets the stage for a new debate between incompatibilists and compatibilists, where the focus is no longer on self-knowledge as such, but on reasoning and rationality: according to the (new) incompatibilist, the possibility of reasoning and rationality (practical as well as theoretical) presupposes transparency of content, and any account that threatens transparency (such as externalism and Millianism) is therefore incompatible with the only plausible account of reasoning. According to the (new) compatibilist, by contrast, a rejection of transparency is perfectly compatible with an acceptable account of reasoning and rationality. Indeed, the compatibilist suggests, externalists (and Millians) can exploit the fact that their theory implies that content is *not* transparent: the subject's reasoning, it is argued, can be accounted for by appealing to the fact that she is mistaken about the sameness and difference of the contents of her own thoughts.[9]

Since I have argued elsewhere that the central objection to externalism concerns not self-knowledge but the role of content in reasoning and action explanation, I think the focus on reasoning is appropriate.[10] However, I do not think that the focus on content transparency is promising; on the contrary, I think that it constitutes yet another detour. Just as it

---

[7] This formulation of the thesis derives from Brown 2003 and 2004a. See also Boghossian 1994, Campbell 1987, Falvey and Owens 1994, Recanati 2012, Sainsbury and Tye 2012, and Schroeter 2007.
[8] See also Boghossian 2011.
[9] See for instance Brown 2003 and 2004a, Millikan 1993, Sainsbury and Tye 2012, and Schroeter 2007.
[10] Wikforss 2006 and 2008a.

is problematic to claim that knowledge of content is of importance to self-knowledge, I argue, so is it problematic to claim that knowledge of content is of importance to reasoning. It is quite correct, of course, that externalism (and Millianism) undermines the transparency thesis, (TrC), and it is at least plausible that internalism (and Fregeanism) supports the thesis.[11] However, the implications for transparency are by-products, as it were, of the theories, and it is a mistake to conclude that transparency is of central significance. In this sense, I suggest, both sides of the debate are mistaken, the new incompatibilists as well as the new compatibilists. Both sides make two central assumptions:

(i) Subjects have meta-level beliefs about the contents of their own thoughts;

and

(ii) These meta-level beliefs play an important role in the subject's theoretical and practical reasoning.

I argue that both assumptions are problematic. The upshot, once again, is that the central point of contention between internalists and externalists is not epistemological; rather, I suggest, it concerns *what role the theory of content should play*.

The chapter is divided into three main sections. In the first section I set the stage by distinguishing between two notions of transparency that are both present in the debate, what I call 'access transparency' and 'functional transparency', and I spell out the motivations behind the contemporary appeal to transparency considerations. In the second section I consider two common construals of the relevant meta-level beliefs and argue that they cannot play the role required of them by both sides of the debate. In the final section I consider a third construal of the transparency thesis and the meta-beliefs it appeals to, according to which the central notion of transparency concerns the transparency of

---

[11] It is important to be clear about the relations between Millianism and externalism on the one hand, and Fregeanism and internalism on the other. As I have argued elsewhere, internalism and externalism are best understood as metasemantic theses concerning the *determination* of content (Wikforss 2008b). Fregeanism and Millianism, by contrast, are *semantic* theories telling us something about the semantics of our expressions and thoughts. Although there are connections between metasemantics and semantics (for instance, Millian theories are paired with a causal, externalist theory of meaning determination), the relations can be quite complex. In particular, it is possible to imagine a version of descriptivism combined with an externalist metasemantics. In what follows I will leave these complexities be, since what matters here is what externalism and Millianism have in common: that they face (prima facie) difficulties capturing the subject's reasoning.

belief (and only implicitly transparency of content). I argue that although this allows for a more plausible construal of the relevant meta-beliefs, it too fails to show that these beliefs play an important role in reasoning. I end with some reflections on the connections between functional and access transparency.

The significance of transparency

Access transparency and functional transparency

The contemporary discussion of content transparency takes its starting point in Dummett's claim that linguistic meaning is transparent. It is an undeniable feature of the notion of meaning, Dummett writes, "that meaning is *transparent* in the sense that, if someone attaches a meaning to each of two words, he must know whether these meanings are the same" (Dummett 1978, p. 131). Boghossian elaborates on Dummett's thesis. First, he argues, the thesis is not merely the weak one that for any two expressions it must be possible for *S* to come to know whether or not they mean the same, but the stronger thesis that "it must be possible for that person to come to know such a fact purely *introspectively*, without the benefit of further empirical investigation" (Boghossian 1994, p. 33). Second, the transparency thesis, in its most interesting form, concerns not the meaning of linguistic expressions, but *mental content*. This is so, Boghossian argues, since the assumption that mental content is transparent is essential to our conceptions of rationality and rational explanations:

> We don't just ascribe thoughts to a person in order to say something true of him. We use such ascriptions for two related purposes: on the one hand to enable assessments of his rationality and, on the other, to explain his behavior. As these matters are currently conceived, a thought must be epistemically transparent if it is to play these roles. (*Boghossian 1994, p. 39*)

The transparency thesis, as understood by Boghossian, is a thesis concerning *epistemic access*: in the case of linguistic meaning, the access speakers have to the meaning of their linguistic expressions; in the case of mental content, the access individuals have to the contents of their own thoughts and attitudes. Let us, consequently, call this type of transparency *access transparency*. Since the concern is with epistemic access, the relevant notion of knowledge is propositional knowledge. This means that if meaning and contents are access transparent, the individual is to be attributed meta-beliefs about the sameness and difference of meanings and contents respectively. Moreover, the beliefs should be *a priori*, in the sense that they should be based on introspection rather than on empirical investigations.[12]

It is of importance to be able to distinguish between access transparency and a second notion of transparency, also found in the literature, what I will call *functional transparency*. The thesis that meaning and mental content are functionally transparent is not an epistemic thesis, but a thesis about the determination of meaning and content. It is motivated by the idea that meaning and content play an important role in explaining the subject's point of view, her reasoning and actions. Thus, François Recanati, defending the transparency of sense, makes clear that transparency boils down to the requirement that content should capture the subject's cognitive perspective, and that transparency construed this way does not require the attribution of meta-beliefs to the subject.[13] Applied to linguistic meaning, therefore, functional transparency does not concern our knowledge of meaning, but is simply a version of the thesis that meaning is determined by the individual's use of a term. For instance, if the speaker assents to 'Hesperus is Hesperus' but dissents from 'Hesperus is Phosphorus', then the terms 'Hesperus' and 'Phosphorus' do not have the same meaning for *S*. Applied to the level of content, similarly, functional transparency does not concern access to contents, but is just the thesis that thought content is determined by cognitive role. Thus, if *S* reasons as if two thought tokens are about distinct objects (as in the case of Hesperus and Phosphorus), then the thoughts have distinct content; conversely, if *S* reasons as if two thought components have the same content (as in the switching scenario), then they do.[14]

Access transparency and functional transparency are therefore importantly different: whereas access transparency concerns propositional knowledge and involves the attribution of meta-beliefs to the subject, functional transparency is not a thesis about (propositional) knowledge

---

[12] In the case of linguistic meaning it does not seem right to say, as Boghossian does, that the beliefs are based on *introspection*. More plausibly, the beliefs would be based on *reflection* (as when one reflects on how one would use a term in various scenarios).

[13] Recanati 2012, pp. 96–110. See also Schroeter 2007. Although Recanati speaks of "epistemic transparency," he makes clear that his notion of transparency does not involve meta-level judgments (see in particular footnote 83, p. 102). And although Schroeter starts with Dummett's thesis and speaks of the idea that we normally have "direct and authoritative access" to the contents of our own thoughts, the central claims made in the paper concern functional transparency.

[14] Recanati actually does not endorse full functional transparency since he argues that in a switching scenario, where a subject equivocates between two distinct concepts, there is failure of reference. On his construal, therefore, the transparency thesis is conditional on successful reference: if the subject treats two mental tokens as co-referring, then they do, *if they refer at all* (2012, p. 109).

of content and does not require the speaker to have meta-beliefs about the sameness and difference of meanings and contents. The focus in this chapter shall be on access transparency. This is the notion of transparency that thesis (TrC) concerns, and it is the notion that plays a central role in the contemporary debate initiated by Boghossian.[15]

Transparency under threat

To illustrate the role of access transparency in the contemporary debate, let us consider theories that are said to violate the thesis that content is transparent. In this context, two aspects of the thesis are commonly distinguished: the transparency of *sameness* of content and the transparency of *difference* of content.[16] Millian theories of content are mentioned as prime examples of theories that are incompatible with transparency of sameness of content: for instance, Pierre is unable to know, a priori, that 'London' expresses the same content as 'Londres'. And Twin Earth externalism is said to pose a threat to transparency of difference of content: Oscar, after being (unknowingly) switched to Twin Earth, is unable to tell that his current 'water' concept is distinct from that of his original 'water' concept (retained in his memories from Earth).[17]

Proponents of transparency take the violation of transparency to be a serious problem for Millianism and externalism respectively since, they argue, it undermines a plausible account of reasoning and rationality. The problem, Boghossian argues, is "that when mental contents violates one or both of these transparency theses, we get cases where a thinker who intuitively looks fully rational, and is merely missing some empirical information, is made to look as though he is committing simple logical fallacies in his reasoning."[18] Thus, in the case of Millianism, the upshot is that the subject is to be ascribed contradictory beliefs, and fails to realize the validity of simple inferences. For instance, Pierre fails to realize that the thought expressed by 'London is not pretty' contradicts that expressed by 'Londres is pretty', and he fails to draw the proper theoretical and practical inferences about the city he lives in. Assuming social externalism, even non-Millian contents may violate the transparency of sameness of content, as illustrated by an example due to Falvey

---

[15] It is an interesting question how access transparency and functional transparency are related. I will return to this question below, in the final section.
[16] See for instance Boghossian 1994, p. 36, and Brown 2004a, p. 160.
[17] As noted in Goldberg 2008b, the situation may be even worse, since, assuming metaphysical realism (that some empirical truths are not knowable to humans), it is possible that some contents are determined by facts that no one (expert or not) will ever be in a position to have knowledge of.
[18] Boghossian 2011, pp. 458–59.

and Owens, involving the terms 'cilantro' and 'coriander'.[19] They imagine an individual, Rudolf, who partially understands these terms and defers to experts for their correct use. As it turns out, the experts treat the terms as synonyms, naming the same herb, although Rudolf fails to realize this. He knows that cilantro and coriander are both herbs, but thinks of cilantro as the fresh herb used in Mexican cooking, and coriander as a dried herb. Thus, Rudolf assents both to 'Cilantro should be used sparingly' and to 'Coriander should not be used sparingly', and he fails to draw some obviously valid inferences.

Similarly, it is argued, when transparency of *difference* of content is undermined, the subject will make some simple invalid inferences. For instance, Oscar is switched to Twin Earth and, as a result, he (eventually) acquires the concept TWATER in addition to the original concept WATER. The new concept is employed in beliefs about current events, the old concept in memory beliefs dating back to Oscar's Earth days. Since Oscar is not able to tell that the concepts are different, he is likely to make simple reasoning errors when current beliefs are mixed with memory beliefs.[20] For instance, Oscar believes:

(1) There was water in the well at my childhood farm;

as well as

(2) There is twater in the well at my new farm;

from which he concludes:

(3) The well at my new farm contains the same liquid as the well at my childhood farm.

Thus he makes a simple invalid inference. This, it is held, illustrates how failures of transparency threaten the ordinary idea that subjects are (by and large) rational and do not make simple reasoning errors.[21]

In both cases, that is, the semantic theory in question mandates that subjects whose capacity for rational thought we have no reason to question, are to be described as being blatantly irrational. Hence, intuitively, the theory fails to capture the subject's cognitive perspective. The source of the trouble, the incompatibilist argues, is precisely that externalism (Millianism) fails to respect the transparency of content thesis, (TrC). According to Boghossian, this illustrates how absolutely central

---

[19] Falvey and Owens 1994. For a discussion of this case see Brown 2004a, p. 161.
[20] It should be noted that not all externalists agree that Oscar retains the old concept. For these externalists, therefore, this problem does not arise.
[21] See for instance Boghossian 2011 and Brown 2004a, chapter 5.

assumptions about transparency are to our ordinary conceptions of reasons and rationality. Indeed, he suggests, it illustrates that the transparency is a crucial (if unstated) premise underlying both internalist and Fregean conceptions of content. This can be illustrated, Boghossian suggests, if we consider Frege's classic argument for the thesis that names have a sense and not merely reference (Boghossian 1994, pp. 46–47).

Boghossian discusses the case of Mary who sincerely asserts 'Ali was a champ' and also asserts 'Clay was not a champ', even though 'Ali' and 'Clay' refer to the same boxer. On the assumption that sincere assertion entails belief, Boghossian argues, we may conclude that Mary believes that Ali was a champ and she believes that Clay was not a champ. However, Boghossian continues, this does not in itself support referential opacity since nothing so far prevents the conclusion that Mary has contradictory beliefs. What is required for the argument to go through is a "reason why an ascription of contradictory beliefs is unacceptable in the present instance" (Boghossian 1994, p. 46). We get such a reason, Boghossian argues, only if we insist that the contents of Mary's beliefs are knowable a priori; that is, only if they are epistemically transparent. Without transparency, Mary would not see the contradiction and so she would be blameless, and the Fregean appeal to sense would lack motivation (ibid., pp. 48–49).

According to Boghossian, therefore, it is not merely the case that there is a connection between internalism (Fregeanism) and transparency, it is also the case that the former *presupposes* the latter. The new compatibilists have been quick to exploit this claim: if, indeed, the arguments for internalism and Fregeanism presuppose that content is transparent, then those very same arguments can be undermined simply by giving up on the transparency thesis. For instance, Jessica Brown has argued that the Fregean arguments for a sense–reference distinction presuppose that sameness of content is transparent, and that, therefore, rejecting transparency undermines the Fregean argument and provides an alternative explanation of the subject's perspective. Thus, she considers Celeste who takes a different attitude toward 'The Morning Star is the Evening Star' than to 'The Morning Star is the Morning Star'. Instead of invoking a difference in content, Brown argues, we can explain this by denying that sameness of content is transparent and appealing to the idea that Celeste thinks, mistakenly, that there is a difference in content: "although Celeste associates thought-constituents having the same content with 'the Morning Star' and 'the Evening Star', she supposes they have different contents since she thinks that the two expressions refer to different planets"

(Brown 2003, p. 444).[22] Similarly, it has been suggested that by giving up on the transparency of difference of content, we can explain why Oscar, in the switching scenario, reasons invalidly: the fallacy is a result of Oscar's mistaken belief that his thought in the first premise ('There was water in the well of my childhood farm') involves the same 'water' concept as that in the second ('There is twater in the well at my new farm').[23]

This means that the new incompatibilists and the new compatibilists both take transparency to play a pivotal role. Moreover, the relevant notion of transparency is that of *access* transparency: it is held that meta-level beliefs about the sameness and difference in content play an important role in the subject's reasoning.[24] The difference between the two camps is that while the incompatibilists take these meta-beliefs to be true and suggest that this is important if we are to explain the subject's reasoning and actions, the compatibilists argue that these meta-level beliefs are often false, and that this provides an alternative explanation of the subject's reasoning. Both sides of the debate therefore share the two central assumptions mentioned in the introduction above: (i) that subjects have meta-level beliefs about the contents of their own thoughts and attitudes; (ii) that this is semantically significant since these beliefs play a central role in explaining the subject's reasoning and actions. Next, let us examine these assumptions.

Content judgments

As we have seen above, the contemporary transparency thesis is intended to go beyond Dummett's thesis in two respects: the transparency concerns *the content of mental events*, not the meaning of linguistic signs, and the relevant knowledge has to be *a priori*, based on introspection. Whether linguistic meaning is transparent in Dummett's sense is controversial.[25] However, even if one grants the transparency of meaning, it is quite another matter to claim that mental content is transparent.

---

[22] A similar idea appears in Sainsbury and Tye 2012. They argue that rejecting transparency provides the Millian with an alternative solution to a set of paradoxes of thought, such as those involving Twin Earth and Kripke's Paderewski case.
[23] Brown 2004a, p. 167.
[24] This might be challenged on the grounds that it is sufficient if the relevant higher-order proposition is merely tacitly presupposed, rather than believed, in which case functional transparency is all that is required. However, since the central idea underlying both lines of argument is precisely that the *rationality* of the subject's reasoning depends on the transparency content (or failure thereof), it is not sufficient that the proposition is tacitly presupposed – it must also play the reason providing role of a *belief*.
[25] For a recent discussion, see Pagin 2012.

The claim that meaning is access transparent implies that speakers are to be attributed metalinguistic beliefs of the following sort:

(i) The meaning of 'cilantro' is the same as the meaning of 'coriander'.
(ii) The meaning of 'water' as used in context C1 is not the same as the meaning of 'water' as used in context C2.[26]

The claim that content is access transparent, similarly, would involve the attribution of beliefs about the contents of thoughts to individuals.[27] In this case, however, it is not so clear how such beliefs are to be understood.

The standard formulation of content transparency in terms of access to contents of thought tokens, as in (TrC), suggests that the relevant judgments are to be construed as a form of 'metalinguistic' judgment. The subject is said to know (introspectively) that a particular thought token, at a time, has a content that is different from (or the same as) the content of another such token. This strongly suggests that thoughts are to be construed as a form of mental expressions that we may have access to independently of knowing their contents, much like we do in the case of linguistic signs, and that the relevant content judgments involve reference to these. Boghossian, in his first discussion of transparency, endorses this construal quite explicitly. Discussing a version of the switching case, where Peter draws an invalid inference involving Pavarotti and twin Pavarotti, Boghossian writes that Peter's externally individuated thought tokens are not epistemically transparent to him: "In particular, Peter's language of thought contains token expressions that possess different semantic values despite being of the same syntactic type ... From the inside, however, there will be no indication of this: as far as Peter is concerned, they will appear to express precisely the same contents" (Boghossian 1994, p. 39).

---

[26] The beliefs could also be tied to the meaning of a word in a particular utterance, capturing the idea that transparency of meaning concerns knowledge of the meaning of one's own words as used on a given occasion.

[27] Dummett formulates the transparency thesis in terms of what the speaker *must know*. Upon this formulation, the claim that meaning is transparent implies that the speaker must have metalinguistic beliefs about the sameness and difference of meaning. But sometimes the transparency thesis is formulated not in terms of what the subject knows, but in terms of what she is in a position to know. For instance, (TrC) appeals to what the subject *can realize*. If so, the subject need not have the relevant meta-beliefs, it is sufficient that she *could* have them. However, the difficulties raised below with respect to access transparency apply equally to the weaker claim that the subject could have these beliefs. Moreover, as noted above, the claim that meta-beliefs about contents play an important role in the subject's reasoning requires not only that the subject *could* have these beliefs but that she does.

If this is how knowledge of content is to be construed, then the claim that content is transparent implies that the subject is able to form beliefs, on the basis of introspection, of the following sort:

(iii) The content of internal expression e_1, as used in thought t_1, is the same as (distinct from) the content of internal expression e_2, as used in thought t_2.

However, this construal is problematic. The trouble is not merely that, understood this way, the thesis would seem to entail a commitment to the controversial language of thought hypothesis. It is, rather, the very idea that subjects are able to introspect the expressions of this language and form judgments about their contents. It is quite clear that we have no such access to anything like symbols of a *lingua mentis*. Indeed, those who accept that there is a language of thought deny that there can be any form of introspective access to this language.[28] The point, of course, is not that the content of the language of thought is *non*transparent, in the sense that subjects have mistaken beliefs about these contents, but that the content of the language of thought is not an object of propositional knowledge in the first place. Indeed, even if the talk of mental expressions does not commit one to the strong claim that there is a full-fledged language of thought, with a language-like syntax and semantics, the very idea that knowledge of content involves having introspective access to the content of mental expressions would seem deeply problematic.

If the proponent of transparency were committed to the claim that subjects are to be attributed meta-beliefs along the lines of (iii), therefore, it would be hard even to get the thesis off the ground. Robert Stalnaker, in discussing self-knowledge and externalism, voices this worry, and argues that "we shouldn't think of access to our thoughts as access to an internal vehicle of representation" (Stalnaker 2008, p. 131). In his 2011 paper, however, Boghossian rejects this reading of the transparency thesis. The proponent of transparency, he argues, is not committed to the idea that mental contents are carried by wordlike components that can be identified independently of their meanings. Concepts, he suggests, are simply to be thought of as propositional

---

[28] The classic discussion of this is in Fodor 1975, chapter 2. He argues that there is no internal representation of the truth conditions of sentences in the language of thought. Rather, he suggests, we simply use these representations in a certain way and that's the end of it. For instance, the answer to the question of how we use the predicates of the language of thought correctly, Fodor suggests, is "that we just do; that we are just built that way" (p. 66).

constituents and hence there is no need to postulate a language of thought "with consciously accessible mental words."[29]

This suggests a rather different construal of the judgments presupposed by the transparency thesis. If knowledge of content is not a matter of knowing the content of mental expressions, but is to be construed as knowledge of propositional constituents, then knowledge of contents would seem to involve knowledge of abstract objects. The relevant judgments, thus, do not involve reference to mental vehicles, but are to be construed as 'bare' content judgments. For instance, S believes that

(iv) The concept CILANTRO is the same as the concept CORIANDER.
(v) The concept WATER is distinct from the concept TWATER.

This avoids the difficulties involved in the idea that we have access to the components of language of thought. However, it also implies a construal of content judgments that cannot play a role in accounting for the subject's cognitive perspective, her reasoning and actions.

The trouble derives from the fact that judgments such as (iv)–(v) are judgments *about concepts and contents* – judgments about abstract objects and not about the subject's first-order thoughts.[30] By denying that transparency involves a commitment to something like a language of thought, 'wordlike components' that can be identified independently of their contents, the link between content judgments and the subject's first-order thoughts is severed. If so, then a subject can know that two concepts are the same or different, without knowing anything whatsoever about the content of her occurrent thoughts. Can this problem be overcome?[31]

Boghossian's idea, it seems, is that we simply need to add a premise about the subject's access to her occurrent thoughts. Criticizing Stalnaker's claim that transparency presupposes that there is a language

---

[29] Boghossian 2011, p. 461.
[30] Nor, notice, is it at all plausible to say that they are based on *introspection*. Even if it were granted that content judgments are a priori in the sense that they are not based on outer experience, it is very difficult to see how they could be based on inner experience. Concepts, on this view, are abstract objects and I cannot discern whether two such objects are the same or not by inspecting my own mind (anymore than introspection reveals whether two numbers are the same or not).
[31] It might be said that even if this is so, we can simply read off facts about transparency from facts about how the subject actually reasons. For instance, if she reasons as if CILANTRO is the same as the concept CORIANDER (and this is false), then the contents are not transparent to her. However, this only holds for *functional* transparency. The point made here is precisely that concepts can be access transparent (in Boghossian's sense) and yet functional transparency will fail. For further elaboration of this point, see below.

of thought, Boghossian argues that the only assumption he needs to make about the internal component is that "a thinker can be introspectively aware that he has an occurrent thought when he has one, something that seems so intuitive as to need no argument."[32] That is, all that is needed is the assumption that subjects have self-knowledge of occurrent thoughts, in the basic sense mentioned above. The claim that content is transparent, then, is to be understood as the conjunction of two separate theses, the transparency of contents and concepts as abstract objects, and the transparency of thought:

(TrC*) For any two contents C_1 and C_2, S can realize a priori whether they are the same or different.

(TrT) For any occurrent thought T that S thinks at time t, S can realize a priori, at t, that she is thinking T.

The trouble is that these combined theses do not add up to the original thesis (TrC): while thesis (TrC*) is about knowledge of contents as abstract objects, it is not about knowledge of one's own thoughts; and while thesis (TrT) is about knowledge of one's own thoughts, it is not about knowledge of contents. Even if it is argued that (TrT) implicitly involves a form of basic 'knowledge of content', it remains the case that theses (TrT) and (TrC*) do not add up to the original transparency thesis. This becomes very clear if one tries to apply the combined theses to the problem cases introduced above: the case of Oscar in the switching scenario, and the case of Mary who fails to know that there is only one boxer involved. That is, even if we assume that content is transparent in Boghossian's sense (combining (TrC*) and (TrT)), this does not remove the difficulties of these scenarios. As a consequence, the claim that content is transparent is rendered insignificant when it comes to accounting for cognitive perspective.

First, consider Oscar in the switching scenario as described above, and assume that Oscar makes correct content judgments and does so purely a priori. That is, he judges, correctly, that the concept WATER is distinct from the concept TWATER. Moreover, he has introspective access to his occurrent thoughts, that is, 'knowledge of content' in the weak sense of (TrT); he self-ascribes both the thought that there was water in the well of his childhood farm and the thought that there is twater in the well of his new farm. However, it should be clear, none of this helps Oscar avoid the invalid reasoning. He knows that the two concepts are distinct and yet he will, as before, move from the premises containing distinct concepts to

---

[32] Boghossian 2011, p. 461.

the invalid conclusion. The bare content judgment simply does not interact with his first-order thoughts in the way required for transparency to play the role allotted to it.[33]

It should be stressed that the problem has nothing to do with Oscar's level of conceptual or theoretical sophistication. We can imagine him being completely infallible when it comes to bare content judgments: he never makes any mistakes about the sameness and difference of concepts. And we can imagine him to have full introspective knowledge: whenever he believes that he is thinking that water is wet, he is thinking that water is wet; and whenever he is thinking that water is wet, he believes that he is thinking that water is wet. Nevertheless, his knowledge of the relations that hold between concepts, in conjunction with his introspective knowledge, does not prevent him from making the basic reasoning errors precisely because this conceptual knowledge does not tell him anything about what concepts are exercised in a particular thought.[34]

Similarly in the case of Mary who sincerely asserts 'Ali was a champ' as well as 'Clay was not a champ'. Let us add, in this case too, that mental content is transparent in Boghossian's sense. That is, assume that Mary has the true meta-belief that the concept ALI is the concept CLAY. As before, this is a pure content judgment and will fail to interact with her introspective beliefs. Thus, she has the correct meta-belief, as well as the correct introspective beliefs (for instance, she believes that she is thinking that Ali was a champ), and yet this will not put her in a position to realize, on reflection alone, that she has contradictory first-order beliefs. Consequently, if the fact that Mary would be contradicting herself did not already provide a reason against a Millian semantics of Mary's terms, adding that content is transparent, in Boghossian's sense, does not provide one either.

The standard construals of the relevant content judgments are therefore problematic: speakers do not have beliefs about the contents of language of thought, as required by the metalinguistic construal, and if,

---

[33] For a related point, see Goldberg 2003a, p. 56, and 2003c, p. 247. Goldberg argues that even if Oscar, on Twin Earth, has a full understanding of the concept TWATER he is not in a position to know a priori that he is thinking with the concept TWATER rather than the concept WATER.

[34] Obviously, this is not to say that it would be *impossible* for him to discover that his thoughts involve different concepts. Perhaps Oscar finds out that he has been switched and that he no longer is on Earth but on Twin Earth where the local liquid is XYZ rather than H_2O. If he adds this piece of empirical knowledge to his knowledge that the concept WATER and the concept TWATER are distinct, plus additional knowledge about the semantics of the term 'water' and how the meaning of a term is related to the concept expressed (in ordinary beliefs as well as memory beliefs), etc. he will eventually be in a position to discover that the inference is invalid. But now, of course, we have gone well beyond what Oscar can know as a result of the transparency of content in Boghossian's sense.

instead, the beliefs are construed as being about contents as abstract objects, then they cannot play any role in accounting for the subject's cognitive perspective. It should be stressed, again, that these difficulties afflict both camps in the debate equally: both the (new) incompatibilists and the (new) compatibilists make the assumption that transparency judgments (whether true or false) play an important role in accounting for the subject's cognitive perspective.

The question is whether there is an alternative, less problematic way of thinking about transparency; one that does not require the attribution of any problematic content beliefs to speakers, but which nevertheless can be said to be central to semantics. Let us consider this question next.

Belief transparency

Central to the standard formulations of the transparency of content thesis is the idea that subjects have a meta-level knowledge of the contents of their thoughts and intentional states. This might seem misguided from the start, however, independently of how one construes the relevant content judgments, since it raises the worry that the transparency thesis is simply too cognitively demanding for it to play a central role in the psychological life of ordinary subjects: after all, having beliefs about the contents of one's own thoughts requires having the semantic concepts of CONCEPT and CONTENT, and it is doubtful that ordinary speakers have these concepts. Most people would probably draw a blank if asked whether 'Hesperus is Hesperus' expresses the same content as 'Hesperus is Phosphorus'. Ordinary reasoning does not require explicit knowledge of content, it would seem, any more than basic self-knowledge does. Perhaps, then, the discussion above is an obvious dead end, and perhaps we must think of transparency differently: not as involving knowledge of the sameness and difference of *contents*, but simply as involving knowledge of sameness and difference of our *mental states*, in particular of our *beliefs*.

This, also, is how the transparency thesis is sometimes formulated in the literature. For instance, David Owen construes transparency as the principle that introspection provides subjects with all they need "to determine sameness and difference in belief."[35] It might therefore be

---

[35] Owen 1990, p. 158. At points, Boghossian also formulates the issue in terms of belief. For instance, discussing Kripke's case of Paul who learns 'cat' and 'chat' separately, Boghossian suggests: "Paul will not be able to tell *a priori* that the belief he expresses with 'All chats have tails' is the same belief that he expresses with 'All cats have tails'" (1994, p. 37).

suggested that we can avoid all the difficulties discussed above simply by sticking to belief transparency:

(TrB) For any two beliefs that S holds at time t, S can realize a priori, at t, whether they are the same or different.

If this is how the transparency thesis is understood, then the relevant transparency judgments are second-order beliefs of the following sort:

(vi) My belief that Hesperus is Phosphorus is the same as (distinct from) my belief that Hesperus is Hesperus.

No doubt, second-order beliefs of this sort involve an *implicit* grasp of the concept of content: if the subject judges that her belief that p is distinct from her belief that q, then this judgment reflects an implicit grasp of the idea that sameness and difference of belief depends on the contents of the states. However, it is not required that the subject has any explicit beliefs involving the concepts of CONCEPT and CONTENT.

The question is whether the transparency thesis understood this way, is 'semantically significant'. In particular: does the Fregean position presuppose (TrB)? Conversely, does rejecting (TrB) provide the Millian (and the externalist) with an alternative account of the subject's cognitive perspective?

To consider this, let us return to Boghossian's argument for why transparency is essential to motivate the appeal to Fregean contents. On the assumption that the relevant notion of transparency is that of belief transparency, the argument has the following form:

(1) The Fregean needs to provide a reason why the attribution of contradictory beliefs is unacceptable.
(2) Transparency provides the reason: only on the assumption that the subject knows that her belief that p contradicts her belief that q, is it unacceptable to attribute contradictory beliefs.
(3) Hence, if transparency is rejected the Fregean argument is undermined.

Premise (1) seems plausible: the Fregean needs to provide some reason why we could not simply say that Mary holds contradictory beliefs about the boxer. The question is why we should accept (2). Why should the required reason concern Mary's capacity to tell the sameness and difference of her beliefs? Belief transparency, I want to suggest, is neither necessary nor sufficient for the Fregean argument.

First, let us assume that Mary does not have any second-order beliefs about the sameness and difference of her first-order beliefs. Perhaps she lacks the concept of belief, and is unable to form second-order beliefs of the sort required for belief transparency.[36] Or perhaps she is just not prone to self-reflection (or philosophizing) and would not know how to answer if we were to ask her whether her beliefs are the same or not. This does not in any way undermine the need to appeal to Fregean contents. We are still faced with the task of giving an account of Mary's perspective, of why she asserts both 'Ali was a champ' and 'Clay was not a champ', and this motivates the appeal to Fregean contents: the difference in attitudes is explained by appealing to a difference in contents. The argument does, of course, presuppose that content ascriptions should serve the role of capturing the subject's cognitive perspective, in this case the fact that Mary reasons and acts as if there are two distinct boxers. This means that the Fregean has to assume *functional* transparency, that is, that relevant differences in use (in conceptual role) imply a difference in meaning and content. But, again, functional transparency is distinct from access transparency (including transparency of belief), and does not involve any meta-beliefs on the part of the subject.

Next, assume that Mary *is* able to form the required meta-beliefs, and that she would be able to tell, a priori, whether her beliefs contradict one another. Why should this, in and of itself, make the attribution of contradictory beliefs unacceptable? If we do not already have a reason to avoid such attributions, adding that Mary knows that her beliefs are contradictory does not provide one either. And, again, we do already have such a reason: the attribution of contradictory beliefs fails to capture Mary's cognitive perspective, it makes it impossible to explain her reasoning and actions. Hence, belief transparency is neither necessary nor sufficient for the Fregean argument.

It might be objected that even if this is so, there is nevertheless a *connection* between the Fregean argument and belief transparency, since there are cases where we do attribute contradictory beliefs and these are, precisely, cases where there are failures of self-knowledge. For instance, a subject may have repressed one of her beliefs and as a result have contradictory beliefs without realizing that she does. Consequently, even if the Fregean argument does not presuppose that Mary has true meta-beliefs about her first-order beliefs, it does presuppose that she does not have *false* such meta-beliefs. The Millian (or the externalist) can simply exploit this and suggest that once the latter presupposition is given up, as Millian contents require, the Fregean argument is undermined: Mary believes

---

[36] As stressed in the literature, small children and some adults (with severe autism) do not have the concept of belief. This poses difficulties for those who claim that second-order beliefs play an essential semantic role. Most people suffering from autism are highly skilled language users and sophisticated reasoners (as long as the reasoning does not involve the beliefs of others).

both that Ali was a champ and that he was not a champ; she just does not know it.[37]

However, while it is quite correct that there are cases where we do attribute contradictory beliefs because there is a failure of self-knowledge, this does not undermine the need for Fregean contents and it does not provide the Millian with an alternative explanation of the subject's cognitive perspective. To bring this out, let us reflect on the trouble caused by the attribution of contradictory beliefs to subjects when it comes to giving an account of the subject's practical and theoretical reasoning. Consider the case where Mary goes to see Ali fight a match. This is explained by her belief that Ali is a champ (in conjunction with her desire to see a champ fight). But, according to the Millian, she also believes that Ali is not a champ. Why, then, does she go to see the match? Contradictory beliefs block all actions: Mary's reason to see the match is undermined by the contradictory belief, giving her equal reason not to see the match. Similarly in the case of theoretical inferences. Mary believes that all champs are hard-working and this belief together with her belief that Ali was a champ supports the conclusion that Ali was hard-working. However, she also believes that Ali was not a champ (according to the Millian), and this should block the inference to her belief that Ali was hard-working. It is of no help at all to add, as the Millian suggests, that Mary does not know that her beliefs are contradictory. This simply does not explain why she acts on one belief but not the other, why she infers from one belief but not from the other.

To explain that, something else would have to be added: it would have to be said that Mary *compartmentalizes*, and that one of her beliefs is 'walled off' from her theoretical and practical reasoning. Such 'walling off' takes place in certain familiar cases of psychological irrationality, such as self-deception and repression, and these typically involve failures of self-knowledge. Compartmentalization restores the subject's rationality, at least partially, and allows us to explain her reasoning and actions. For instance, assume that Mary had a painful childhood and believes both that her father is a nice man, and that her father is not a nice man at all. However, she has managed to repress the latter belief, and acts as if her father is a nice man. In this case, there is a failure of self-knowledge: while Mary self-ascribes the first-order belief that her father is a nice man, she does not self-ascribe the contradictory first-order belief (she might even

---

[37] This is the explicit strategy used by Sainsbury and Tye 2012. By ascribing false second-order beliefs about the sameness and difference of first-order beliefs, they argue, "we can explain how it is that someone with normal powers can nonetheless be in no position to detect the contradictory character of a pair of his beliefs" (p. 135).

have the explicit but false second-order belief that she does not believe that her father is a horrid man).

There is therefore a grain of truth in the claim that there is a connection between the issue of self-knowledge of belief and the question of when it is acceptable to attribute contradictory beliefs to a subject: there are cases, involving compartmentalization and failure of self-knowledge, in which rational subjects hold contradictory beliefs. By the same token, there is a connection between the Fregean argument and assumptions about self-knowledge: the Fregean must assume that the difference in attitude (in the case under consideration) cannot be explained as involving compartmentalization and repression. This, however, is an assumption that falls far short of (TrB), and it is an assumption that seems to be very obviously fulfilled in the Fregean cases: in these cases there are no signs of compartmentalization. On the contrary, Mary expresses her beliefs in sincere assertions, and she self-ascribes both of the first-order beliefs correctly: she believes that she believes that Ali was a champ and she believes that she believes that Clay was not a champ. Hence, Mary's failure to notice the contradiction cannot be said to involve any 'walling off' or repression, allowing us to explain why she reasons and acts as she does despite holding contradictory beliefs.[38] And it is precisely because we lack an explanation of this sort in the Fregean cases, that the attribution of contradictory beliefs is unacceptable.

For this reason the existence of cases of compartmentalization cannot be exploited by the Millian to provide an alternative explanation of the subject's cognitive perspective by rejecting belief transparency. No doubt, it follows from the Millian view that Mary does not know that her beliefs are contradictory. But this cannot in itself be used to explain why Mary acts and reasons as she does. It does not, for instance, explain why she goes to the boxing match. At most, the assertion that she does not know what she believes *absolves* her from her irrationalities. Since Mary's error is not a result of some psychological irrationality on her part but, rather, a result of the semantics, she is not to be criticized. In this sense Mary is perfectly 'rational': although she holds irrational beliefs (and acts irrationally), this does not show that she has any cognitive shortcomings and it does not provide grounds for criticism. However, the important question does not concern *culpability* but *explanation*.[39] What we were looking

---

[38] For a related discussion of when compartmentalization can plausibly be invoked, see Glüer 2009, p. 303.

[39] It should be clear that being irrational is not the same as being culpable or subject to criticism. In general, just as in ethics, we must distinguish the question of what is correct (rational or morally right) from the question of when a subject is blameworthy. The distinction is even more important in the case of belief, since the problems with doxastic

for, and what motivates the Fregean, is not absolution, but an explanation of the subject's reasoning and actions.

Similar remarks apply to the case of Twin Earth externalism. Here the problem, again, is not that the theory implies that the subject has to be attributed contradictory beliefs, but that it implies that she has to be attributed different beliefs despite reasoning and acting as if the beliefs were the same. Thus, in the case of Peter above, he reasons as if his beliefs about water involved the same concept as his beliefs about twater, and yet externalism implies that the beliefs are different. As a result, he is to be described as making a simple invalid inference, despite being perfectly capable cognitively and not in any way confused. Of course, on the externalist view it follows that Peter does not *know* that he is reasoning invalidly, and this may absolve Peter from his irrationality: he is not to be criticized. However, what the internalist is asking for is not absolution, but an account of content that serves to capture how Peter reasons. And the assertion that he does not know how he reasons does not meet this demand.

This brings us closer to the real, underlying conflict between Millian and Fregean accounts of content, as well as between internalist and externalist accounts. The real conflict, I submit, concerns *the role of the theory of content*: are content ascriptions constrained by the requirement that they should serve to explain the subject's reasoning and actions? The Fregean (internalist) accepts this requirement while the Millian (externalist) rejects it.[40] Indeed, the Millian (externalist) appeal to failures of transparency is, in effect, simply a rejection of this requirement: saying that there is 'transparency failure' whenever the semantics implies the attribution of problematic beliefs, is to deny that there is any need for the semantics to capture the subject's cognitive perspective, allowing us to explain her reasoning and actions.[41]

voluntarism suggest that it is very doubtful that we are responsible for what we believe in the first place. If so, we are never to be blamed for what we believe (in contrast with our *actions*, which are the concern of ethical blame and praise) and the issue of culpability drops out altogether, All that matters to rationality is whether the belief is inferentially supported and coheres with the subject's other beliefs. For a defense of this conception of rationality, see Glüer and Wikforss 2013.

[40] Some externalists, in fact, accept the requirement (see e.g. Burge 1979). As I have argued elsewhere, however, the requirement is in serious tension with externalist theories of content (Wikforss 2006). This is not to say, however, that the internalist must accept the requirement. Although internalism is typically motivated by the need to account for the subject's reasoning and actions, it need not be (see footnote 42).

[41] Of course, not all Millians appeal to failures of transparency to account for the discrepancy between Millian contents and the subject's reasoning. An alternative strategy consists in appealing to pragmatic factors, beyond the theory of content (see e.g. Soames 2002). Since the topic of this paper is transparency, not Millian theories per se, I shall not discuss this alternative proposal.

Concluding remarks

I have argued that the transparency of content thesis does not have the semantic significance it is widely assumed to have. Both sides in the debate, compatibilists as well as incompatibilists, assume that subjects have meta-level beliefs about their first-order thoughts and states, and that these meta-beliefs play an important role in accounting for the subject's reasoning and actions. I have considered three alternative construals of the relevant meta-level beliefs and have argued that none of them supports this assumption.

It should perhaps be stressed that I do not wish to deny that there is a *connection* between semantics and transparency issues. It is no doubt true that certain semantic theories are in conflict with the transparency of meaning and content, while other theories are not. In the case of linguistic meaning, for example, the Fregean theory supports meaning transparency, whereas the Millian does not, and it is easy to see why. On the Fregean view, reflection on the use of S's terms is a good source of metalinguistic beliefs. For instance, if the subject reflects on the fact that she is willing to assent to 'Hesperus is Hesperus' but not to 'Hesperus is Phosphorus', on the Fregean view this justifies the subject in inferring that there is a difference in meaning between her terms. This is a direct result of the fact that on the Fregean view meaning is functionally transparent.[42] On the Millian view, however, reflections of this sort do not show that there is a difference in meaning – one would also have to know whether or not 'Hesperus' and 'Phosphorus' indeed refer to the same thing and this is not, normally, something one can know on the basis of reflection alone. That is, if meaning is not functionally transparent (as on the Millian view) then the speaker will not be able to form true, metalinguistic beliefs merely by reflecting on how she uses and is disposed to use her terms. Consequently, functional transparency is a necessary condition for access transparency. However, again, the converse does not hold. Access transparency is not a necessary condition for functional transparency, and the Fregean view does not *require* that meaning is access transparent: even if the subject is not able to form metalinguistic beliefs about sameness and difference in meaning, the fact that she takes a

---

[42] Notice that it is less clear that there is a direct connection between meaning transparency and *internalism*: the claim that meaning is determined by internal features does not automatically imply that sameness and difference of meaning is access-transparent. Rather, whether meaning is transparent depends on how the particular internalist position is spelled out – in particular, on whether the internalist accepts rationality constraints, such as Frege's principle. Indeed, internalism need not even be committed to functional transparency. I shall have to leave further discussion of this complex issue for another occasion.

different attitude toward the two sentences suffices to motivate the appeal to Fregean senses.

Similar remarks apply to belief transparency. If we assume, with the Fregean, that belief contents are functionally transparent, then we have reasons to think that beliefs are access transparent: a subject can determine whether two beliefs are the same or not simply by reflecting on her first-order attitudes. For instance, asked whether she thinks that 'Clay was a champ' expresses the same belief as 'Ali was a champ', reflection on her attitudes tells Mary that she holds the first to be false and the second to be true and she can conclude from this that they express different beliefs. On the Millian view, however, it is clear that such reflection would not tell Mary anything about the sameness and difference of her beliefs. However, again, it would be a mistake to think that because there cannot be access transparency without functional transparency, functional transparency presupposes access transparency.

In conclusion, the semantically significant thesis is not the thesis that content (or belief) is access transparent but the thesis, underlying functional transparency, that it is essential to content that it serves to explain the subject's reasoning and actions. This is an important, and disputed, thesis within foundational semantics, but it is not a thesis concerning knowledge of content.

9 On knowing what thoughts one's utterances express

Gary Ebbs

To have what I call *minimal self-knowledge* is (in a sense to be clarified) to know without empirical investigation what thoughts one's own utterances express. According to the thesis of *minimalism about minimal self-knowledge* that I have developed and endorsed elsewhere,[1] to have minimal self-knowledge is just to exercise one's ability to use one's words competently in discourse – to raise and address questions, evaluate one's own and others' claims, answer challenges to one's claims, express one's conjectures, and so on. The idea is that by competently using one's sentence "Water is a liquid at room temperature," for instance, one expresses the thought that *water is a liquid at room temperature,* and one thereby (and in that first-order, practical way) also counts as 'knowing' what thought one's utterance of "Water is a liquid at room temperature" expresses, even if one has no substantive (i.e. nondisquotational) metalinguistic knowledge of this.

In this chapter I shall try to clarify and defend minimalism about minimal self-knowledge (or minimalism, for short) by addressing two main objections to it. The first objection is that minimalism does not address what appears to be the main question we should be asking about minimal self-knowledge, namely, "How do we attain substantive, second-order, or metalinguistic, knowledge of what thoughts our utterances express?" To address this first objection, I propose (in the first section) a way of formulating the main question about minimal

---

I presented earlier versions of this chapter at the University of Texas at Austin in October 2013 and at the Anthony Brueckner Memorial Conference in Santa Barbara in February 2015. On both occasions I received comments that tested my conclusions and helped me to clarify my arguments. Thanks, especially, to Dorit Bar-On, Tyler Burge, Robin Jeshion, Cory Juhl, David Sosa, and Ernie Sosa. Thanks also to Sandy Goldberg for helpful and constructive comments on my penultimate draft. My greatest debt is to Tony Brueckner, who pressed me for years to clarify my account of minimal self-knowledge. I think he would have agreed with my conclusions here, even if he might not have liked the way I argue for them. I dedicate this chapter to him.

[1] Ebbs 1996, 1997, 2001, 2003, 2005, 2009, 2011, and Ebbs and Brueckner 2012.

self-knowledge that does not by itself imply that minimal self-knowledge is substantive second-order, or metalinguistic, knowledge, and explain (in the second section) why, given some additional constraints, minimalism about minimal self-knowledge is an attractive and plausible answer to the main question about minimal self-knowledge, thus formulated.

One might accept my formulation of the main question about minimal self-knowledge, yet reject some of the additional constraints on which my explanation and defense of minimalism about minimal self-knowledge rests. I pose and address (in the third section) an objection of this second kind, adapted from Gareth Evans's argument (in Evans 1982) that there are ordinary, nonskeptical circumstances in which one could use one's words to express thoughts *without* thereby having the sort of understanding of those thoughts that is required for minimal self-knowledge. I argue that contrary to the view of minimal self-knowledge that lies behind the second objection, if the main question about minimal self-knowledge is formulated in the way I propose in the first section, then there is no space between one's use of one's words to raise and address questions, on the one hand, and the sort of understanding of those thoughts that goes with minimal self-knowledge, on the other.

A framework for elucidating minimal self-knowledge

The phrase "minimal self-knowledge" is not part of ordinary language, but a term of art that may be applied in a number of different ways. We therefore cannot hope to elucidate the notion of minimal self-knowledge until we know why we are interested in ascribing minimal self-knowledge in the first place. When does the question of whether or not a speaker "knows what thoughts her utterances express" come up? Why is it of interest to us? Before we try to answer the questions, we need to specify our motives in raising them, so that we can make clear how we interpret them.

I shall assume that (a) we are interested in ascriptions of minimal self-knowledge insofar as we are interested in characterizing the deliberative, first-person point of view of a person engaged in rational inquiry; (b) to engage in rational inquiry is (at least) to construct a theory in a language and to express the questions, conjectures, and claims of one's theory in that language; and (c) an inquirer has the vocabulary to self-ascribe beliefs, and to ask herself what to believe.

When an inquirer of this sort asks herself what to believe about a given topic, how should she address this question? In a widely quoted passage, Gareth Evans writes:

In making self-ascriptions of belief, one's eyes are, so to speak, or occasionally literally, directed outward – upon the world. If someone asks me "Do you think there is going to be a Third World war?", I must attend, in answering him, to precisely the same outward phenomena as I would attend to if I were answering the question "Will there be a third world war?" I get myself in a position to answer the question whether I believe that p by putting into operation whatever procedure I have for answering the question whether p... If the judging subject applies this procedure, then necessarily he will gain knowledge of one of his own mental states: even the most determined skeptic cannot find here a gap in which to insert his knife. (*Evans 1982, p. 225*)

One might say (following Evans 1982, Edgely 1969, and Moran 2001, among others) that if S is a sentence that we can directly use to raise the question of whether or not to believe that *S*, this question is *transparent* for us, in the sense that we pass directly *through* it to the question whether or not *S*.[2] This point about transparency may be formulated less metaphorically as follows:

> *Transparency of Belief* If S is a sentence that an inquirer can directly use to raise the question of whether or not to believe that *S*, her deliberation about whether or not to believe that *S* is *transparent* for her to the question whether or not *S*, in the sense that she can address the question about whether or not to believe that *S* by applying whatever procedure she has for answering the question whether or not *S*.[3]

This point of view on belief is often emphasized in discussions of how a person can come to know what to believe without relying on any observations about her mental states or her behavior. As Moran puts it, "A statement of one's belief about X is said to obey the Transparency Condition when the statement is made by consideration of the facts about X itself, and not by either an 'inward glance' or by observation of

---

[2] Here and throughout this chapter I use a capital S as standing in for the name of a sentence in a given person's language, and an italicized capital S, written *S*, to represent a particular *use* of that sentence to raise a question, make an assertion, or express a belief. What thought a particular use of a sentence S expresses depends of course on many factors, including whether S contains indexicals, ambiguous predicates, and quantified expressions whose domains are fixed by the context of use. I shall abstract away from such complications by focusing on 'eternal' sentences that do not contain indexicals or ambiguous expressions.

[3] This formulation avoids an objection to taking the procedure Evans describes to be our best answer to the question of what we actually believe. The objection (raised, for instance, by Gertler 2011b) is that sometimes what we actually believe is not what we would believe if we approached the question of what to believe in the way that Evans recommends. The proposal in the text focuses only on how we should think about what *to* believe, not on how we know what we actually now believe.

one's behavior" (Moran 2001, p. 101). I depart here from this standard emphasis, however, by taking Transparency of Belief as a guide to clarifying minimal self-knowledge.

My leading idea is that if, as I assume, we are interested in ascriptions of minimal self-knowledge insofar as we are interested in characterizing the deliberative, first-person point of view of a person engaged in rational inquiry, then the sense of "minimal self-knowledge" that matters most to us is one that can only be clarified by investigating what it is for a person to be in a position to use her sentences to pose questions and try to answer them in a context in which she is deciding what to believe in the world-directed way that goes with Transparency of Belief. I therefore propose the following constraint on a proper elucidation of minimal self-knowledge:

> *Transparency Constraint* An inquirer has minimal self-knowledge of what thought her utterances of a sentence S of her language expresses if and only if the question whether or not to believe that S is *transparent* for her to the question whether or not S, in the sense of "transparent" described by Transparency of Belief.

A central virtue of the Transparency Constraint is that it helps to clarify minimal self-knowledge without settling whether or not minimal self-knowledge is second-order or metalinguistic knowledge. On the one hand, the Transparency Constraint leaves open for now the possibility that an inquirer's belief that *water is a liquid at room temperature*, for instance, is transparent for her to the question whether or not water is a liquid at room temperature, in the sense of 'transparent' described by Transparency of Belief, only if she can know by introspection, without appealing to any knowledge about how things stand 'external to' her mind, that her utterances of "Water is a liquid at room temperature" express the thought that water is a liquid at room temperature. Following Boghossian 1989, one might think, for instance, that self-knowledge is based on introspection – a process of examining with the mind's eye 'inner' mental states or events, including mental states or events that we bring into being by uttering particular sentences, such as "Water is a liquid at room temperature." If one begins with this assumption, then we may be inclined to agree with Boghossian that if we do not engage in any special empirical inquiry into what thoughts our utterances express, our knowledge of what thoughts our utterances express must be restricted to our introspective knowledge of properties that are intrinsic to the sentences (or other vehicles of content) that we utter. If we understand our access to what thoughts our sentences express in this introspectionist way, then we will find it difficult to avoid the skeptical conclusion that minimal self-knowledge is impossible to attain. Boghossian's approach to understanding minimal self-knowledge appears mandatory, however, if we take the metalinguistic surface grammar of claims to minimal self-knowledge at face value. Nothing we have yet observed about the Transparency Constraint rules it out.

On the other hand, we may come to be convinced, for reasons I present in the next section, that the question whether or not to believe that S can be transparent for a given inquirer to the question whether or not S even if she has no substantive second-order knowledge of what thoughts her utterances of S express. The leading idea behind this more minimalist alternative is that Transparency of Belief requires only that an inquirer be able to use her sentences to raise and address questions, not that she have any substantive knowledge, independent of her practical ability to use the sentences themselves, of what the sentences express. If we accept a version of this idea, then, for reasons I shall explain below, we should conclude that an inquirer may have minimal self-knowledge – that she may (in the relevant sense) "know what thought her utterances of her sentence S express" – even if she has no explicit or nontrivial second-order knowledge of what thoughts her utterances of S express.

Minimalism about minimal self-knowledge

In order to develop an account of minimal self-knowledge that satisfies the Transparency Constraint, we need to investigate when a person is in a position to use one of her sentences S in such a way that the question whether or not to believe that S is transparent for her to the question whether or not S. I propose that we do so by investigating our ordinary practices of attributing thoughts and beliefs to inquirers who construct and express their theories in language. I assume that a central aim of these practices is to attribute beliefs and thoughts that characterize such an inquirer's own evolving first-person point of view – how the inquirer takes things to be – where to have such a point of view is to be in a position to use some of one's sentences S in such a way that the question whether or not to believe that S is transparent for one to the question whether or not S. Following Putnam 1975 and Burge 1979, I also assume that (first) our ordinary practices of attributing thoughts and beliefs to inquirers provide us with our best grip on an inquirer's point of view, and (second) that our attributions of thoughts and beliefs to an inquirer often (though not always) rely on our ordinary practices of identifying words of her language with words of our own language, which we take ourselves to share with her. When our attributions of thoughts and beliefs to an inquirer rely on our ordinary practices of identifying words of her language with words of our own language, they go hand in hand with our judgment that for some sentence(s) S in which those words occur, she is minimally linguistically competent to use S in such a way that the question whether or not to believe that S is transparent for her to the question whether or not S.

I therefore propose that we adopt the following additional constraint on a satisfactory elucidation of minimal self-knowledge:

> *Thought Attribution and Word Identification Constraint* Our ordinary practices of attributing thoughts and beliefs to an inquirer and of sometimes identifying words of her language with words of our own language provide us with our best grip on whether or not, for some sentence(s) S in which those words occur, she is minimally linguistically competent to use S in such a way that the question whether or not to believe that S is transparent for her to the question whether or not S.

As I understand this constraint, it fits naturally with the observations about belief attribution and thought attribution that are central to standard arguments (due to Putnam 1975 and Burge 1979) for anti-individualism – the thesis that the contents of a person's beliefs and thoughts are not determined solely by physical or psychological states of the person that can be individuated independently of his or her social or physical environment. Hilary Putnam famously observed, for example, that an English speaker who cannot discriminate, whether perceptually or by means of substantive descriptions, between elms and beeches may nevertheless be minimally competent in the uses of the English words 'elm' and 'beech', in the sense that she is in a position to use sentences that contain tokens of the English words 'elm' and 'beech' to raise questions or express her thoughts or beliefs about elms or beeches. If Alice, for instance, is such a speaker, she may ask, "Are there many elm trees in Indianapolis?" and thereby raise the question, *Are there many elm trees in Indianapolis?* Alice knows too little about elms to answer the question on her own. By relying on the testimony of others, however, Alice may be able to discover whether or not there are many elm trees in Indianapolis. She may ask an expert about trees or consult an authoritative book, arriving at an answer by trusting what she is told or what she reads. If we accept the Thought Attribution and Word Identification Constraint, then, we will therefore judge that Alice is able to raise the question whether to believe that there are many elm trees in Indianapolis in a way that is transparent for her to the question whether there are many elm trees in Indianapolis.[4]

These observations have consequences for the question of whether or not the speaker has minimal self-knowledge only if she has substantive second-order knowledge of what thoughts her utterances express. To see why, note that before Alice consults experts or authoritative books about trees, she is able to raise the question whether there are many elm trees in Indianapolis. At that point, however, she has no substantive second-order knowledge of what thoughts her utterances of "There are many elm trees in Indianapolis" express. If she asks herself the metalinguistic question "What thoughts do my utterances of 'There are many elm trees in Indianapolis' express?", then she can of course give the trivial (and correct) answer that her utterances of that sentence express the thought that there are many elm trees in Indianapolis. By hypothesis, however, she does not know what distinguishes elms from other trees, and hence she could not provide any accurate and specific characterization of the conditions under which the sentence is true without simply and directly using it.

Alice's situation is not unusual. In many familiar and ordinary cases in which an inquirer is able to use a sentence S to ask herself whether to believe that *S* and to address that question in a way that displays the transparency of belief, she could not provide any accurate characterization of the conditions under which S is true without simply and directly using it.[5]

---

[4] Tyler Burge writes: "The fundamental reasoning in 'Individualism and the Mental' [Burge 1979], and in subsequent thought experiments that support anti-individualism, is not reasoning about language. The fundamental reasoning concerns conditions under which one can be in certain sorts of mental states, or have certain concepts" (Burge 2007, p. 162). Burge's understanding of his thought experiments in Burge 1979 is fully compatible with the Thought Attribution and Word Identification Constraint, which does not rest on "reasoning about language," or imply that language is in some way constitutive of thought or belief content.

[5] As part of his clarification and defense of an argument for anti-individualism due to Burge, Sanford Goldberg argues for what he calls minimalism about conceptions, according to which "the characterization of the conception expressed by a speaker's use of an expression E employs (= uses or mentions) that very expression in characterizing the conception" (Goldberg 2002, p. 616). Goldberg 2009 develops a closely related minimalist thesis about a speaker's understanding of what she is told by others. Both of Goldberg's minimalist theses can be interpreted in a way that fits well with my proposal that we attribute minimal self-knowledge to a person who exercises (at least) minimal competence to use her words. My method of clarifying and defending something like what Goldberg calls minimalism about conceptions and understanding is fundamentally different from his, however. One of my central goals is to resist the second-order surface grammar of philosophers' ascriptions of minimal self-knowledge. To reach this goal what we need, and what I offer in this section, is a principled account of why minimal self-knowledge matters to us that does not imply that minimal self-knowledge is second order. It is only in the context of such an account, I believe, that minimalism about conceptions or understanding can be properly motivated and clarified.

These observations support the conclusion that when the Transparency Constraint is combined with the Thought Attribution and Word Identification Constraint, it implies

> *Consequence 1* An inquirer may have minimal self-knowledge of the thought expressed by a given sentence S that she can use even if she could not provide any accurate characterization of the conditions under which S is true without simply and directly using it, and, in that sense, has no substantive second-order knowledge of what thoughts her utterances of S express.

This is not to say, however, that an inquirer may have minimal self-knowledge of the thought expressed by her utterances of a given sentence S if she has no *first-order beliefs* that she would express by using sentences that contain words that occur in S. If a subject, let us call him Burt, has no beliefs at all that he would express by using sentences that contain the English word 'el', then if Burt utters a question that sounds very much *like* the English question, "Are elms airplanes?", for instance, we would not take him to have raised the question whether elms are airplanes. More generally, we would not take Burt to be minimally linguistically competent to raise questions about elms by uttering sentences that contain the word 'elm'.

These third-person judgments are inextricably linked with our understanding of Burt's own first-person point of view. In particular, the judgments are correct only if Burt does not (and cannot now) take himself to be in a position to pose a question about what to believe about elms – a question that is transparent for him to a question that he can directly raise by using the English word 'elm'. By hypothesis, he has no idea what elms are, and hence no idea where to begin any inquiry, or whom to ask about it, or why any such question could matter to him at all. He is not even able to express the *thought* that he has no idea what elms are, or the thought that he cannot use the word 'elm' to express thoughts about elms, since in order to do so he would need to be competent to use the English word 'elm' to express thoughts about elms, but, by hypothesis in this example, he is not.

In contrast, despite Alice's ignorance of the difference between elms and beeches, our taking her to be minimally competent to use 'elm' to raise and try to address the question whether there are elm trees in Indianapolis, goes hand in hand with attributing to her at least some beliefs that she expresses by using the word 'elm'. These beliefs need not all be true. It may be, for instance, that she affirms such sentences as "Elms are deciduous trees," that "Elms grow only in North America," and "Elms cannot grow to be over fifty feet tall," thereby expressing her beliefs that elms are deciduous trees, that elms grow only in North America, that elms cannot grow to be over fifty feet tall. Such third-person belief attributions are inextricably linked with our understanding of Alice's own first-person point of view, especially the first-order beliefs she takes for granted when she poses for herself the question whether there are many elm trees in Indianapolis.

Cases like this are both familiar and plentiful. There is no need to multiply examples in order to be convinced that

> *Consequence 2* Typically, to be able to inquire into whether or not S, an inquirer must have some first-order beliefs that she expresses by using some of the words that occur in S.[6]

Some, possibly all, of the first-order beliefs described in Consequence 2 are those that a person acquires by accepting testimony from others. As J. L. Austin emphasizes, "Reliance on the authority of others is fundamental ... for corroboration and for the correctness of our own use of words, which we learn from others."[7] More recently, the psychologist Paul Harris observes that "many of the classifications that we make ultimately depend on the testimony of other people. Whether the entity is a palpable object such as a fruit or a tool, or something more abstract such as a neighborhood or a college, we often turn to others to learn how to classify it and what its properties are."[8]

The first-order beliefs that we acquire by accepting testimony from others may be purely logical, but are typically nonlogical, or 'empirical', and may be easily overturned by new testimony or by our own observations. How then does Consequence 2 fit with our preliminary characterization of what it is to have what I call *minimal self-knowledge* – namely "to know without empirical investigation what thoughts one's own utterances express"? The answer, I suggest, is that in this context "without empirical investigation" means "without going through any special or new empirical investigations of one's own." We can summarize this point in a way that relates it to the conditions described in the Transparency Constraint, as follows:

> *Consequence 3* An inquirer can raise the question whether or not to believe that S in a way that is transparent for her to the question

---

[6] This consequence does not imply that for some sentence S there are first-order beliefs (expressed by using words that occur in S) that any person who is able to inquire into whether or not S must accept. It is compatible with Consequence 2 that for a given sentence S, if a person x is able to inquire into whether or not S, then x has some first-order beliefs or other that she expresses by using words that occur in S. Consequence 2 therefore does not imply that there are any linguistic stereotypes in the sense of Putnam 1975. See Ebbs 1997, p. 346, n. 48.
[7] Austin 1979, p. 83, n. 1.   [8] Harris 2012, p. 64.

whether or not S only if she can raise this question without going through any special or new empirical investigations of her own.

I propose that we elucidate minimal self-knowledge by defining the most minimal account of it that satisfies both the Transparency Constraint and the Word Identification and Thought Attribution Constraint, understood in such a way that they together imply Consequences 1–3. The result is

Minimalism about Minimal Self-Knowledge To know what thoughts one's utterances express is to exercise (at least) minimal competence in the use of one's words, in a sense of "minimal competence" that is elucidated by a description of our ordinary practices of attributing thoughts and beliefs to an inquirer, in accord with the Transparency Constraint and the Thought Attribution and Word Identification Constraint, understood in such a way that they together imply Consequences 1–3.[9]

If we accept Minimalism about Minimal Self-Knowledge, then we have no reason to expect that there are any informative necessary or sufficient conditions for minimal linguistic competence in the use of a given word or sentence. We have no reason to expect, for instance, that we will be able to provide informative necessary or sufficient conditions for using the sentence "There are many elm trees in Indianapolis" to express the thought that there are many elm trees in Indianapolis, or for using the word 'elm' to express thoughts about elm trees. The descriptions of minimal linguistic competence that I have sketched in this section do not aim to provide such independent criteria, but, instead, to *elucidate* the sort of minimally competent language use that goes with the Transparency Constraint and the Thought Attribution and Word Identification Constraint, by investigating and describing typical thought attributions and generalizing from these descriptions, as I have done here by sketching examples that support Consequences 1–3.

By eschewing the metalinguistic surface grammar of attributions of minimal self-knowledge and focusing our attention on whether particular speakers are able to use their sentences to raise and address questions, Minimalism about Minimal Self-Knowledge allows us to bypass, and to regard as irrelevant, Boghossian's questions about what we can know

---

[9] Minimalism about minimal self-knowledge, and especially Consequences 2 and 3, imply that, contrary to Stanley and Williamson 2001, practical knowledge (know-how) is inextricable from, but not reducible to, propositional knowledge (know-that). For a similar view, sketched more broadly and supported in a very different way, see Wiggins 2012. I evaluate Stanley and Williamson's claims about knowledge of meaning in section 9.8 of Ebbs 2009.

about what thoughts our sentences express by examining with our minds' eyes the intrinsic properties of the 'inner' mental states or events that we bring into being by uttering particular sentences. Some philosophers, including Davidson 1987 and Burge 1988, have rejected the introspectionist model of minimal self-knowledge without rejecting the second-order surface grammar of ascriptions of minimal self-knowledge. Unless such approaches are supplemented by an account of why it is illegitimate to require that second-order or metalinguistic knowledge of what thoughts our utterances express be *substantive*, and not, for instance, just disquotational, then they are vulnerable to the objection (pressed by Brueckner 1995) that they do not provide substantive accounts of our second-order or metalinguistic knowledge of what thoughts our utterances express. My approach is not vulnerable in this way, since it implies that the second-order surface grammar of ascriptions of minimal self-knowledge, which sustains the appearance that we must provide a substantive account of our second-order or metalinguistic knowledge of what thoughts our utterances express, is misleading, and disappears when the ascriptions are properly paraphrased.

Of the other proposals for clarifying minimal self-knowledge that are currently available in the literature, my approach is perhaps closest to that of Robert Stalnaker, who also rejects Boghossian's introspectionist approach to minimal self-knowledge, and who recommends an alternative that focuses on attributing beliefs and thoughts to a person, that characterize how the person takes the world to be. Stalnaker writes:

we shouldn't think of access to our thought as access to an internal vehicle of representation ... We should think of the representation of states of knowledge and belief, and the content of occurrent thoughts, in this way: Thinkers are things with the capacity to make their actions depend on the way the world is, and with dispositions to make their actions depend on the way they take the world to be. Theorists and attributors of thought characterize these capacities and dispositions by locating the world as the thinker takes it to be in a space of relevant alternative possibilities ... A principle of epistemic transparency is satisfied, according to this picture, not because the thinker is directly acquainted with an inner object that has an inner content essentially, but because an apt description of a thinker's cognitive state, if it is to explain the rational capacities and dispositions it is intended to explain, must represent the way the world is according to the thinker in a way that satisfies it. (*Stalnaker 2008, p. 131*)

Unlike Stalnaker, however, I develop this sort of rough sketch of an alternative to introspectionist accounts by explicitly laying down the Transparency Constraint and the Thought Attribution and Word Identification Constraint, understood in such a way that they together imply Consequences 1–3. Taken together, these constraints allow us to explain a person's minimal self-knowledge in terms of her practical ability to use her sentences in discourse, in such a way that she can count as having minimal self-knowledge even if she lacks substantive metalinguistic knowledge of what thoughts her utterances express.

Evans on crediting a subject with the thought that *p*

There are of course many different objections one could raise about Minimalism about Minimal Self-Knowledge. I shall focus here on an objection to it that takes the Transparency Constraint for granted but which challenges the Thought Attribution and Word Identification Constraint. The objection is based on Gareth Evans's neo-Russellian account of when a speaker can be credited with a thought.[10]

Evans endorses a version of what he calls Russell's Principle, according to which "a subject cannot make a judgment about something unless he knows which object his judgment is about" (Evans 1982, p. 89).[11] According to Evans, "[t]here is [also] a principle parallel to Russell's Principle, to the effect that in order to have the concept of a given natural kind one must have some way of distinguishing its members from all other things. (This could perhaps be regarded as an application of the same principle.)" (p. 92, n. 5). I will use the term "Russell's Principle" in this more general sense, so that it applies both to singular referring expressions (demonstratives and proper names) and natural kind term.

Evans acknowledges that Russell's Principle may seem either trivially false or trivially satisfied:

> If the principle is interpreted as appealing to the colloquial use of the expression "knows which", then it is surely incorrect, since a subject may make a judgment about an object which he sees, or about himself, even when it would be correct to say that he does not know which item he is seeing, or who he is. If on the other hand, no restriction is placed upon the kind of answers the subject may be able to give to the question "Which item are you thinking about?", then the principle appears trivial, since anyone who is prepared to ascribe to a subject the thought that *a* is *F* in the first place will also be prepared to ascribe to him the thought, and presumably the knowledge, that it is *a* that he is thinking about. (p. 89)

Evans tries to avoid this dilemma for Russell's Principle by theorizing, to begin with, that in order for a subject to be credited with the judgment

---

[10] Evans's neo-Russellian views of when a speaker can be credited with a thought have been discussed many times before (by Bach 1987 and Burge 2010, for instance), but not as part of an evaluation of an account of minimal self-knowledge that is subject to the Transparency Constraint.

[11] All subsequent references to Evans 1982 are cited parenthetically within the main text using page number only.

that *p*, he "must have a capacity to distinguish the object of his judgment from all other things" (p. 89). This formulation still leaves us with two difficult questions:

> (Q1) What does it take for a subject to possess a capacity to distinguish the object of a judgment that *p* from all other things?

and

> (Q2) Why should we accept that a subject must have such a capacity to be credited with the judgment that *p*?

To address these questions, Evans investigates and generalizes from (1) a range of circumstances in which we attribute to an inquirer thoughts that she expresses by using demonstratives, (2) a range of circumstances in which we attribute to an inquirer thoughts that she expresses by using proper names, and (3) a range of circumstances in which we attribute to an inquirer thoughts that she expresses by using natural kind terms.

I shall argue that given the sort of answer Evans offers to Q1, his answer to Q2 is unconvincing.

Consider, to begin with, Evans's example of the indistinguishable steel balls:

> Suppose ... that on a certain day in the past, a subject briefly observed two indistinguishable steel balls suspended from the same point and rotating about it. He now believes nothing about one ball which he does not believe about the other. This is certainly a situation in which the subject cannot discriminate one of the balls from all other things, since he cannot discriminate it from its fellow. And a principle which precludes the ascription to the subject of a thought about one of the balls surely has a considerable intuitive appeal. Certainly, if one imagines oneself in this situation and attempts to speculate about one of the balls rather than the other, one finds oneself attempting to exploit some distinguishing factor or other. (*p. 90*)

Evans goes on to note that even if in fact all of the subject's memories of the ball are memories causally linked to perceptual experiences of just one of two balls, if the subject is unaware of this causal link, then he might wonder, at least, whether he is able to entertain a thought that is about one of the balls and not about the other (p. 90). Evans suggests that since "the subject will certainly behave as though he subscribed to Russell's Principle, interpreted as requiring discriminating knowledge," we should conclude that in the circumstances described the subject does not have any thought that is about one of the balls. Here Evans's argument is aided by an assumption that I highlighted above in my presentation of Minimalism about Minimal Self-Knowledge — the assumption that part of the point of ascribing a thought to an inquirer is to capture his first-person point of view. There may be good reason to reject or qualify this assumption in the case of small children and nonhuman animals. In the present context, however, where we are investigating ascriptions of thoughts to inquirers who use language to express their theories, the assumption is attractive and plausible, and I shall not question it. I shall focus instead on presenting and evaluating Evans's view that this assumption, together with observations about when we ascribe thoughts and beliefs to particular subjects, supports Russell's Principle, and (in effect) thereby conflicts with Minimalism about Minimal Self-Knowledge.

The main source of the conflict between Russell's Principle and Minimalism about Minimal Self-Knowledge can be inferred from Evans's explanation of why he is interested in investigating the requirements for thought and judgment about particular individuals:

> Why does the investigation of the requirements for thought and judgment about particular individuals matter? It matters because the concept of thought about an individual is tied to the concept of *understanding* a statement about an individual. I hold that it is in general a necessary condition for understanding an utterance of a sentence containing a referring expression, say "*a* is *F*", that one have a thought, or make a judgment, about the referent, to the effect that it is being said to be *F*. This is not a necessary condition for making such an utterance in such a way as to say of the referent that it is *F*. The divergence arises because of the possibility that a subject may exploit a linguistic device which he does not himself properly understand ... Given the divergence between the requirements for *understanding* and the requirements for *saying*, it would be absurd to deny that our primary interest ought to be in the more exigent conditions which are required for understanding. (p. 92)

Evans takes for granted, in effect, the Transparency Constraint – that the sort of understanding that he seeks to explain is precisely the sort of understanding that is required of a subject if she is to be able to regard the question of whether or not to believe that *a* is *F* as transparent to the question whether *a* is *F*. Another point on which Evans at least *appears* to agree with minimalism is that by ordinary standards for linguistic competence, an inquirer may be able to *use* a linguistic expression (or, as Evans says, "exploit a linguistic device") to *say* that *a* is *F*, where *F* is a natural kind term (e.g. "That (demonstrated *x*) is an elm") even if she cannot discriminate between *a*, or the natural kind *F*, and all other things. Evans proposes that we

> think of individuating the words of a language not only phonetically and also by reference to the practices in which they are used. In these terms, the requirement on a speaker using a proper name is not that he indicate which *object* he intends to be (taken to be) referring to, but that he indicate which name he intends to be (taken to be) using. (p. 384)

He concludes, as I do, that "if a speaker uses a word with the manifest intention to participate in such-and-such a practice, in which the word is used with such-and-such semantic properties, then the word, as used by him, will possess just those semantic properties" (p. 387).[12] To this superficial extent, Evans's approach to linguistic interpretation and thought attribution is compatible with the Thought Attribution and Word Identification Constraint.

According to Evans, however, if a subject cannot discriminate between *a*, or *F*s, and all other things, then she has no *thoughts* about *a*, or *F*s, and, in particular, no thought with the content that *a* is *F*. He thinks a subject can have minimal linguistic competence to use a word or sentence to say something or to raise a question, yet lack the sort of understanding of what she is thereby saying or asking that is required for minimal self-knowledge according to the Transparency Constraint. He distinguishes between participating in a practice, and thereby 'using' a given name or kind term, on the one hand, and entertaining thoughts about the referent of the name or kind term, on the other.[13] "It is a perfectly intelligible possibility, occasionally realized," he writes, "that someone can use an expression to refer without being himself in a position to understand the reference" (p. 398).

In support of this claim, Evans offers the following argument-by-example:

Suppose someone is maliciously introduced into the practice of using the name "Harold Macmillan" by being told "Harold Macmillan is a bachelor, was leader of the Conservative Party, plays the organ, took Britain into the Common Market,

---

[12] How to describe such linguistic practices is a complex and difficult question that I cannot get into here. I offer a deflationary account of them in chapter 9 of Ebbs 2009.
[13] Evans assumes that in any ordinary practice of using a proper name or natural kind term, there is a group of speakers who have been introduced to the practice by their *acquaintance* with the person or natural kind to which the name or kind term refers. Evans calls such members of the name-using practice "producers" (Evans 1982, p. 376). In some practices using name kind or natural kind terms, there is also a group of speakers who participate in the practice of using a particular name or natural kind term, even though they are not acquainted with the person to which the name or kind term refers. Evans calls such members of the name-using practice "consumers" (ibid., p. 377). Consumers of a proper-name-using practice have no role in connecting the name with the person to whom it refers. In contrast, "It is the actual patterns of dealings the producers have had with an individual – identified from time to time by the exercise of their recognitional capacities in regard to that individual – which ties the name to the individual" (ibid., p. 382). In a similar way, according to Evans, there are producers and consumers of practices of using natural kind terms: "it is a central feature of the practices associated with terms like 'elm', 'diamond', ' leopard', and like that there exist members – producers – who have ... an effective capacity to distinguish occasions when they are presented with members of that kind, from occasions when they are presented with members of any other kinds which are represented in any strength in the environment they inhabit" (ibid.).

has a yacht". It would surely not be supposed that this person understands the name "Harold Macmillan", because in interpreting uses of it he would be thinking of Edward Heath. (*p. 402*)

I am not convinced. Suppose Clara is introduced to the practice of using the name 'Harold Macmillan' in the way Evans describes, and that she does not know that Edward Heath has all the properties that she is (wrongly) told that Harold Macmillan has; suppose also that, in fact, Edward Heath is the only person who has all those properties. Does it follow that in using the name 'Harold Macmillan' Clara is thinking of Edward Heath? Not, it seems, unless Clara regards 'Harold Macmillan' as short for a definite description, such as "The person who is a bachelor, was leader of the Conservative Party, plays the organ, took Britain into the Common Market, has a yacht." But in another part of *Varieties of Reference*, Evans himself rightly rejects the view that speakers who can participate in a name-using practice treat those names as definite descriptions in this way. He emphasizes that speakers who participate in a name-using practice are "in a position of permanent deference – sensitive to information which [they] . . . do not possess about the person whose name [they] are using" (p. 396). Even if Clara believes that Edward Heath is the only person who has all the properties listed above, her deference to those who know more about Harold Macmillan than she does should lead her to *wonder*, at least, whether Harold Macmillan is indeed Edward Heath. Perhaps she is wrong that there is only one person who satisfies the description. Or perhaps she is misinformed about Harold Macmillan. It would be irresponsible of her simply to assume that Harold Macmillan is Edward Heath. The example does not support the conclusion that if Clara is introduced to the practice of using the name 'Harold Macmillan' in the way described, then, in interpreting uses of it, she would be thinking of Edward Heath.

Perhaps, however, the example can be used to illustrate Evans's view that, even though Clara is in a position use the name 'Harold Macmillan' to *say* that Harold Macmillan is a bachelor, she does not *understand* what she is thereby saying. There is surely some sense of 'understand' in which this claim is true. One could insist, for instance, that in one demanding sense of 'understand', to understand the claim that Harold Macmillan is a bachelor, one must be in a position to discriminate between Harold Macmillan and all other people *without either using or mentioning the name 'Harold Macmillan'*. Similarly, one might insist that in this same demanding sense, to understand the claim that there are many elms in Indianapolis, one must be in a position to discriminate between elms and other trees *without using or mentioning the word 'elm'*.

These negative claims do not provide a complete answer, on Evans's behalf, to Q1 (What does it take for a subject to possess a capacity to distinguish the object of a judgment that p from all other things?), but at least provide us with an informative necessary condition for a complete answer to that question. The necessary condition that Evans demands is that a satisfactory account of what it takes for a speaker to be able to discriminate an object or a kind from all other things does not rely on the speaker's ability to use or mention a name of that object or kind.[14]

This negative claim is of a piece with the demanding the sense of 'understanding' that is relevant to evaluating Evans's claim that "it is a perfectly intelligible possibility, occasionally realized, that someone can use an expression to refer without being himself in a position to understand the reference" (p. 398). Why is Evans so interested in this demanding sense of 'understanding'? Part of the answer is already clear from a passage quoted above. Evans holds that "the concept of thought about an individual is tied to the concept of *understanding* a statement about an individual" (p. 92). But this account of his interest in the demanding sense of 'understanding' presupposes that there is a "divergence between the requirements for *understanding* and the requirements for *saying*" (p. 92). He believes there is such a divergence because he accepts Russell's Principle, understood in the way sketched above. Why does he accept this principle?

I am not sure how to answer to this question. The answer is not, I believe, that a person who does not satisfy Russell's principle and is therefore, according to Evans, only in a position to say that p, is not able to say of herself that she is saying that p. Self-reference may occur equally in cases of such sayings and in what Evan's would describe as genuine cases of second-order self-ascriptions of the thought that p. What distinguishes the two kinds of cases must be something else. One possibility is that Evans is thinking of understanding in a way that requires that it be elucidated by reflections about how a person's use of a sentence determines and thereby also conveys, in a publically observable way, what thoughts are expressed by it. In the passage quoted above, Evans writes: "It would surely not be supposed that this person understands the name 'Harold Macmillan',

---

[14] Evans argues that to reject Russell's Principle is to accept that "there may be no difference, in respect of what they can do, between a thinker who knows what it is for some proposition to be true, and one who does not" (ibid., p. 106). But isn't the difference between being able to use a sentence to *say* (and, on my view, also to think) that *there are many elms in Indianapolis*, for instance, and not being able to do so, a difference in respect of what two speakers can do? To answer no, one must be able to characterize what a person can do in way that is independent of her ability to use a sentence to say something. I am unable to formulate a plausible characterization of this kind that supports Russell's Principle, as Evans understands it.

because in interpreting uses of it he would be thinking of Edward Heath" (p. 402). This way of describing the situation suggests that Clara (in the Evans-like case I described above) should be seen as trying to figure out how to interpret the expression 'Harold Macmillan' by looking at evidence about how it is used by the person who introduced the name to her, taking for granted her use of the words (namely, "is a bachelor, was leader of the Conservative Party, plays the organ, took Britain into the Common Market, has a yacht") in terms of which the reference of the name 'Harold Macmillan' is explained. Evans's description of his 'Harold Macmillan' example thereby suggests that he presupposes the following general principle about understanding:

(*) A speaker understands the reference of a given w that she learns from another only if she has enough evidence about how w is used by the other speaker to arrive at a correct interpretation of w that she could express solely by writing or uttering *other* words that she has *already* learned to use, hence without using or mentioning w.

It should be uncontroversial that without directly *using* the name 'Harold Macmillan', or employing a description that *mentions* it, such as "The person who others in my linguistic community call 'Harold Macmillan'," Clara cannot specify who or what "Harold Macmillan" refers to from the little she has observed, or can independently state, about the conditions under which other speakers utter sentences that contain the name. This fact, together with (*), implies that Clara does not understand the reference of 'Harold Macmillan'. Similar reasoning implies that Alice does not understand the reference of 'elm'.

There are two related problems with (*). First, (*) rules out a natural way to understand some cases in which a speaker learns a new word – namely, that the speaker learns how to use the new word directly, by learning to utter sentences that contain it in conversationally appropriate circumstances, without translating it into other words that she can already use. Second, (*) is incompatible with the evident possibility that there are some words that can *only* be learned in this direct way.

To reject Evans's demanding account of 'understanding', however, we need not insist on either of these points. It is enough, instead, to reject the background assumption that (*) provides us with our best and only grip on the sense of 'understanding' that goes with a speaker's participation in a name- or natural-kind-using practice. It is enough to accept, for instance, that despite her ignorance about Harold Macmillan, Clara can pose the question whether Harold Macmillan did all those things that she was told that he did, she can ask others who know more than she does about Harold Macmillan, she can do Google searches to get information about Harold Macmillan, and so on. Similarly, even though Alice knows very little about elm trees, she can raise the question of whether to believe there are many elm trees in Indianapolis, and she can address this question by asking others who know more than she does about elms. Neither Clara nor Alice understands the questions they are asking in the demanding sense of 'understand' that Evans presupposes. One can grant this, however, without agreeing that Clara and Alice must understand their questions in Evans's demanding sense in order to be in a position to regard the question whether or not to believe that Harold Macmillan is a bachelor or that there are many elm trees in Indianapolis, for instance, as transparent to the questions whether Harold Macmillan is a bachelor or that there are many elm trees in Indianapolis.

Evans is aware that "[There are some] who would agree that understanding a use of the proper name requires of thinking of the reference, but would argue that extreme misinformation of the kind we have been discussing does not prevent a subject from thinking of the referent" (p. 401). He also grants that "there are uses of the idioms 'believes that' or 'thinks of' which might appear to support these views" (p. 401). He insists, however, that "these linguistic data cannot by themselves be taken to settle anything" (p. 401). His view therefore amounts to a rejection of the Thought Attribution and Word Identification Constraint.[15]

For reasons I have sketched above, however, if our goal is to provide an account of minimal self-knowledge that satisfies the Transparency Constraint, we have no good reason to take Evans's neo-Russellian account of understanding to be a satisfactory account of the sort of understanding that goes with minimal self-knowledge. We therefore have no good reason to take Evans's neo-Russellian account of understanding to discredit the Thought Attribution and Word Identification Constraint. I conclude that despite first appearances, Evans's neo-Russellian account of understanding does not undermine Minimalism about Minimal Self-Knowledge. On the contrary, by challenging us to reflect on what sort of understanding matters for minimal self-knowledge, Evans's account of understanding helps us to see that there is no space between a person's uses of her words to raise and address questions, on the one hand, and the sort of understanding of those thoughts that goes with minimal self-knowledge, on the other.

---

[15] One might think that to take seriously the "linguistic data" he dismisses would be to "reason from language" in an illegitimate way that implies that beliefs and thoughts are somehow essentially linguistic. This is not so, however, for reasons I explain in note 4 above.

10 Anti-individualism, comprehension, and self-knowledge

Sanford C. Goldberg

1

In the 1990s, into the early 2000s, the topic of anti-individualism's implications for first-person authority[1] was much discussed.[2] Less discussed was the topic of anti-individualism's implications for the epistemology of understanding.[3] Less discussed still is the connection between these two topics.[4] This might encourage the idea, natural enough anyway, that there is no connection between them. In this chapter I aim to argue that they are intimately connected.

I am not the first person to advocate such a view. In his 1999, Tyler Burge himself suggests as much. He writes: "comprehending standing, conceptual aspects of one's own thought and idiolect is itself, as a matter of psychological and sociological fact, normally dependent on having comprehended thoughts (one's own) that were shaped and expressed through the words of others" (p. 243). I think Burge's point here is both true and important. In this chapter I aim to develop it in defense of the following thesis: a plausible account of the epistemology of linguistic comprehension will provide further support for a 'minimalist' view of the knowledge each of us has of our own standing states of mind. If this is correct, then it gives us a new angle on the old debate about the compatibility of anti-individualism and first-person authority. The fact that a good deal of what we know comes from accepting what others tell us – a fact about our relations to *other* subjects – tells us quite a bit about our relations to *our own* minds.

---

[1] Or some other doctrine articulating the authoritative knowledge each one of us has of our own thoughts.

[2] Various volumes treat this topic: see e.g. Ludlow and Martin 1998; Wright, Smith, and MacDonald 2000; Frapolli and Romero 2003; Nuccetelli 2003; Schantz 2003; Hahn and Ramberg 2004; and Goldberg 2007a. In addition see Brown 2004a, which treats this topic at length.

[3] It is not that there was no discussion. See e.g. several of the entries in Barber 2003. See also Burge 1999 and Goldberg 2004, 2007a, 2008a, 2009.

[4] Of the papers cited in the previous footnote, only Burge 1999 connects the two issues.

2

Let us begin with the humdrum fact that a good deal of what we know comes from accepting what others tell us. I am going to be making four simplifying assumptions about this phenomenon, in an attempt to argue for 'minimalist' conditions on comprehension.[5]

The first two assumptions have to do with the process of language understanding itself. First, I will be assuming a doctrine of Content Preservation, to the effect that

> (CP) In many central cases in which one acquires knowledge through accepting what another tells one, what one comes to know is the very knowledge expressed in the telling itself. (Content is preserved in the communication.)[6]

Second, I will be assuming that CP itself reflects a fact about the Nature of our Understanding of others' speech acts:

> (NU) For the central cases in which CP holds, what the hearer comes to know – the content of her knowledge – is what she understood the speaker to have asserted in the telling.

The idea behind NU is simple. In cases of content-preserving communication, it is one's understanding of the telling that plays the role of content preserver: understanding another's telling is a matter of recovering the very content of the telling, so that (other epistemic conditions being satisfied) one is then in a position to acquire the very knowledge expressed in the telling itself. Taken together, CP and NU imply that, in the central cases for which CP holds, we have the following Triple Identity:

> (TI) The content of the hearer's knowledge = the content recovered by the hearer's understanding of the telling = the content of the telling.

As I say, TI follows from our two assumptions having to do with the process of language understanding itself.

TI describes the correctness of the hearer's representation of the content of the telling. But it is worth noting that, in cases in which communication preserves (not only content but also) *knowledge* of the

---

[5] What follows is a very abbreviated version of the argument I tried to make in chapter 4 of Goldberg 2007a.

[6] Here I am using the phrase "accepting what another tells one" in a way that does not presuppose that *what* is accepted – the content accepted – is the very content of the telling. (Otherwise CP itself would be trivial.) If this is not a happy use of the phrase "accepting what another tells one," I ask the reader to substitute the phrase she thinks best captures my intended meaning.

preserved content, we can make a claim stronger than TI. This is owing to the fact that knowledge requires more than true belief – it requires reliability in the process(es) that produced the true belief. Consider, then, what it is for a belief through another's say-so to have been formed through a reliable process. This would require that the process produce a preponderance of true beliefs. On the other hand, a belief formed through another's say-so is *not* reliable if the process itself would produce too great a ratio of false beliefs. Now one way to form a false belief through a telling is for the telling itself to have presented-as-true what in fact was a false proposition.[7] But I ignore this complication as not central to my concerns here, which focus on linguistic understanding rather than monitoring for credibility.[8] So let us restrict ourselves to cases in which the speaker's telling is not only true but also knowledgeable. Our question is how, in *these* cases, it can happen that the hearer comes to form a false belief. The answer is obvious: the envisaged condition obtains if the hearer H *misunderstood* the telling – that is, took it as presenting as true something other than what it presented as true – where the content H took the telling to have presented as true is in fact false, yet where H still goes on to accept that content. To illustrate: suppose that, wishing to communicate your knowledge that p to me, you tell me that p, and I guess correctly that what you told me is that p. But suppose too that I might just as easily have guessed that what you told me was that q, where [q] is some false proposition which I would then have gone on to accept. Then even though the belief I formed through accepting your telling was the belief that p, all too easily I could have relied on the same method yet formed a *false* belief.[9] In that case, even though the belief I actually acquired through your telling is a belief in the very content you expressed in your telling, and even though your telling itself was knowledgeable, even so, I fail to know, for the simple reason that my belief was not formed in a reliable fashion. To avoid this, the hearer's recovery of the attested content in these cases must be not merely correct but also the result of a reliable process. In short: given our two assumptions of CP and NU, we arrive at the conclusion that whenever we have a "central case," the hearer must have recovered the

---

[7] If you think 'tell' is a success verb, so that 'S told me that p' implies 'p', then replace my talk of telling with talk of apparent tellings.
[8] I discuss the complications arising from the need to monitor for credibility in Goldberg and Henderson 2006.
[9] There are complications over the conditions on 'same method'. To sidestep these, let me stipulate that the (part of the) method I care about is that involving linguistic comprehension of an uttered sentence. (For some of the complications that arise owing to the conditions on method individuation, see Goldberg 2010.)

very content of the telling through a process that itself was reliable. Whenever this twofold condition is met, I will speak of the hearer as having *comprehended* the telling. Together, CP and NU imply that in central cases, the hearer comprehends the telling.

This brings me to my third and fourth assumptions, which have to do with the conditions under which communication takes place.

My third assumption has to do with the Doxastic Diversity of Knowledge Communities:

> (DDKC) There is a great diversity of belief among members of a single linguistic community.

What I have in mind by 'doxastic diversity' are cases in which two or more people's belief sets – and here I include not only what they believe and disbelieve, but also what they are agnostic about – differ from one another. So understood, DDKC is almost platitudinous. Its truth reflects the fact that people within a single linguistic community have different experiences, different expertise, and different informational resources. Thus a dentist has beliefs about dental health that we would not expect a dancer to have; an historian has beliefs about the causes of the War of 1812 that we would not expect an accountant to have; and so forth. My fourth and final assumption is that Comprehension in the sense characterized above – correct representation of the content of a telling, produced by a reliable process of language understanding – standardly happens even in cases of Doxastic Diversity:

> (CDD) Even substantial doxastic diversity between speaker and hearer does not prevent the hearer's comprehension of the speaker's telling.

I think CDD is also almost platitudinous as well: dancers comprehend dentists, accountants comprehend historians, and so forth.

CDD can be brought to bear on an account of the conditions on comprehension. For if CDD is true, then whenever we have a "central case" in which knowledge is acquired through another's telling, the process of comprehension implicated in the hearer's recovery of the content of the telling was reliable, *no matter how much doxastic diversity there was between the speaker and the hearer*. No doubt, there can be cases in which there is too much doxastic diversity, or doxastic diversity of a particularly drastic sort (more on which in a moment) – with the result that the prospects for knowledge communication itself are undermined. One form of drastic doxastic diversity which can undermine the communication of knowledge concerns beliefs about word meanings: if you think that 'Stockholm' means *orange juice*, you won't be in a position to learn what I aim to tell you when I assert "Stockholm was founded in the early thirteenth century." Perhaps this is not the only form. Such scenarios are not the "central cases" of which CP speaks. But there is reason to think that such scenarios are not particularly common.

To see this, it will be helpful to consider how we might determine the conditions on comprehension. In particular, we want to know when doxastic diversity is so great as to overwhelm the prospects for a hearer's comprehension of a speaker's telling. Following a suggestion in Evans (1982, pp. 310–11), I submit that we approach this question by using our sense of when knowledge is communicated in particular cases.[10] In any case in which, following our sense of things, we say knowledge was communicated, the result is that we can count such a case as one in which the hearer comprehended the telling. In this way we can use verdicts regarding knowledge communication in particular cases as a way to discern the conditions on comprehension itself.

I submit that when we follow this procedure, we find that the conditions on comprehension are 'minimalist' in the sense that they require very little in the way of the hearer's ability to explicate the concepts that figure in the propositions in question. I offer some paradigmatic cases as support. Consider these cases:

> NEOPHYTE STUDENT Henry is taking his first physics class, and so knows very little about electrons and is completely ignorant of the present state of theory regarding electrons. When Professor Ginsburg asserts, "Electrons are significantly smaller and less massive than nucleons," he accepts her say-so, and comes to express his belief using the very same form of words. Verdict: Henry has come to know (through her say-so) that electrons are significantly smaller and less massive than nucleons, where the content of his knowledge is *that electrons are significantly smaller and less massive than nucleons*.

---

[10] Evans writes:

> [C]ommunication is *essentially* a mode of the transmission of knowledge ... If the speaker S has knowledge of x to the effect that it is F, and in consequence utters a sentence in which he refers to x, and says of it that it is F, and if his audience A hears and understands the utterance, and accepts it as true (and there are no defeating conditions), *then A himself thereby comes to know of x that it is F*. If we are prepared to take for granted our grasp of the semantical concepts which this principle employs, we can use it to yield epistemological dividends. But it is possible to use the principle the other way round, bringing our intuitions about *knowledge* to bear upon the explicitly semantic concpets – the concepts of reference, saying, and understanding – in the middle. We shall then be thinking of communication as a relation between speaker and hearer which can constitute a link in a chain of knowledge-transmission. (*Evans 1982, pp. 310–11*)

NEWSPAPER READER Henrietta, a life-long resident of Juneau, Alaska, is reading an online version of an English-language newspaper from Thailand, the *Changrai Times*. She has never before been to Thailand, and knows nothing of its culture, politics, geography, or history. She reads that "Thai authorities incinerated 10 billion baht worth of narcotics on Wednesday (June 26, 2013) in Ayutthaya, Thailand in a bid to tackle their reputations as hubs for illicit substances and mark World Drug Day."[11] She immediately forms a belief that he expresses using the same form of words. Verdict: Henrietta has come to know (through the newspaper report) that Thai authorities incinerated 10 billion baht worth of narcotics on Wednesday (June 26, 2013) in Ayutthaya, Thailand in a bid to tackle their reputations as hubs for illicit substances and mark World Drug Day, where the content of this knowledge is *that Thai authorities incinerated 10 billion baht worth of narcotics on Wednesday (June 26, 2013) in Ayutthaya, Thailand in a bid to tackle their reputations as hubs for illicit substances and mark World Drug Day*.

NEW BASEBALL FAN Hank, a young man who grew up knowing nothing of baseball, goes to a Yankees game with Sally, a life-long fan of the New York Yankees. Over the course of the game, Sally makes various remarks to Hank about the state of play. On one occasion toward the end of the game, as the top of the ninth inning is due to start, Sally asserts: "It is the top of the ninth inning, with the Yanks up 2–1, and the Yankees are bringing in Mariano Rivera to pitch." Hank comes to accept what she says, and so forms a belief that he would express (at least for this short while before the game restarts) with the same form of words. Verdict: Hank has come to know (through Sally's telling him so) that it is the top of the ninth inning, with the Yanks up 2–1, and the Yankees are bringing in Mariano Rivera to pitch, where this is the content of her knowledge.

These examples could be multiplied, of course.

In each of them, there is a recipient who comes to acquire the very piece of knowledge expressed in the telling or the report, despite substantial doxastic diversity between the speaker and the hearer deriving from the hearer's minimal background knowledge of the subject matter

---

[11] Taken directly from the *Changrai Times* online (English) edition, cited on June 26, 2013. (References to the city and date were added.)

in question. But more than this: in each case the recipient/hearer, owing to his or her minimal background knowledge of the subject matter, *is not in a position to explicate the very concepts that figure in the propositional content of the very knowledge she acquires*. Henry cannot explicate the concepts ELECTRON or NEUCLEONS; Henrietta cannot say exactly where in Thailand the city of Ayutthaya is, nor can she explicate NARCOTIC so as to distinguish this category of drugs from others (her life in Juneau having been that sheltered); and Hank could not explicate the concepts of INNING or PITCH, nor can he distinguish Rivera from any other player in Yankees' pinstripes. Still, none of this doxastic diversity undermines the successful communication of a very specific piece of knowledge.

If this is correct, then we have an argument for a minimalist account of comprehension. The argument is as follows:

(Premise 1) The above cases are ordinary, everyday cases of which there are many other examples.
(Premise 2) In the above cases and the others like them, a very specific piece of knowledge is communicated from source to recipient.
(Premise 3) The hearer/recipient's knowledge is underwritten by his or her comprehension of the source message.
(Premise 4) The hearer/recipient attains such comprehension despite an inability to explicate each of the concepts that figure in the propositional content of her knowledge.
(Conclusion) Comprehension of the sort required by ordinary, everyday knowledge communication does not require the ability to explicate each of the concepts that figure in the propositional content of the knowledge one acquires through accepting another's telling.

I have argued elsewhere that this sort of argument can be resisted only at the cost of a rather wholesale rejection of standard accounts of knowledge communication (Goldberg 2007a). The important result for my purposes here, however, is simply this: when it comes to the sort of grasp one has of the contents of *others'* thoughts and the utterances or inscriptions that express them, we have excellent reason to allow that one can comprehend those thoughts and utterances/inscriptions – one can correctly and reliably represent their content – without being able to explicate each of the concepts that figure in them. I now want to use this conclusion to argue that precisely the same point holds for one's grasp of *one's own* thoughts (and the utterances/inscriptions that express them).

3

The simplest point to make here is the obvious one: since in the "clear central" cases of the sort described above one comes to know the very content expressed in the telling, it follows from the assumption that knowledge entails belief that one comes to *believe*, and hence to think, the very content of that telling. This is precisely what Burge had in mind in the quote I cited above: "comprehending standing, conceptual aspects of one's own thought and idiolect is itself, as a matter of psychological and sociological fact, normally dependent on having comprehended thoughts (one's own) that were shaped and expressed through the words of others" (Burge 1999, p. 243). If this is correct, then insofar as one's grasp of the concepts involved in the other's statement was partial, one's grasp of the concepts involved in one's own thought, when one comes to comprehend and accept their statement, is partial. This point is straightforward.

At the risk of developing what is already obvious, it is worth spelling out the context in which this point is being made.

It is widely acknowledged that insofar as we allow that there are public languages and sociolects, and so allow that there are concepts expressed by the lexical items in public languages and sociolects, the phenomenon of partial or incomplete grasp will be widespread. (By 'partial grasp' here I mean to designate the phenomenon whereby a hearer is unable to explicate in a correct and illuminating way the application conditions of the concept(s) in question.) While this point itself is widely acknowledged, there is great debate about its significance for the study of mind and language. On the one hand, Tyler Burge and others have famously argued that the significance of this point is great indeed, since it is typically the case that *these very (partially grasped) concepts* (i) are expressed in the linguistic acts of individual speakers and (ii) figure in the propositional contents of the attitudes of such speakers. On the other, many who have resisted Burge's "anti-individualistic" approach to mind and language have denied Burge's contention. Some have held that there really *are* no public languages and sociolects in the first place (Chomsky 1992, 1995; Davidson 1986b). Others have held that such concepts rarely if ever figure in the speech acts of speakers or the thoughts of thinkers (Davidson 1999). A slightly more concessive ('hybrid') view is held by still many others. According to this hybrid view, while public language concepts are expressed in the *speech acts* of speakers, few if any of these speakers actually *think thoughts involving* propositional contents whose concepts are those of the public language (Loar 1988; Patterson 1990;

Elugardo 1993; McKinsey 1994 and McKinsey 1999; Bach 1988 and Bach 1997; Byrne and Thau 1995).[12]

Now I want to suggest that those who resist Burge's position here face one of two unattractive options. The first option, which involves rejecting the very idea that public language concepts (typically) figure in the speech acts and thoughts of subjects in a language community, will result in the forced repudiation of the idea that there are simple cases of successful communication involving a very specific piece of knowledge that is passed between subjects exhibiting doxastic diversity. In that case, our theorist will be forced to deny at least one of the four assumptions I made in section 2. The latter option, which involves endorsing something like the hybrid view just described, will result in a 'split' account of communication, whereby the contents that are expressed in the use of language are precisely those associated with the public language lexicon, whereas the contents that are believed when one believes another's telling are distinct contents (which in the best case have the same truth conditions as the contents expressed by the speaker). But both views are unattractive.

To bring this out, I begin by noting how such views are often defended. They are often defended on the grounds that views of this sort best capture the agent's epistemic perspective – roughly, how she takes things to be. The implicit assumption behind such a defense is this:

(IA) How a subject S takes things to be is determined by S's explications of the concepts that figure in the propositions she avows.

That IA lies behind this defense of the views above is clear when we consider an alternative conception of how a subject takes things to be. On this alternative conception, how a subject S takes things to be is often determined by how *other subjects* take things to be, for the simple reason that S often accepts that things are as they are represented to be in another's telling. Since we have already seen that subjects are often not in a position to explicate the concepts expressed in another's telling, the result is that if this alternative conception is correct, then IA is false. And so we see that, for those who wish to resist Burge's picture in one of the two ways above, it will not do simply to defend their alternatives as the best way to capture how a subject takes things to be. What is needed is an explicit independent defense of IA itself.

The present point can be approached from a slightly different perspective. Part, and perhaps the main part, of the motivation behind individualist and internalist views of content is that they seem to square

---

[12] Against such a view see Heck 1995 and 1996, as well as Goldberg 2007a, chapter 4.

with a certain view of authoritative self-knowledge: each of us is authoritative about what we currently consciously think, and we cannot make mistakes about this. Hence one of the original objections to anti-individualism was its failure to square with first-person authority.[13] In response, Burge (1988) argued that the sort of first-person authority that people worried about in this context is the result of a perfectly general mechanism of self-verification in *cogito*-like thoughts of the form '*(With this very thought) I am thinking that p*'. Still, many continued to worry that, even if Burge is correct in the point he is making, his response fails to capture something crucial to the subject's epistemic perspective on the world. Thus, Bach (1988), Elugardo (1993), Wikforss (2001, 2004, 2008), and others have argued that, even as supplemented with Burge's point about the self-verifying mechanism involved in *cogito*-like thoughts, the anti-individualistic position fails to capture *how the agent is conceiving of things*. Now if we fail to have in mind the role others play in our attempts to learn about the world, this response to Burge can seem strong. For it can seem curious to suppose that how one conceives of things is determined in part by facts about the norms of usage for items in the public language – since, after all, one may be ignorant or (worse still) wrong about those norms. It is this curiosity, I think, that underlies the perennial attraction of individualistic views of meaning and content. But once we see that such views fail to jibe with our profound dependence on others for what we know of the world – in particular, once we see that such views fail to square with the simplest, most plausible account of the content dimension of accepting another's telling, as spelled out in section 2 above – we see that such a view ought to be questioned. For this view is underwritten by an assumption, IA, which itself should be denied by anyone who accepts that account of knowledge communication.

In fact, it can seem that we do injustice to the theory of meaning and content if we continue to approach this domain from the blinkered perspective of the individual in isolation from her community. Such a blinkered perspective is implicit in arguments that proceed *from* (highly individualistic) assumptions about the nature of self-knowledge, or about the nature of a subject's conceptions of things, to conclusions about the nature of meaning and content. Such assumptions come in simple forms, dressed as accounts of first-person authority. But such assumptions also come in more sophisticated forms, dressed as accounts as to what is

---

[13] The worry goes back at least as far as Burge 1988 and Heil 1988. See also the various entries in Ludlow and Martin 1998; Wright, Smith, and MacDonald 2000; Frapolli and Romero 2003; Nuccetelli 2003; Schantz 2003; Hahn and Ramberg 2004; and Goldberg 2007c. In addition see Brown 2004a, which treated this topic at length.

involved in capturing "the subject's perspective."[14] As against this sort of approach, I submit that a subject's take on her own mental life is best seen as part and parcel of her take on the world itself – a take which, given the social sort of creature we are, implicates others' take on the world. Once this is seen, it is no more strange to suppose that a subject might fail to be able to explicate her own concepts than it is to suppose that she might fail to be able to explicate the concepts expressed in another's telling. What she loses in explicational capacity is more than made up for by the extension in knowledge that is enabled when she takes the words of her peers (Goldberg 2009). An insistence on IA, on the contrary, jeopardizes precisely this extension in knowledge.

4

My aim in this chapter, in effect, has been to urge that we take a broader perspective on the debate about anti-individualism and authoritative self-knowledge. In particular, when we see the question regarding a subject's relation to her own thoughts as part of a bigger picture in which she acquires quite a bit of what she thinks about the world from the tellings of others, we see that there is no good reason to suppose – and there is good reason to deny – that she will be able to explicate in a correct and complete way all of the concepts that figure in her thoughts. What has been known as the doctrine of incomplete grasp, then, appears to be part and parcel of our best account of the sort of knowledge we get from others through their say-so. Complete grasp can no more be a requirement on thinking a thought for oneself, than it can be a requirement on the sort of understanding that puts one in a position to get knowledge through what others tell one.

---

[14] Perhaps the most sophisticated version of this I have seen is Farkas 2008.

Part 3

Metasemantics and the Nature of Mental Content

11 Externalism, self-knowledge, and memory

Jordi Fernandez

This chapter discusses Paul Boghossian's 'memory argument' for the incompatibility of externalism and self-knowledge. The argument raises the question of whether or not, assuming externalism, the contents of our past thoughts are accessible to us through memory. I concede that there is a sense in which memory does not give us access to the contents of our past thoughts if externalism holds. However, I argue that, in the relevant sense, the view that the contents of our past thoughts are inaccessible to memory cannot be used to establish incompatibilism through the memory argument. Drawing on some tools from two-dimensional (2D) semantics, I suggest that one of the premises in the argument trades on an ambiguity between two notions of mental content.

Introduction

In this chapter I will discuss a certain use that has been made of the notion of memory to motivate incompatibilism in the literature on externalism and self-knowledge. Self-knowledge is understood in this literature as the view that our beliefs regarding our thoughts enjoy a special type of epistemic justification; special in that we are not supposed to rely on either reasoning or empirical evidence for such beliefs. Externalism is understood as the view that thinking something is a matter of being related to some objects or substances in our environment (as opposed to having some intrinsic property). We may abbreviate this by saying that the contents of our thoughts 'depend on' certain environmental conditions. The incompatibilist position is that externalism and self-knowledge cannot both be correct: how can we have any sort of epistemically special access to the contents of our own thoughts if those contents really depend on our environment? After all, whether we are on, let us say, Earth or Twin Earth, is not something that we can determine without substantial empirical investigation and reasoning.

Paul Boghossian has been a prominent advocate of incompatibilism.[1] One of his incompatibilist arguments was originally meant as a response to Tyler Burge's account of self-knowledge, but the argument has received much attention in its own right. Boghossian's argument relies on some views about the content of memories, and it has sparked a debate on the proper understanding of memory within an externalist framework.[2] In this chapter I will discuss Boghossian's 'memory argument' and offer a response to it based on a distinction between two types of belief content. I will begin by sketching Burge's account of self-knowledge. Next, I will examine Boghossian's argument against it. Then, I will put forward the distinction between two types of belief content. I will introduce the distinction by drawing on some ideas from 2D semantics and, finally, I will apply the distinction between two types of belief content to tackle the memory argument. The conclusion will be that the memory argument cannot be used to bolster incompatibilism in response to Burge's account of self-knowledge.

Basic self-knowledge and the memory argument

Tyler Burge's account of self-knowledge focuses on the special entitlement that we have to beliefs of a particular type.[3] Let us consider the class of beliefs expressed by utterances of the form 'I am thinking that P'. Following Burge, we may call these beliefs 'basic self-knowledge'. Beliefs that amount to basic self-knowledge have a peculiar structure. In basic self-knowledge, the content of my belief about my own thought is partly constituted by the content of that thought which my belief is about. As a result of their peculiar structure, beliefs that qualify as basic self-knowledge are self-verifying in that they are made true just in virtue of being instantiated. Given that I must think that P in order to believe that I am thinking that P (in order, that is, to attribute the thought that P to

---

[1] See Boghossian 1989 and McKinsey 1995 for the two main defenses of incompatibilism.
[2] Some of the relevant literature can be found in Ludlow and Martin 1998. The type of memory that is relevant for this debate is semantic (or factual) memory, as opposed to episodic (or experiential) memory. Semantic memory is the type of memory that one has when one remembers a fact that one learnt in the past. Episodic memory is the type of memory that one has when one remembers a fact that one experienced in the past. Whereas episodic memories are quasi-perceptual experiences, semantic memories are beliefs; beliefs that were acquired in the past and have been maintained up to the present time by memory. As we will only be concerned with semantic memories in what follows, I will occasionally refer to memories as beliefs. Hopefully this will cause no confusion.
[3] For details of his account of self-knowledge and his compatibilist proposal, see Burge 1988.

myself), my belief that I am thinking that P must be true whenever I have it. The self-verifying character of basic self-knowledge is, according to Burge, what entitles us to those beliefs in an epistemically special way: for any proposition P, I can be certain that my belief that I am thinking that P is true just in virtue of having that belief. Other people, by contrast, may believe that I am thinking that P, but their beliefs about my thoughts will not be true just in virtue of their having those beliefs. This is the sense in which beliefs expressed by utterances of the form 'I am thinking that P' enjoy the special type of epistemic justification that characterizes self-knowledge.

This account of self-knowledge suggests a straightforward compatibilist proposal. How can we be especially entitled to believe that we have thoughts with certain contents if the contents of those thoughts depend on the environment we are in? The reason why we are entitled to our beliefs about the thoughts that we have is that, whether we are on Earth or Twin Earth, those beliefs are guaranteed to be true. Consider the belief that I would express by uttering 'I am thinking that water contains hydrogen'. If I am on Earth, I am expressing the belief that I think that water contains hydrogen. And, in that scenario, I will indeed think that water contains hydrogen, since having such a thought is a necessary condition for me to believe that I am having that thought. Conversely, if I am on Twin Earth, the belief that I am expressing by uttering 'I am thinking that water contains hydrogen' is the belief that I think that twater contains hydrogen. And, in that scenario, I will indeed think that twater contains hydrogen. For thinking that twater contains hydrogen is necessary for me to believe that I am thinking it. Either way, then, my belief about the thought that I am having is guaranteed to be true, which is meant to account for my special entitlement to it even if we assume externalism.

One difficulty with Burge's account concerns our knowledge of our recent mental states. Boghossian points out that nothing in Burge's account guarantees that if I believe that I was thinking a certain proposition just a moment ago, then I must have been doing so. The point is meant to threaten Burge's account in two ways. First of all, it is intended to reveal that its scope is too narrow, since our entitlement to our beliefs about many of our own thoughts (very recent ones) is left unexplained by the account. Furthermore, on the basis of this shortcoming, Boghossian builds an interesting argument for the more damaging objection that Burge's account cannot even explain our entitlement to beliefs which do qualify as basic self-knowledge.

In order to build this argument, Boghossian relies on a certain view about the nature of knowledge, that is, the 'relevant alternative' theory of knowledge.[4] According to this view, true belief amounts to knowledge if one is able to rule out all the relevant alternatives to what one believes. Whether or not an alternative to what one believes counts as relevant depends on facts about the context in which one's belief occurs. The thought is that one can possess knowledge in the face of some uneliminated possibilities of error because some of those possibilities are, in the context in which one is placed, not relevant. However, in a different context, those possibilities of error might become relevant, which would require one to rule them out in order to possess knowledge. The possibility that Boghossian is going to use for evaluating Burge's account of self-knowledge arises within the following 'slow-switching' scenario:

> Unbeknown to her, subject S undergoes a series of switches between Earth and Twin Earth. In every switch, S stays on either Earth or Twin Earth as long as needs be for her conceptual repertoire to change completely (Earthian concepts wholly replace Twin Earthian concepts, or vice versa).[5]

Boghossian uses the slow-switching scenario to argue for incompatibilism as follows. Consider two times t_1 and t_2. Suppose that, at t_1, S is on Earth having the belief that she would express by uttering 'I am thinking that water contains hydrogen'. Suppose that, at t_2, S is also on Earth having the belief that she would express by uttering 'I was thinking that water contains hydrogen'. Let us stipulate that S does not forget anything between t_1 and t_2. Thus, S remembers, at t_2, what she knew at t_1. Is S especially entitled, at t_1, to the belief that she is thinking that water contains hydrogen? Burge's remarks about the self-verifying character of basic self-knowledge suggest that she is. And yet, Boghossian thinks that, despite that feature of basic self-knowledge, S is not especially entitled to her belief at t_1. In support of this view, Boghossian offers the following argument:[6]

(1) If S forgets nothing between t_1 and t_2, then what S knows at t_1, S knows at t_2.
(2) S forgets nothing between t_1 and t_2.
(3) At t_2, S does not know that she was thinking that water contains hydrogen.

---

[4] On relevant alternatives, see Fred Dretske 1970.
[5] There is a version of the slow-switching scenario in which S's conceptual repertoire is enlarged to include both Earthian and Twin Earthian concepts. I will need to leave this version of the scenario aside for reasons of space.
[6] The reconstruction of the argument is due to Peter Ludlow in his 1995.

Therefore,

(4) At t_1, S does not know that she is thinking that water contains hydrogen.

Let us call this the 'memory argument'. Premise 1 in the memory argument is supposed to follow from a platitude about memory, namely, that memory stores our knowledge over time.[7] Premise 2 is meant to be a stipulation.[8] Much of the weight in the memory argument, therefore, is carried by premise 3.

Premise 3 is motivated by an appeal to the slow switching scenario and the relevant alternative theory of knowledge as follows: Since S finds herself in the slow switching scenario, there is a certain possibility that becomes a relevant possibility of error for S at t_2. This is the possibility that S was on Twin Earth at t_1, thinking that twater contains hydrogen, and S is now having, while being on Earth at t_2, the belief that she would express by saying that she was thinking that water contains hydrogen. Let us refer to this possibility as 'Switch'. If Switch is a relevant alternative possibility for S at t_2, then S needs to rule it out in order for her belief at t_2 to constitute knowledge. But S's memory does not allow her to rule out Switch at t_2, since it does not allow S to discriminate between the thoughts that she actually had at t_1 and those which she would have had at t_1 if she had been in Switch. Thus, S needs to rely on reasoning in order to rule out Switch; hence premise 3.[9]

The conclusion of the memory argument tells us that, in the slow-switching scenario, a subject does not know the thoughts that she has in the way required for her to possess self-knowledge. But slow-switching scenarios are acknowledged to be common by externalists. Thus, the argument suggests, more generally, that we do not have self-knowledge about the contents of our thoughts if externalism holds.

It is worth highlighting that, even though the memory argument was originally conceived as a response to Burge's account of self-knowledge, the argument allows for a broader incompatibilist use. Notice that the argument simply relies on the idea that memory preserves knowledge through time, and the relevant alternative theory of knowledge. Both of these views seem prima facie plausible whether or not one endorses

---

[7] However, the premise has been challenged, for example, in Brueckner 1997.
[8] And yet, this premise has also been challenged. For an illuminating discussion of the notion of forgetting, see Nagasawa 2002.
[9] Notice that, strictly speaking, the claim motivated by these considerations cannot be that, at t_2, S does not know that she was thinking that water contains hydrogen. After all, S might be able to reason her way to the conclusion that she is not in Switch. Premise 3 therefore needs to be read as the weaker claim that S does not have, at t_2, the kind of knowledge that qualifies as self-knowledge, namely, noninferential a priori knowledge.

Burge's self-verification account of self-knowledge. A theorist of self-knowledge might alternatively endorse, for example, an inner-sense account of self-knowledge, a transparency-based account, or an expressivist account of self-knowledge.[10] As long as neither the notion of knowledge nor the conception of memory underlying the argument is called into question, such a theorist will have trouble endorsing externalism about mental content in the face of the memory argument. In the next two sections I will put forward a response to the argument that focuses on the conception of memory presupposed by it.[11]

Memory and content

The memory argument raises an analogous question to that of whether the contents of our current thoughts are accessible to introspection (broadly understood as our capacity for self-knowledge (whatever that capacity amounts to)) if externalism is right. It raises the question of whether the contents of our past thoughts are accessible to memory if externalism is right. Boghossian's line of reasoning for premise 3 of the memory argument seems to assume that they are not. The idea that I cannot tell by memory alone whether my past thoughts were, for instance, about water or about twater suggests that I do not have access to the contents of my past thoughts through memory if externalism is right. For if memory did give me access to the contents of my past thoughts, then it should allow me to discriminate between my past thoughts about water and my past thoughts about twater. And yet, we are told, memory does not allow me to carry out such discriminations. Thus, Boghossian's strategy in the memory argument seems to be that of using, as a foothold, the view that the contents of our past thoughts are inaccessible to memory if externalism holds in order to eventually lift himself to the conclusion that the contents of our current thoughts are inaccessible to introspection if externalism holds.

My aim in this section is to pull apart two strands of our notion of mental content that seem to be responsible for the idea that I cannot tell by memory alone whether my past thoughts were about water or about twater. The main intuition behind this idea seems to be that if I had been on Twin Earth in the past, then what I would have thought in the past would have been different from what I did think. And yet, what I would now remember having thought in the past would be the same. Why is

---

[10] For an in-depth discussion of the various approaches to self-knowledge, see Gertler 2011a.
[11] See Goldberg 2005a for an attack on the memory argument that focuses instead on the notion of knowledge involved in the argument.

that? Presumably, the reason is that the contents of our memories do not depend on past environmental conditions; conditions that obtained at the time that those memories were formed. If there is no such dependence, then it does seem natural to think that, even if those environmental conditions which obtained at the time that I had my thoughts in the past had been different from what they actually were, what I would now remember thinking at the time would have been the same.[12] I will argue that, in a sense, the contents of my past thoughts would have differed depending on whether, in the past, I was having my thoughts on Earth or Twin Earth. And, in a sense, those differences would admittedly not be reflected in the contents of my current memories. But those are, I will claim, two different types of mental content. By distinguishing between these two types of content, we will be able to clarify the precise role that memory plays in Boghossian's incompatibilist argument. For the sake of simplicity, I will concentrate on the case of *belief* content, though the distinction should generalize to the contents of other mental states provided that those contents can be cashed out in terms of satisfaction conditions.

Two types of belief content can be differentiated by using a distinction that is present in the literature on 2D semantics.[13] The main idea in 2D

---

[12] There is a certain tension between Boghossian's position here and his position about the contents of memory in the context of a different argument for the incompatibility of self-knowledge and externalism. The argument in question (Boghossian 1992a, 1992b, 1994) is aimed at showing that externalism is incompatible with the view that we have a priori knowledge of whether an argument is logically valid or not. A subject in a slow-switching scenario, the argument goes, may see Luciano Pavarotti bathing in Lake Taupo while being on Earth. Later, while being on Twin Earth, she may see twin Luciano at a concert. Suppose that the day after the concert, the subject has two memories; one formed on Earth and another on Twin Earth. She would express them by uttering, respectively, 'Pavarotti once swam in Lake Taupo' and 'The singer I heard yesterday is Pavarotti'. And, on the basis of those two beliefs, the subject infers that the singer she heard yesterday once swam in Lake Taupo. Boghossian claims that, even though the inference will appear valid to this subject, it isn't. For the first premise expresses a memory about Luciano Pavarotti whereas the second premise expresses a memory about twin Luciano (1992a, p. 22). Notice that this is only true if, assuming externalism, the contents of our memories depend on environmental conditions that obtained at the time that those memories were formed. But if this is the correct externalist way of construing the contents of memories, then it is hard to see why, in the memory argument, I cannot tell by memory alone whether my past thoughts were about water or they were about twater. After all, my memories of what I was thinking at the time should be different in each case.

[13] The 2D framework is aimed at reconciling some convincing metaphysical and semantic views put forward by Saul Kripke in 1972, and some apparently conflicting, though equally appealing, views about the epistemology of modality. Kripke proposed that expressions such as indexicals, demonstratives, proper names, and natural kind terms designate the same thing with respect to every possible world. As a result, any true identity formulated with terms of those kinds is necessary. However, many of them (such as 'Hesperus is Phosphorus' or 'Water is H_2O') appear to be contingent. This

frameworks is the distinction, for any utterance or belief, of the context where it occurs from the context relative to which it is to be evaluated. In the case of belief, the distinction may be drawn as follows. We take beliefs to be mental states of the type that can be evaluated as true or false. For each belief, then, there are conditions under which it is true and conditions under which it is false (for short, 'truth conditions' of it). Thus, it is reasonable to think that if you want to know what the content of a belief is, you should ask yourself what its truth conditions are. The main tenet of this section is that there are two kinds of truth conditions that can arguably be used to specify the content of a belief. To capture this distinction, it will be convenient to represent the truth conditions of beliefs by means of certain abstract objects, namely, propositions. For the purposes of our discussion in this chapter, I will construe propositions as sets of possible worlds.

If we think of propositions as sets of possible worlds, then we can individuate one kind of truth condition for an occurrent belief by reference to the proposition that only contains those possible worlds such that, if the belief in question had occurred there, it would have been true of that world. Let us call this type of truth condition the 'subjective content' of the belief. We can also individuate a different kind of truth condition for the occurrence of the belief by reference to the proposition that only contains those possible worlds such that the state of affairs that is needed to make the belief true in the world in which the belief actually occurs obtains in those worlds. Let us call this type of truth condition the 'objective content' of the belief.[14]

To illustrate the distinction, consider the following example. In possible world W_1, I am lost in the university campus on January 1, 2013. A fire has started in the Napier building and, unbeknownst to me, I am located inside that building. Suddenly I see a lot of smoke in the building and, at a time that happens to be noon, I form the belief that I would express by uttering 'there is a fire here'. Not wanting to die, I immediately run out of the building. Let us also stipulate that, in W_1, no other fire is taking place on campus. In the terminology introduced above, the objective content of the belief that I have in W_1 is constituted by the proposition that only contains those worlds in which there is a fire in the Napier building at

conflicts with the prima facie plausible idea that we have a reliable access to possible worlds: if our epistemic access to counterfactual situations is trustworthy, then why are we prone to such modal illusions? Two-dimensional semantics tries to build a notion of meaning that accounts for this fact. There are, however, a number of different versions of two-dimensionalism, most of which have other interesting applications as well. Chalmers 2006 offers a useful taxonomy of various two-dimensionalist systems.

[14] The distinction is not new. It is essentially David Chalmers's (2002) distinction between the 'subjunctive' and 'epistemic' intensions of a thought.

noon on January 1, 2013 (whether I am in those worlds, having the belief in question, or not). By contrast, its subjective content is constituted by the proposition that only contains those worlds in which, at the time that I have my belief, I am located at a place where there is a fire (whether there is a fire in the Napier building at noon on January 1, 2013, or not).

It is easy to appreciate the difference between the objective content of my belief in W_1 and its subjective content by considering two other possible worlds, W_2 and W_3. In both W_2 and W_3, I suddenly see a lot of smoke at noon on January 1, 2013, and I have a belief that I would express by uttering 'there is a fire here'. However, in both W_2 and W_3, I am not in the Napier building at that time. Unbeknownst to me, I am instead, let us say, in the Hughes building. The difference is that, whereas in W_2, there is no fire there but there is a fire in the Napier building, in W_3, there is a fire in the Hughes building but there is no fire in the Napier building. It seems that W_2 belongs to the objective content of the belief that I have in W_1, since there is a fire in the Napier building at noon on January 1, 2013 in W_2. But W_2 does not belong to the subjective content of the belief that I have in W_1, since that belief occurs in W_2 at a place and a time at which there is no fire. Conversely, W_3 does not belong to the objective content of the belief that I have in W_1, since there is no fire in the Napier building at noon on January 1, 2013 in W_3. But W_3 does belong to the subjective content of the belief that I have in W_1, since that belief occurs in W_3 at a place and a time at which there is a fire.

Now, how does the distinction between objective and subjective content illuminate the question of whether the contents of my past thoughts are accessible to memory if externalism holds? The distinction helps us pull apart a sense in which, assuming externalism, the contents of my memories depend on past environmental conditions from a sense in which they do not. And, by doing so, it will allow us to isolate the precise sense in which I cannot tell by memory alone whether my past thoughts were about water or they were about twater.

Let us consider, first of all, the sense in which the contents of our memories depend on past environmental conditions assuming externalism. Suppose that, in the three possible worlds that we have considered, I am on 1 January, 2014 now, and I remember the reason why I once had to run out of a university building. The memory that, in all those worlds, I have on 1 January, 2014 is, then, a belief that I would express by uttering 'there was a fire there'. Now consider the objective content of that memory in W_1 in particular. What is needed for my memory to be accurate in W_1 is that at noon on 1 January, 2013 there is a fire in the Napier building. Whether I remember those details or not, my memory causally originates on a belief through which I originally referred to that place and that time. And the fact that my memory bears a causal relation to that belief is enough to secure the reference of my memory to a fire in the Napier building at noon on 1 January, 2013. That event, whether I can describe it in those terms or not, is what it takes for my memory to be correct in W_1. Thus, the objective content of my memory contains those possible worlds in which there is a fire in the Napier building at noon on 1 January, 2013.

Notice that the objective content of my memory in W_1 and the objective content of the belief on which that memory originates coincide in this example. This is what we should expect. For if the reference-fixing mechanism of our memories is parasitic on that of our original beliefs in the way that has just been alluded to, then, for any memory, the possible worlds which that memory is true of will always turn out to be those possible worlds which its corresponding original belief was true of. The upshot of these considerations, therefore, is that the objective contents of our memories are identical with the objective contents of the beliefs on which those memories originate. There is, therefore, a sense in which the contents of our memories do depend on past environmental conditions if externalism is right: the *objective* contents of our memories depend on them, since they are identical with the objective contents of our corresponding past thoughts, and those depended on environmental conditions in the first place.[15]

Let us now consider the sense in which the contents of our memories do not depend on past environmental conditions. Take, once again, the possible world W_1 in which, on 1 January, 2014, I remember why I once had to run out of a university building. I remember it by having a belief that I would express by uttering 'there was a fire there'. What is the subjective content of that memory? My memory would be true if it occurred in a certain range of possible worlds, namely, those possible worlds in which the memory originates on the belief that I would express by uttering 'there is a fire here' in the past, and there is a fire at the place and the time at which I am having that belief, whatever that place and that time is. The subjective content of my memory in W_1, therefore, is the proposition that only contains those possible worlds.[16] Compare that

---

[15] The claim that our memories inherit their objective contents from those beliefs on which they originate fits nicely with the view, put forward by Tyler Burge (1993), that memory preserves the contents of our beliefs through time. (See, however, note 16 for the main difference with the view offered here.)

[16] Recall that the subjective content of the belief on which my memory originates is constituted by the proposition that only contains those worlds in which, at the time at which I have that belief, I am located at a place where there is a fire. It seems, then, that the subjective content of my belief is different from the subjective content of the memory that derives from it, simply because my memory provides me with more information than my

proposition, now, to the subjective content of a different memory. This is the memory that I have in, let us say, W_3 when, in that world, I have the belief that I would express by uttering 'there was a fire there' on 1 January, 2014. It seems that my memory in W_3 would also be true if it occurred in those possible worlds in which it originates on the belief that I would express by uttering 'there is a fire here' in the past, and there is a fire at the place and the time at which I am having that belief. Thus, it seems that the subjective content of my memory in W_1 and that of my memory in W_3 coincide.

And yet, the objective contents of the beliefs on which my W_1 and W_3 memories originate are different. As we have seen, in virtue of the fact that my original belief in W_1 takes place in the Napier building, its objective content is constituted by the proposition that only contains those worlds in which there is a fire in the Napier building at noon on 1 January, 2013. But the objective content of my original belief in W_3 seems to be constituted by the proposition that only contains those possible worlds in which there is a fire in the Hughes building at noon on 1 January, 2013. For that is the building in which my original belief took place in W_3. There is, therefore, a sense in which the contents of our memories do not depend on past environmental conditions even if externalism is right: the *subjective* contents of our memories are not sensitive to past environmental conditions even if, in accordance with externalism, the objective contents of the past thoughts on which those memories originate are indeed sensitive to such conditions. This proposal about the subjective content of memories squares with the intuition that I cannot tell through memory alone whether, when I had a belief that I would have expressed by uttering 'there is a fire here', my past belief was about a fire in the Napier building at noon, or it was about a fire in some other building at some other time. For if the proposal is right, there is indeed a sense in which the memories that I would now have in each of the two possible situations would be the same, namely, my memories would have the same subjective contents.

Thus, the distinction between the objective and subjective contents of our past beliefs, as well as those of our resulting memories, yields a precise sense in which the contents of our past beliefs are inaccessible to memory: they are inaccessible in that, when our beliefs are preserved by memory, there are environmental conditions other than those in which our beliefs

original belief did. Not only does my memory tell me about a fire, but it also tells me that I now believe something about a fire because I formed that belief in the past. With regards to subjective content, therefore, memory does not seem to perform a purely preservative function. Instead, it seems to perform a generative function. (See note 15 for the contrast with memory for objective content.)

actually took place such that, if they had obtained, the objective contents of our past beliefs would have been different. And yet, the subjective contents of our resulting memories would have been the same. What remains to be seen, however, is whether the view that the contents of our past beliefs are inaccessible to memory, thus understood, can be used to motivate premise 3 in the memory argument. Let us therefore approach the memory argument with the distinction between objective and subjective content in mind now.

The memory argument revisited

Recall Boghossian's line of reasoning in the memory argument. A subject S who is in a slow-switching scenario may, at a time t_1, be on Earth having the belief that she would express by uttering 'I am thinking that water contains hydrogen'. And, at a later time t_2, S may also be on Earth having the belief that she would express by uttering 'I was thinking that water contains hydrogen'. Assume that to be the actual situation. In that situation, Boghossian argues, S does not know, at t_2, that she was thinking that water contains hydrogen. And this, in turn, is meant to show that S did not know, at t_1, that she was thinking that water contains hydrogen. For if S had possessed that knowledge at t_1, memory would have made it available to her at t_2, and we can stipulate that S has not forgotten anything between t_1 and t_2. Thus, S lacks self-knowledge if she is in a slow-switching scenario. But such scenarios are supposed to be pervasive if externalism holds. Thus, S lacks self-knowledge if externalism holds.

The distinction between objective and subjective content may shed some light on what is problematic about this argument. Specifically, the distinction reveals a difficulty with the premise that S does not know, at t_2, that she was thinking that water contains hydrogen. The reason why S is supposed to lack that knowledge at t_2 is that S is in a slow-switching scenario. That scenario is intended to make a certain possible situation a relevant possibility of error for S when she believes, at t_2, that she was thinking that water contains hydrogen. The possible situation in question is possible situation Switch, in which S is, at t_1, thinking that twater contains hydrogen on Twin Earth and, at t_2, S is on Earth, having the belief that she would express by saying that she was thinking that water contains hydrogen. Since S's memory does not allow her to tell apart Switch from the actual situation in which she was on Earth at t_1, S cannot rule out Switch without relying on reasoning. And, for that reason, at t_2 S lacks the type of noninferential knowledge that qualifies as self-knowledge. This was essentially the rationale for premise 3 in the memory argument.

My contention is that Switch is not a relevant alternative possibility which S has failed to rule out when S believes, at t_2, that she was thinking that water contains hydrogen. In order for a possible situation to constitute a relevant alternative possibility which S has not ruled out when S has her belief at t_2, the possibility in question must be such that if it obtained, then S would be mistaken in her belief. And in order for S's belief to be mistaken at t_2, what S remembers at t_2 to have thought in the past must be different from what she did think at t_1. As Boghossian sees it, possibility Switch does meet those requirements. For if Switch had obtained, then S's belief at t_2 regarding her past thought would have been false: what S thought at t_1 would have been different, and yet S's memory of what she thought would have been the same. That is why, on Boghossian's view, S has not been able to rule out Switch at t_2.

Let us look more closely, however, at the claim that if S had been on Twin Earth at t_1, then what S thought at t_1 would have been different, and yet S's memory of what she thought would have been the same. I suggest that the plausibility of this claim trades on an ambiguity concerning the notion of 'what S thought', an ambiguity that can be dispelled by using the distinction between objective and subjective content. There is a sense of 'what S thought' in which if Switch had obtained, then what S thought at t_1 would have been different, and there is a sense in which S's memory of what she thought would have been the same. But those are, I propose, different senses of the expression 'what S thought'. With that expression, we may either refer to the subjective content of S's thought at t_1, or refer to the objective content of S's thought at t_1. In the former case, it seems correct to say that, had Switch been the case, what S remembers at t_2 to have thought in the past would have been the same. However, what S thought at t_1, in the relevant sense, would have been the same too. In the latter case, it seems right to say that, had Switch been the case, what S thought at t_1 would have been different. However, what S remembers at t_2 to have thought in the past, in the relevant sense, would have been different as well. Let me explain.

Consider the thought that, in the situation assumed to be actual within the memory argument, S would express with 'water contains hydrogen' at t_1 while being on Earth. What is S thinking with that thought? The objective content of S's thought seems to be the set of possible worlds in which H_2O (the transparent, odorless, tasteless liquid that actually fills rivers and seas in the environment in which S has her thought) contains hydrogen. The subjective content of S's thought, by contrast, seems to be the set of possible worlds in which S is having her thought in an environment in which the transparent, odorless, tasteless liquid that fills rivers and seas contains hydrogen. Is what S actually thinks at t_1 different, then, from what S would have thought at t_1 in Switch? It depends on whether we focus on the objective content of S's thought, or on its subjective content.

Take the thought that S would have expressed with 'water contains hydrogen' at t_1 if S had been in Switch. The subjective content of that thought is the set of possible worlds in which S is having that thought in an environment in which the transparent, odorless, tasteless liquid that fills rivers and seas contains hydrogen. Thus, the subjective content of S's actual thought at t_1 and that of her thought in Switch at t_1 do not differ. If we construe the notion of 'what S thought' in terms of subjective content, therefore, it seems incorrect to say that if S had been in Switch when she had the thought that she would express by uttering 'water contains hydrogen' at t_1, then she would have thought something different from what she actually thought at t_1. The upshot is that, in this case, Switch does not constitute a relevant alternative possibility which S has failed to rule out at t_2 because, as far as the subjective content of S's thought at t_1 is concerned, it constitutes no alternative at all.

What about the objective content of the thought that S would have expressed with 'water contains hydrogen' at t_1 if S had been in Switch? The objective content of it is the set of possible worlds in which XYZ (the transparent, odorless, tasteless liquid that actually fills rivers and seas in the environment in which S has her thought) contains hydrogen. Thus, the objective content of S's actual thought at t_1 and that of S's thought in Switch at t_1 do differ. If we construe the notion of 'what S thought' in terms of objective content, therefore, it seems correct to say that if S had been in Switch when she had a thought that she would express by uttering 'water contains hydrogen' at t_1, she would have thought something different from what she actually thought at t_1. Hence, it is tempting to think that the possibility that S might have been on Twin Earth at t_1 is, as Boghossian claims, a relevant alternative possibility which S has failed to rule out when she has her belief at t_2.

However, we should resist that temptation. For it turns out that S is in fact ruling out Switch at t_2. The reason is that, in Switch, S's memory of what she thought in the past matches what S did think at t_1. We have seen that, in Switch, what S thinks at t_1 (in the sense of the expression that concerns objective content) can be captured by the proposition that contains those possible worlds in which XYZ contains hydrogen. Consider now S's memory of what she thought in the past, that is, the belief that she would express at t_2 by saying that she was thinking that water contains hydrogen. What is the objective content of that memory in Switch? As we saw in the third section, memories inherit their objective contents from those beliefs on which they originate. Let us turn our attention, therefore, to the belief on which S's memory originates in Switch.

In Switch, S's memory originates on a belief of the type that Burge labeled 'basic self-knowledge'. It is the belief that, at t_1, S would express with an utterance of the form 'I am thinking that water contains hydrogen'. To determine what the objective content of that belief was at t_1 in Switch, recall that, in basic self-knowledge, what a subject believes to be thinking incorporates as part of it, as it were, what she is thinking. It seems, then, that the objective content of S's belief about her own thought at t_1 should bear the same kind of relation to the objective content of that thought, whether S is on Earth at t_1 or not. This consideration suggests that, in Switch, the objective content of the belief that S would express by uttering 'I am thinking that water contains hydrogen' at t_1 is constituted by the set of possible worlds in which, at t_1, S is thinking a thought with a certain objective content. What content specifically? It is the objective content of the thought that, in Switch, S would express at t_1 by uttering 'water contains hydrogen', namely, the set of possible worlds in which XYZ contains hydrogen.

Now, the reason why, in Switch, S has been able to report at t_2 what she thought in the past is that her piece of basic self-knowledge has been preserved by memory from t_1 to t_2. As a result, the objective content of her memory at t_2 is, in Switch, identical with the objective content of her original piece of basic self-knowledge; the set of possible worlds in which S is thinking, at t_1, a thought with the content constituted by the set of possible worlds in which XYZ contains hydrogen. That is, in other words, what S remembers at t_2 to have thought (in the sense of the expression that concerns objective content) when she is in Switch. But notice that Switch belongs to the objective content of that memory. Switch is one of the possible situations in which S did have, at t_1, a thought with the content constituted by the set of possible worlds in which XYZ contains hydrogen. Thus, in the possible situation in which S is on Twin Earth at t_1 and, at t_2, S is on Earth remembering what she thought, there is a match between what S thought at t_1 and what S remembers at t_2 to have thought in the past. The upshot is that possibility Switch is indeed a relevant possibility of error for S at t_2 since, in that possible situation, the objective content of S's thought at t_1 would have been different from that of her actual thought at t_1. But it is not a possibility of error which S has failed to rule out at t_2 since, in that possible situation, what S would believe at t_2 to have thought in the past would turn out to be correct.[17]

---

[17] This is essentially the compatibilist line adopted by Kevin Falvey and Joseph Owens (1994, pp. 116–18). Notice that if one works with the notion of objective content exclusively, then all that is needed in order to defend Burge's account of self-knowledge from the memory argument is two things: Burge's idea that memory preserves the contents of our beliefs over time; and his idea that, in basic self-knowledge, the contents

The outcome of our discussion in this section is that, when S believes at t_2 that she thought that water contains hydrogen, the possibility that she might have been on Twin Earth at t_1 is not a relevant alternative possibility which S has failed to rule out. This outcome casts doubt on the plausibility of premise 3 in the memory argument. For the main consideration in support of the view that S does not know, at t_2, that she was thinking that water contains hydrogen is that, at t_2, S is not in a position to rule out the possibility that she might have been thinking that twater contains hydrogen at t_1. If the possibility in question is not a relevant alternative possibility which S has failed to rule out when she has her belief at t_2, then it is hard to see why we should challenge S's knowledge at t_2. The moral from our discussion of the memory argument, therefore, seems to be that premise 3 in Boghossian's argument is in need of further support.

Conclusion

The 2D approach to the memory argument does more than just identifying the weakness in the grounds provided for premise 3 in the memory argument. It also provides an explanation for why, at first glance, premise 3 *seems* true to us. Premise 3 seems true because the idea that the contents of my past thoughts are inaccessible to memory if externalism is right does make sense. But, as we saw at the end of the third section, the idea makes sense because it involves two different types of content: The contents of my past beliefs are inaccessible to memory in that, when my beliefs are preserved by memory, there can be differences in the objective contents of my past beliefs due to alternative environmental conditions which would not generate differences in the subjective contents of my resulting memories. What we have seen in the fourth section is that, once the operative notion of content is disambiguated, the inaccessibility idea loses its appeal. If we employ the notion of objective content throughout the memory argument, then it is false that, when my beliefs are preserved by memory, there can be differences in the contents of my past beliefs due to alternative environmental conditions which would not generate differences in the contents of my resulting memories. For my memories inherit their objective contents from my corresponding original beliefs. And if we

of our beliefs about our own thoughts are partly constituted by the contents of those thoughts which our beliefs are about. However, this line of defense is not enough to account for the intuitive appeal of premise 3 in the memory argument. To explain why it seems right to think that memory does not give us access to the contents of our past thoughts if externalism holds, one needs to appeal, as we saw in the third section, to a combination of the notions of objective and subjective content.

only employ the notion of subjective content to run the argument, then it is also false that, when my beliefs are preserved by memory, there can be differences in the contents of my past beliefs due to alternative environmental conditions which would not generate differences in the contents of my resulting memories. For differences in past environmental conditions would not affect the subjective contents of my original beliefs in the first place. The diagnosis of the memory argument provided by the 2D approach, therefore, explains why the argument fails to establish incompatibilism. And, importantly, it also explains why the argument can mislead us into thinking that incompatibilism has been established.

12 Externalism, metainternalism, and self-knowledge

Jussi Haukioja

Introduction

In joint work (Cohnitz and Haukioja 2013), Daniel Cohnitz and I have argued that two quite different kinds of externalist thinking about reference have not been properly distinguished in recent philosophy of language. One kind of externalism, *first-order* externalism, concerns the question of what determines the reference of linguistic expressions: an externalist of a familiar kind holds that the reference of at least some expressions is determined partly by factors external to a speaker. Another kind of externalism (which we dub *meta*externalism) holds, roughly, that *whether* and *how* external factors enter into the determination of reference is also, at least in part, externally determined. We have also argued that, while there are good reasons to be a first-order externalist, we should not embrace metaexternalism, but rather be meta*internalists*.

In this chapter I will argue that this distinction, when extended to the case of thought contents, can help to dispel worries about content externalism and self-knowledge. I will first show, in the section that follows, how the distinction between two kinds of externalist views can in a natural way be extended from the case of language to the case of thought. I will also argue that, for reasons analogous to the ones Cohnitz and I have given in the case of language, we should be first-order externalists, but not *meta*externalists, about thought content. Roughly, this means holding that the contents of at least some of our thoughts are partly externally determined, but that the fact *that* our thought contents are externally determined in this way, is wholly determined by our individual psychology.

Second, I will (in the third section) explore the relevance of this distinction to the problems of content externalism and self-knowledge.

An earlier version of this chapter was presented at the CCCOM workshop in Trondheim in 2013; I want to thank the audience, in particular Åsa Wikforss, for helpful feedback. I am especially grateful to Sandy Goldberg for comments on an earlier written version. Research for this work was supported by the Norwegian Research Council grant 212841.

First-order externalism and self-knowledge are not incompatible, I think, at least not for the kinds of reasons standardly discussed. Moreover, a certain kind of metainternalism – one which I think is independently plausible – gives direct support for a specific line of response to McKinsey-style problems about self-knowledge. A *dispositionalist* version of metainternalism can account for our knowing that a concept is a natural kind concept (in one sense of "natural kind concept") without being committed to the problematic a priori entailments that McKinsey's argument relies on.

Finally (in the last section) I will consider whether the kind of dispositionalist metainternalism I am advocating might raise problems of its own, by making our knowledge of the natures of our thoughts hostage to empirical facts concerning our own dispositions. I will look at two sources of potential problems and conclude that they, at most, place certain limits on the extent and security of our knowledge concerning the natures of our own thoughts, but do not seriously undermine it, even if content externalism is true.

The view I am defending in this chapter is based on an overall dispositionalist view of meaning and content, including a dispositionalist explanation of how externalism about meaning and content can be true of at least some of our terms and concepts. I will not be able to defend the view in full detail here. Nor do I pretend to have a complete and detailed theory at hand, although I have taken some steps toward giving one in earlier work. However, I do think such an overall view is independently highly plausible. My main aim here is to show that if a view along the lines I am sketching can be rigorously formulated and defended, then problems of content externalism and self-knowledge will be far less severe than many authors have taken them to be.

Content externalism and self-knowledge

The discussion in this chapter is, as far as I can tell, quite neutral with respect to the precise formulations of content externalism and self-knowledge: unless otherwise noted, the views I am putting forward do not presuppose one or another particular content externalist theory, or one or another particular conception of self-knowledge. Therefore I can afford to be fairly general in my characterizations of the two doctrines.

By content externalism, I mean here the widely held view that some thought contents do not supervene on the internal psychology of the thinker in question. According to widely shared content externalist views, for example, the fact that I am thinking that *water is wet* (rather than that *twater is wet*) is partly determined by factors external to me: by the fact that I am, or have been, surrounded by samples of water rather than twater. This is the familiar kind of externalist view about content that is fueled by Twin-Earth-style thought experimentation (the *locus classicus* of which is Putnam (1975); the extension from language to thought contents was first made by McGinn (1977)).

What, then, about self-knowledge? The problems concerning content externalism and self-knowledge are often presented as problems for combining content externalism and a priori knowledge about one's own thought contents. However, I would prefer not to take a stand on the question of whether self-knowledge deserves to be called 'a priori'. It suffices for my purposes to assume that self-knowledge is *introspective* knowledge. To accept the thesis of self-knowledge about our own thoughts is to hold that we can attain knowledge of our own thought contents through *introspection*, without relying on empirical information about ourselves, or our surroundings.

The McKinsey argument

The alleged problems with combining content externalism with self-knowledge have been highlighted with various different arguments. I will here concentrate on the one that is often taken to be the strongest argument against their compatibility, the so-called "McKinsey argument," or "McKinsey's recipe," put forward by Michael McKinsey (1991).

The argument can be presented as a *reductio*. If both content externalism and the thesis of self-knowledge were true, then it should be possible for one to arrive at some paradigmatically empirical truths merely by relying on logic and introspection: therefore, they cannot both be true. For ease of exposition, I will here discuss the following, fairly simple formulation of the argument:

(1) I am thinking that water is wet.
(2) If I am thinking that water is wet, then my environment contains samples of water.
(3) My environment contains samples of water.

Depending on the precise version of externalism that we are assuming, premises 2 and 3 might have to be reformulated or replaced with more complicated ones, making reference to past states of affairs, membership in a speech community, or what have you (cf. Brown 1995). For my purposes here, these complications do not matter. The comments I am about to make will, as far as I can tell, be just as effective or ineffective, regardless of such details.

The alleged incompatibility arises as follows. Premise 1, and the fact that one should be able to know it via introspection, is a straightforward consequence of the thesis of self-knowledge. Premise 2, on the other hand, is supposed to be conceptual truth: it follows from externalist theories of content, which in turn are argued for by thought experimentation, rather than empirical investigation. That externalism is true for my concept of water (and thereby for my thoughts about water), is supposed to be a conceptual truth, at least in principle available to me by introspection. Yet, (1) and (2) jointly imply (3), and if (1) and (2) are knowable without empirical investigation, (3) should be so knowable as well. But (3) is a paradigmatically empirical truth, so something must have gone wrong. The argument is valid, so we need to either deny the introspective knowability of (1) or (2), or possibly find a way of living with the introspective knowability of (3). A range of strategies for responding to the argument have been suggested: for helpful reviews of the various options, see Kallestrup (2011) and Parent (2013).

Externalism and metaexternalism

I will now present the distinction between first-order externalism and metaexternalism in more detail, first for the case of language, then extended to the case of thought contents.

Externalism and metaexternalism about reference

In Cohnitz and Haukioja (2013) the distinction is made between first-order externalism and metaexternalism about the reference of linguistic expressions. First-order externalism is a familiar externalist view concerning how the reference of expressions is determined.

First-Order Externalism: The reference of (at least some) linguistic expressions used by a speaker S, is determined (at least partly) by factors independent of the individual psychological states of S. (*Cohnitz and Haukioja 2013, p. 476*)

This is, again, the kind of view many philosophers of language have been convinced of by Kripke's (1980) and Putnam's (1975) celebrated thought experiments, and by others like them. However, sometimes it appears that a much stronger externalist view is assumed without being clearly distinguished from first-order externalism. According to the stronger view, the fact *that* a given linguistic expression is to be given a (first-order) externalist semantics can also be determined, at least partly, by external factors. Cohnitz and I dub this view *metaexternalism*:

Metaexternalism: How a linguistic expression E[1] in an utterance U by a speaker S refers and which theory of reference is true of E is not determined by the individual psychological states of S at the time of U. (*Cohnitz and Haukioja 2013, p. 482*)

Note that the two kinds of externalist views are clearly concerned with very different kinds of questions. First-order externalism is a view about what kinds of factors are involved in determining the reference of an expression. The stronger view is concerned with the question of what *makes it the case that* such factors are so involved. Because the two kinds of externalism have generally not been distinguished from each other, explicit statements of this stronger view are not easy to find: however, some fairly clear commitments to metaexternalist views can be found for example in Cappelen and Winblad (1999), Ludlow (2003), and Devitt (2011).[2]

First-order externalism and metaexternalism are logically independent views: neither entails the other. And Twin-Earth-style thought experiments, we argue, give no support for metaexternalism. The thought experiments are merely concerned with what determines the reference or extension of various expressions: as such, they do not shed any light on the question of what makes it the case *that* reference and extension are so determined. Indeed, if metaexternalism were true, then it would be quite difficult to see how the kinds of referential intuitions or judgments that are elicited by thought experimentation could give very good evidence for theories of reference in the first place.[3] Furthermore, we argue that metaexternalism should be rejected. The main problem, we claim, is

---

[1] "How a linguistic expression E refers" is shorthand for, roughly, "whether external factors can play a role in determining what E refers to, and if so, which kinds of external factors: causal chains, or underlying essences, or the judgments of experts, or . . ."

[2] Cappelen and Winblad (1999) commit themselves to externalism in taking "reference" to be 'Twin-Earthable', thereby assuming that the individual psychology of a speaker is not sufficient for determining which theory of reference is true of the speaker's usage of referring terms. Ludlow (2003) argues that even the logical forms of our utterances can be externally determined, "completely independently of facts about our linguistic intentions" (p. 405). Devitt's (2011) commitment to metaexternalism is apparent in his insistence that the *causal history* of a deferential speaker's relevant, causally efficacious mental state is enough to secure reference to a particular individual, making the speaker's current deferential intuitions and dispositions irrelevant.

[3] Of course, one might deny that such intuitions *are* very good evidence for theories of reference – this is, of course, exactly what Devitt (2012) does, and what some recent experimental philosophers have done. But if metainternalism is true, we claim, much better sense can be made of the standard methodological practices in philosophy of language (cf. Cohnitz and Haukioja 2013).

that if metaexternalism were true, then reference, and theories of reference, could not play the kind of role in the explanation of successful communication that they *should* play: the kind of external reference-determining facts that the metaexternalist is committed to would be completely idle in the explanation of communication, thus leaving open the possibility of unacceptable systematic mismatches between the semantic content of sentences and the contents successfully communicated by using them (Cohnitz and Haukioja 2013, pp. 484–85).

Having rejected metaexternalism, we advocate metainternalism:

Metainternalism: How a linguistic expression E in an utterance U by a speaker S refers and which theory of reference is true of E is determined by individual psychological states of S at the time of U. (*ibid., p. 482*)

According to metainternalism, the fact *that* first-order externalism is true, of a token expression uttered by me, obtains *because* of some features that have to do with my individual psychology. Metainternalism, having been formulated as merely the negation of metaexternalism, is in itself neutral with respect to the question of *which* kinds of internal factors do enter into the determination of reference. But the most promising version of metainternalism by far, we think, locates the internal factors in a speaker's linguistic dispositions. If, for example, a natural kind term like "water" is to be given a first-order externalist semantics, it is because a speaker using the term is disposed to apply and interpret it in certain distinctive ways (which I'll say more about below). Similarly, if social externalism about reference is true of a token expression, it is because the speaker in question has the proper kinds of deferential dispositions: she is, for example, disposed to re-evaluate her applications of the expression in the light of disagreements that may arise between her usage and the usage of other members of her speech community.

Externalism and metaexternalism about content

The above points were made for the case of reference and linguistic expressions, but the distinctions carry over naturally to the case of content. Again, first-order externalism about *thought* is the kind of externalism standardly supported by Kripkean and Putnamian thought experiments, only this time presented for thought contents instead of word extensions. First-order externalism about thought can be formulated as follows:

First-order Externalism about Thought The contents of at least some of the thoughts of a cognitive agent A are partly determined by factors independent of the individual psychological states of A.

Again, this should be clearly separated from *meta*externalism about thought:

> *Metaexternalism about Thought* The question of whether first-order externalism about thought is true, about the thoughts of A, is partly determined by factors independent of the individual psychological states of A.

I will not try to develop a direct argument against metaexternalism about thought here. Rather, my aim is to show that, if metaexternalism is rejected, there are no serious problems for combining content externalism (i.e. first-order externalism about thought) and self-knowledge. (Of course, if I'm successful in this, this might be taken as an indirect argument against metaexternalism about thought.) I do want to point out, however, that standard Twin-Earth-style arguments do not provide any support for metaexternalism about thought. And again, to the extent that Twin-Earth-style thought experiments support first-order externalism, this can be much better made sense of, if meta*internalism* about thought is true:

> *Metainternalism about Thought* The question of whether first-order externalism about thought is true, about the thoughts of A, is determined by the individual psychological states of A.

As in the case of reference, metainternalism can be combined with first-order externalism. According to this combination of views, at least some of our thought contents are partly externally individuated, but the fact *that* they are so individuated, is wholly due to the thinker's individual psychology. Again, metainternalism as such is silent on the question of *which* individual psychological states determine whether, and how, thought contents *are* externally individuated. I will now outline a specific, dispositionalist version of metainternalism.

The metainternalist answer to McKinsey

Recall the McKinsey argument:

(1) I am thinking that water is wet.
(2) If I am thinking that water is wet, then my environment contains samples of water.
(3) My environment contains samples of water.

How does a metainternalist view help us answer the argument?

Premise 1, I take it, can be known by introspection because of its self-verifying nature (cf. Burge 1996). Metainternalism comes in to help us see how we can have introspective knowledge concerning the external conditions of individuation for our thoughts about natural kinds, without premise 2 in the McKinsey argument turning out to be knowable by introspection.

I will now first say more about how, exactly, a metainternalist will explain why content externalism is true of the contents of at least some of our thoughts. I will then go on to argue what consequences this explanation has for how we *know* that externalism holds of our own thought contents. Finally, I will show where, exactly, the McKinsey argument goes wrong, according to my metainternalist view.

A metainternalist explanation of content externalism

Once again, metainternalism is merely the denial of metaexternalism: as such, metainternalism is not committed to any particular view about *which* kinds of internal factors determine thought contents. In this section I will outline *one* possible, and in my view plausible, metainternalist explanation of content externalism.

This explanation builds on the same kind of dispositions as mentioned earlier, in the second section of this chapter. My claim is that the questions of *whether* and *how* a given concept or thought is to be at least partly individuated by external factors are to be grounded in dispositional facts concerning us, such as the following: our dispositions to interpret thought contents (both of others and our own) in counterfactual situations, our dispositions to (re-)evaluate the truth or falsity of thoughts (both of others and our own) in the light of new empirical information, and so on.

To illustrate, let us consider an example. Take our thoughts about bachelors, on the one hand, and about water, on the other. Suppose, as seems plausible, that the contents of our water thoughts depend on external matters of fact in a way that our bachelor thoughts do not – this difference is based on the fact that first-order natural kind externalism is true of our water concept, but not of our bachelor concept.[4] Why is this? Something like the following explanation seems overwhelmingly plausible. We are disposed to revise our judgments concerning claims about water in the light of new empirical information about

---

[4] This difference between the concepts of water and bachelors is directly parallel to the semantic differences between 'water' and 'bachelor': the former is actuality-*dependent*, while the latter is actuality-*independent* (cf. Haukioja 2012).

water. Were it to turn out that all water is actually XYZ, this would, if first-order externalism holds of our concept of water, immediately affect the way we categorize samples as water or nonwater, and how we evaluate and re-evaluate our classifications, not just in the actual world, but also in counterfactual worlds. Nothing like this holds for our concept of a bachelor. Suppose it turned out that, in the actual world, all and only bachelors possessed a certain neural structure, N. Would this affect the way we categorize persons as bachelors or nonbachelors? Would we reconsider our past classifications of adult married men as bachelors, using newly available neural data to confirm that they really were bachelors? No, we wouldn't: we would continue to rely on age, gender, and marital status in our categorizations, without any inclination to reconsider and revise our judgments. Our concept of a bachelor, one might say, has no aspirations whatsoever to be a natural kind concept. This is why first-order natural kind externalism holds of our concept of water, but not of our concept of a bachelor.

It is of course quite plausible that first-order *social* externalism holds also of our concept of a bachelor. If so, this will be explained by recourse to the agent's dispositions to revise her application of the concept of a bachelor, but now not in response to empirical findings about *bachelors*, but in response to how other people in one's community are categorizing things as bachelors and nonbachelors.

Obviously, what I've presented above is just a rough sketch of how such dispositions determine contents, externally determined or not. A major obstacle to any such theory is, of course, the Kripkensteinian paradox of rule-following (Kripke 1982). I will not try to resolve this paradox here. However, I have in earlier work (Haukioja 2005) defended a dispositionalist solution to the rule-following problem, making use of dispositions on two levels: dispositions to apply concepts to entities, as well as dispositions to re-evaluate and correct one's concept applications in the face of new empirical evidence and/or disagreement across agents and times. The general structure of such a theory was first formulated by Philip Pettit (1996): I am here claiming that such a theory already has the resources for a plausible explanation of why, and how, some concepts are in a certain way externally individuated while others are not.

A metainternalist explanation of our knowledge *of content externalism*

Suppose that the dispositionalist view sketched above is right. How, on this picture, can we come to know *that*, and *how*, the content of a given thought content is externally determined?

The first thing to notice is that the relevant dispositions seem to be introspectively accessible to us. Indeed, Twin-Earth-style thought experimentation is precisely a project in which one *does* introspectively access such dispositions. Thought experimentation of this kind can be understood as a kind of mental simulation: we imagine finding ourselves in various metaphysically possible situations and ask ourselves whether or not we would be disposed to apply a given concept to a given entity (or substance, state, process, etc.), and how, if at all, we would reconsider our classifications in the face of various imaginable empirical findings, or in the face of finding ourselves disagreeing with others in our community, and so on. In doing this, we are not relying on empirical evidence, but rather activating our own dispositions in simulation.

By engaging in such simulation, I can come to know, by introspection, how the contents of my externally individuated thoughts and concepts depend on certain details of the environment. I can come to know that, *given* that the actual world is thus-and-so, my concept of water is the concept of H_2O; given that the actual world is different in certain respects, it is the concept of XYZ; given that it is yet different in a certain way, it is the concept of a mixture of the two, or maybe even a concept of a functional kind, and so on (for more details, see Haukioja 2009). What I cannot know by introspection is *which* of these various possibilities is realized in the actual world; that we can only know by empirical investigation.

Any first-order externalist should, of course, be happy to accept that I cannot know by introspection whether my concept of water is the concept of H_2O or of XYZ. But it might be objected (cf. Häggqvist and Wikforss 2007) that the kind of view I am defending extends our ignorance too far: after all, I am claiming that I cannot know by introspection whether my water concept is the concept of *any* uniform chemical kind, rather than a mixture, or a functional kind, and so on. According to Häggqvist and Wikforss, this is to say that I do not even know, by introspection, the key *semantic properties* of my water concept: I do not know whether it should be given an externalist or an internalist semantics. But I think this would mischaracterize my position. My water concept would, as it were, continue to *prefer* a natural kind as its referent, even if it turned out that in the actual world there is no interesting uniformity among the samples of watery stuff. We have introspective access to what our water concept would denote, were any of a variety of epistemically possible situations to be actual: but even if water turned out to be a motley kind, our water concept would still *aim* to denote a natural kind, in a sense to be clarified in the next section.

It is precisely here that the metainternalist view delivers a crucially different picture from the metaexternalist one. According to metaexternalism, as noted before, whether my water thoughts are to be individuated internally or externally is determined by factors external to me. According to metainternalism, however, my water thoughts are externally individuated *even if* I find myself in a world where "water" names a motley kind: it is precisely the fact that the watery stuff in that world *is* a motley kind – an external fact – that would then determine that my concept of water would refer on the basis of surface features. But, again, according to the metainternalist, the facts that determine that my concept of water would, in those circumstances, be so individuated, are facts concerning my individual psychology, and at least in principle are introspectively available to me.

Denoting vs. aiming to denote

The kind of view outlined above, combining metainternalism with first-order externalism about content, lends quite direct support for a specific line of response to McKinsey first suggested by McLaughlin and Tye (1998a, 1998b). The response begins by distinguishing between two senses of a natural kind concept. A concept can be a natural kind concept by *aiming* to denote a natural kind or by *in fact denoting* a natural kind. A natural kind concept in the first sense somehow includes a preference – possibly a defeasible one – that it should denote a natural kind, while a natural kind concept in the latter sense in fact succeeds in this aim. Plausibly, a concept cannot in fact denote a natural kind without *aiming* to denote one, but not the other way around. For example, the phlogiston theorists' concept of phlogiston, it appears, aimed to denote a natural kind, but failed. McLaughlin and Tye suggest that we can plausibly know through introspection that a given concept aims to denote a natural kind, but not that it in fact succeeds.

In knowing, through introspection, that I am thinking that water is wet, then, I know only that my thought *aims* to be about a natural kind. No credible version of externalism, however, will claim that a thought that merely *aims* to be about a natural kind necessitates the existence of samples of that natural kind. Premise 2 in the McKinsey argument, in other words, is not introspectively knowable in the sense that would be needed for the argument to be valid.

This kind of a response has seemed promising to many. However, more should be said about what, precisely, it is for a concept to *aim* to denote a natural kind. It is here, I think, that the metainternalist view outlined above can help us make progress. A concept aims to denote a natural kind when roughly the following holds (again, the precise details will depend on which externalist theory of natural kind concepts is true): should it turn out that (at least most of) the actual samples categorized as falling under the concept share a causally relevant underlying feature, then the agent who possesses the concept will be disposed to apply the concept, and evaluate its usage (actual and counterfactual), on the basis of whether the objects that the concept is being applied to share this feature with the actual samples. We saw earlier that our concept of water is a concept that aims to denote a natural kind in this sense, while our concept of a bachelor is not. The kind of dispositionalist metainternalism I have outlined above can give us a plausible account of what it is for a concept to aim to denote a natural kind, as well as of how we can *know*, of a given concept, that it aims to denote a natural kind.

Metainternalism and knowledge of content

I've argued, then, that there is no serious worry about the compatibility of content externalism and self-knowledge. In this final section I will look at whether metainternalism might run into problems of its own concerning our knowledge of the natures of our own thoughts. I will look at two potential sources of problems: similar worries have been previously raised in a slightly different argumentative context, concerning whether a dispositionalist theory of concept possession and content makes a priori conceptual analysis possible (Melnyk 2008). First, as already briefly mentioned above, any dispositionalist view will somehow have to account for the distinction between correct and incorrect dispositions: the worry is that to explain knowledge of the nature of our thoughts, a dispositionalist would have to make problematic assumptions about our knowledge of *which* dispositions are content-constitutive. Second, the explanation of knowledge about contents via simulation sketched above raises worries about possible mismatches between simulated dispositions and "true" dispositions.

Let us take the problem of correct and incorrect dispositions first. As noted above, any dispositionalist account of meaning or content will have to address the Kripkensteinian problem of rule-following. A central facet of this is the problem of error. *All* of one's conceptual dispositions cannot be content-constitutive, because we have dispositions to make errors. Somehow or other, a dispositionalist will have to give an account of what distinguishes the correct, and thereby content-constitutive dispositions, from the erroneous dispositions. Kripke (1982) argued forcefully that the dispositionalist will not be able to do this in a noncircular way.

However, various different suggestions about how this could be done have been made in the massive literature that has followed.

Even if it turns out that the dispositionalist can answer Kripke's challenge, it may appear that the possibility of error will cause problems for the view I've outlined above. On my view, a cognitive agent can attain knowledge of how the contents of his or her thoughts are determined by introspecting his or her own dispositions in a process of mental simulation. Since we are every now and then disposed to make errors in our actual application of concepts, we will also presumably be disposed to make errors in applying our concepts in mentally simulated situations. So, in addition to having introspective access to one's own dispositions, one should have introspective access to *whether a given disposition is content-constitutive*. But why should we think we have introspective access to *that*?

We do not, I agree, have introspective knowledge of whether a given disposition is content-constitutive. But I do not think such knowledge is needed for my view to work. It is enough that we have access to *what the criteria of being content-constitutive* are, and I think it is plausible to think that we do possess such knowledge.

A standard dispositionalist strategy is to specify a set of conditions that are *favorable* for the application of a given concept, and claim that the content-constitutive dispositions are those that are manifested in such conditions. The worry just raised can then be reformulated as the worry that we do not have introspective access to which conditions are favorable, for the application of a given concept. My response is that it is enough that we have introspective access to *how* the favorability of conditions is determined, even if the question of which conditions in fact *do* turn out to be favorable may depend on external factors not available to us via introspection. The dispositionalist view of rule-following I have elsewhere defended (Haukioja 2005) maintains that the favorability of conditions is determined in interpersonal and intertemporal practices of negotiation, where disagreements across times and persons are resolved (cf. Pettit 1996; see also Haukioja 2007)[5]. On this view, it is part of being competent in the use of a concept to know how disagreements are resolved, and thereby how the favorability of conditions is determined.

The second problem arises as follows. Suppose a subject S, in mental simulation, has the disposition that she would categorize x, in conditions C, as F. But suppose also that, were S *in fact* confronted with x in C, she would reliably categorize it as non-F. There is no reason to suppose that such mismatches could not occur. Which dispositions, then, constitute the identity of S's concept F: S's dispositions to apply F in *simulation*, or

---

[5] A similar idea is explored, in another context, by Ebbs (2001).

S's dispositions to apply F, were S *truly* to find herself in C? I do not have a good argument one way or another, but pretheoretically, I would incline toward the latter. But this view raises some potential problems for simulationist view.

Here, I think, it will simply have to be admitted that our introspective knowledge, concerning whether and how our thought contents are externally determined, falls short of certainty. I cannot know through introspection, of any given simulated disposition, that it corresponds to how I would in fact be disposed to act if I were to encounter the situation simulated. Our introspective knowledge about the determination of our own thought contents is, then, in a certain way empirically defeasible. However, I think we do have good reason to think that our simulations are, in general, quite reliable. We simulate various imaginable situations all the time, not only in philosophical thought experiments, but also in everyday life. We simply do not find massive discrepancies between how we are disposed to categorize things in simulation, and how we in fact do categorize things when we encounter similar situations: we do not find ourselves, surprisingly, categorizing things in a different way than we expected when we encounter situations that we have previously only imagined. At the very least, I would say that the burden of proof is on those who would want to claim that such discrepancies are common enough to cause problems for introspective knowledge of how the contents of our thoughts are determined.

Conclusion

I have argued that at least some of the problems of content externalism and self-knowledge can be dispelled when we distinguish between first-order externalism about thought – which any content externalist will have to accept – and metaexternalism about thought, and embrace metainternalism. I have also outlined a metainternalist view, building on dispositionalism about meaning and content. Such a view, I've argued, can make good sense of why first-order externalism is true, and at the same time provide a plausible response to McKinsey-style problems about content externalism and self-knowledge. A more detailed development of the metainternalist view, as well as the question of its relevance to other ways of raising problems about externalism and self-knowledge, are for the time being left for future work.

13 Externalism, metasemantic contextualism, and self-knowledge

Henry Jackman

Introduction

This chapter examines some of the interactions between holism, contextualism, and externalism, and will argue that an externalist metasemantics that grounds itself in certain plausible assumptions about self-knowledge will also be a *contextualist* metasemantics, and that such a contextualist metasemantics in turn resolves one of the best known problems externalist theories purportedly have with self-knowledge, namely, the problem of how the possibility of various sorts of 'switching' cases can appear to undermine the 'transparency' of our thoughts (in particular, our ability to tell, with respect to any two occurrent thoughts, whether they exercise the same or different concepts).

Metasematics, self-interpretation, and contextualism

Philosophers of language can be understood as offering two sorts of semantic theory. On the one hand, they can present an account of what the semantic values of the words in our language *are* and how the values of complex expressions are a function of the semantic values of their parts (what we can simply call a *semantic* theory). On the other hand, they can present an account of how our words came to *get* those particular semantic values (what we can call a *metasemantic* theory).[1] Often, they will present theories of both sorts.

Thanks to Anne Bezuidenhout, Sanford Goldberg. Michael Lynch, Mark McCullaugh, Ram Neta, and Arthur Zucker (as well as audiences in Toronto, Chicago, New Orleans, Barcelona, Lisbon, Paris, and Athens (Ohio)) for comments on earlier versions of this chapter.

[1] Davies (2006) also describes the distinction in these terms, though it is described elsewhere as the distinction between "Descriptive" and "Foundational" semantics (Stalnaker 1997, 1999), "Formal" and "Philosophical" semantics (Brandom 1994), "semantic theories" and "foundational theories of meaning" (Speaks 2011), semantics in the "linguist's" and the "metaphysical" sense (Block 1998), and "formal semantics" and "Philosophical Meaning Theory" (Glüer 2011, 2012).

Externalism, metasemantic contextualism, and self-knowledge   229

For instance, within the broadly 'Davidsonian' framework presupposed here one's semantic theory (his "truth theory") understands meaning in terms of truth and satisfaction,[2] with, say, "Chicago" being satisfied by *Chicago* and "city" being satisfied by members of the set of *cities*, and "Chicago is a city" being true if the object that satisfies the first term is among the set of objects that satisfies the second. In contrast to this 'atomistic' semantic theory, Davidson's metasemantics (which takes the form of his "theory of interpretation") is unapologetically holistic, with the ultimate explanation of how each word gets its meaning being dependent on how other terms in the language get theirs.[3] The Davidsonian understands the satisfaction conditions of any word in a speaker's language as determined by the set of assignments that would maximize the truth of *all* of that speaker's commitments.[4]

Davidson isn't always clear about why one's metasemantics should maximize the amount of truth that the subject believes,[5] but I think that such maximization can be motivated in terms of what will here be referred to as the "Self-Interpretation Principle," namely, when faced with conflicting commitments on an agent's part, we should assign semantic values to his or her words in a way that preserves the truth of the commitments that he or she would hold on to were he or she aware of the tension.[6] So, to take an example from Burge that we will return to later, if a speaker believes both that, say, (1) he has "arthritis" in his thigh, and (2) doctors study how to treat "arthritis" in medical school, then whether his "arthritis" utterances refer to *arthritis* or *tharthritis* (the latter picking out a larger set of ailments including both arthritis and similar pains occurring beyond one's joints) will be determined by which of these two he would treat as mistaken were he made aware of the conflict.[7]

---

[2] See, for instance, Davidson 1965/1984, 1967/1984.
[3] See, for instance, Davidson 1973/1984, 1974/1984, 1975/1984, 1977/1984, 1979/1984, 1986a.
[4] This is usually explained in terms of the Davidsonian's commitment to the 'Principle of Charity'. For a more complete discussion of this, see Jackman 2003.
[5] Davidson argues that "if we want to understand others, we must count them right in most matters" (Davidson 1974/1984, p. 197), but this only requires that beliefs be *mostly* true, it doesn't explain why *maximization* is required, that is, why, when faced with two interpretations according to which the subject's beliefs are mostly true, we should pick the interpretation that attributes to him or her *the most* true beliefs.
[6] For a more extensive discussion of Davidson's conception of the Principle of Charity, and how it relates to what this self-interpretation principle, see Jackman 2003.
[7] See Burge 1979. We are assuming for the sake of argument that the rest of his 'arthritis' beliefs were true of both *arthritis* and *tharthritis*, and that "treating as a mistake" is more substantial than simply giving up the practice of asserting the sentence. One could "give up" one of the beliefs that one had arthritis in one's thigh because one wanted to bring one's usage into line with one's community without thinking that the original belief was false (just as I might "give up" my belief that someone moving from the United Kingdom

The Self-Interpretation Principle thus leads to a type of truth maximization and motivates it in terms of a form of self-knowledge that is underwritten by the fact that it is precisely the agent's point of view that we are trying to capture in interpretation. It leads to a type of maximization frequently associated with the Principle of Charity because it has always been assumed that what is to be maximized is not just the *total number* of true beliefs, but rather some *weighted* total of them.[8] Some beliefs will be more important to the speaker than others, and preserving the truth of these beliefs may have a higher priority than preserving the truth of multiple beliefs that are assigned less weight. It is precisely such weighing that would be revealed in the way the speakers revise their beliefs when conflicts become manifest,[9] and so assigning truth to the belief(s) that are preserved through such conflicts maximizes the (weighted) amount of truths the subject believes.

A holistic metasemantics that draws on the Self-Interpretation Principle can be shown to both leave meaning comparatively stable, and be compatible with semantic externalism,[10] and it will be argued here that it also underwrites a type of *contextualism* that is given less emphasis in the literature than it could. In particular, if the function which maximizes the number of truths believed by the speaker works on weighted totals governed by something like the Self-Interpretation Principle, then we can account for some contextual variations in the semantic values of our words in terms of the fact that how much weight a particular belief has can vary from context to context.[11]

---

to the United States might "give up" his practice of referring to what American's call "cookies" as "biscuits" in order to be better understood in his new environment without thinking that any of his previous "that's a biscuit" utterances were mistaken).

[8] For more on the importance of such weighing in understanding anything like Charity as being remotely plausible, see Glüer 2011, Jackman 2003, Pagin 2006.

[9] Subject to some idealization relating to the fact that in practice speakers won't be aware of all of the incompatibility relations that exist among their various commitments, and so may in practice favor belief *A* over belief *B* simply because they were unaware that *A* was also incompatible with beliefs *B* and *C*.

[10] For an extended discussion of this, and whether the Self-Interpretation Principle should be understood as an explication or replacement of the 'Principle of Charity', see Jackman 2003.

[11] It is important to remember that the type of contextualism defended here is of a *metasemantic* sort. *Semantic* Contextualism treats the semantic value of a term as itself making reference to some feature of the context. Indexicals are paradigms of this ("I" means "the person making the utterance"), but accounts of, say, "tall" or "flat" that tie them to 'hidden parameters' (e.g. tall = 'tall for an f', where f is determined by the context) that are implicitly marked at the level of logical form do this as well. *Metasemantic* Contextualism, on the other hand, simply tells a story about how our terms get their semantic values that suggests that they may have different semantic values in different contexts (though the resulting semantic values themselves may make no reference to context). Consequently, one should not expect the sorts of syntactic markers associated with more familiar sorts of semantic

For example, we can see a type of context sensitivity by considering the following two sentences about a freckle-faced 7-year-old (Frank) who has just covered his school with graffiti.

(1) The principal should call Frank's mother.
(2) Frank probably gets those freckles from his mother.

Now if Frank is adopted, then (whether the speaker knows about the adoption or not) the extension of these two instances of "mother" will probably be different. (Assuming that we are acquainted with Frank but with neither of his 'mothers'.) We typically should contact the woman bringing Frank up if he is in trouble, but assume that the woman who contributed to his genetic make-up is responsible for his freckles. Somebody uttering the two sentences may thus refer to two different groups of people with the word "mother" not because they have added or lost any 'mother beliefs' but because the comparative importance of those beliefs changes from context to context.

The variance in the semantic value for "mother" can thus be understood as being produced by our various interests resulting in different 'mother beliefs' being more-or-less heavily weighed. When I am talking about Frank's disciplinary problems, my belief that Frank is being brought up by his mother will be weighed more heavily than my belief about his mother contributing to his genetic make-up. When I am talking about his freckles, the opposite will usually be the case. Different aspects of our 'mother prototype' are given greater weight in the two contexts.

An obvious alternative understanding of such cases would be to explain them in terms of ambiguity, that is, in terms of their being multiple words in one's lexicon that just happen to sound the same. Just as there are two distinct meanings for "bank," there would be multiple meanings for "mother." However, even if we were to admit that most of us had at least two separate "mother" entries in our mental lexicon,[12] there seem to

---

contextualism (for some discussion of these, see Stanley 2007) to be found if the contextualism involved is at the metasemantic level. Indeed, the contextualism defended here will be in many respects closer to the 'cheap' contextualism defended by Peter Ludlow (Ludlow 2008), and the view would suggest that the lexicon is 'dynamic' in much the way that he suggests (Ludlow 2008, 2014).

[12] And one might doubt whether two would be enough. Cases like the pair of sentences above could be created to show that "mother" would have to be ambiguous between the woman bringing up the child, the woman who contributes its genetic material, the woman who actually gives birth to the child, the woman who provides the egg, etc. We can certainly creat separate terms to explicitly distinguish birth mothers, biological mothers, traditional surrogate mothers, adopted mothers, stepmothers, and the rest, but it is hard to imagine that these are simply labels for separate items that existed in our mental lexicon as soon as we started talking about "mothers" at all.

be cases where this sort of response couldn't be appropriate (as when the two sentences were uttered by someone brought up in so sheltered an environment that they hadn't been aware that the two sorts of mothers ever came apart, and so had no reason to put two entries for the term in their mental lexicon). Further, even if one were to think that this sort of case is best handled by ambiguity, there are others where this seems harder to do.

For instance, consider a speaker who, when Venus rises at the beginning of the evening, will reliably point to it and say "there is Venus." He does the same in the morning, and never 'misapplies' the term to any other star or planet. The putative extension (those items that the term is *actually* applied to) of "Venus" in his language consists only of the planet Venus. However, while the putative extension of Venus in his language is much like it is in ours (assuming – falsely in my case – that we can identify Venus in the night sky), the general characterization he associates with the term is very different. In particular, while we believe that Venus is a lifeless planet, that we have sent satellites to gather information about it, and so on, this speaker believes that Venus is the goddess of love, that she is married to Vulcan, is the lover of Mars, responds to the prayers of her followers (of whom the speaker is one), and so on.

For such a speaker, there is a serious lack of fit between the general characterizations associated with "Venus" and what he actually applies the term to, and we could imagine his background to be shaped in three different fashions, each of which may lead us to interpret his use of "Venus" in different ways. If the speaker is a particularly devout worshiper, who was only interested in looking up at the night sky because he took himself to be viewing the distant goddess herself, then he may be much more willing to give up everything in the putative extension rather than his general beliefs. If he is informed that the distant star is a lifeless planet, he will be inclined, correctly, to think that he misapplied the term "Venus" every morning and evening when he looked at the sky.[13] On the other hand, if he were not at all devout, and his interest in 'Venus' was primarily as a guide to navigation, with the myths just providing interesting background about the light that happens to guide him, then he might give up all of his goddess-friendly general beliefs if he found them not to be true of

---

[13] There may be some temptation to treat utterances of his such as "Venus is looking especially bright tonight" as still being true (provided that the planet is especially bright on that night), but this may just be because (1) it is true in the sense that my utterance of "John looks hurt" might be considered true if I mistake Peter for John and Peter looks hurt, so that the speaker's reference for such utterances may be Peter or the planet, while the semantic reference remains John or the Greco-Roman goddess, or (2) one is implicitly moving on to a case more like the third type of Greek who shifts from one reference to the other depending upon what is most important to him in various contexts.

the celestial body that he applied the term to, and so his use of "Venus," even in sentences like "Venus is a goddess," would refer exclusively to the planet. Finally (and this may have put him in the largest group at some point), he may be someone in between, whose goddess-friendly beliefs are more important in some contexts, and whose navigation-friendly beliefs are more important in others. In this final case, it may be that what he refers to by the term switches form context to context, sometimes picking out a planet, sometimes a fictional goddess, and so on.[14]

It should hopefully be clear at this point how this sort of metasemantic context-shifting is intended to work,[15] and it will be argued below that we see a similar kind of context-shifting in a number of familiar philosophical thought experiments, and a lack of recognition of the 'shiftiness' of these cases can lead to the intractability of the disputes about what to say about them.

Metasemantic contextualism, ambiguity, and externalist intuitions

The literature on semantic externalism is often driven by intuitions about particular cases (finding "water" on Twin Earth, Bert's complaining to his doctor about his "arthritis", etc.), but philosophers have never

---

[14] In much the same way, who, if anyone, we refer to by "Moses" may depend upon how heavily our beliefs are weighed. Someone who is interested in the history of the Middle East may weigh heavily the belief that Moses led the Israelites out of Egypt, but not put much weight on beliefs relating to the miracles Moses purportedly performed (even if he does believe that they were, in fact, performed). On the other hand, someone who is only interested in the miraculous aspects of the story might weigh the miracles the most heavily, and if there turns out to be no one who took the tablets containing the Ten Commandments from God and parted the Red Sea, then his term "Moses" would not refer to anyone. Finally, someone may be both of these, interested sometimes in history, and sometimes in miracles, and the reference of the name may shift for him accordingly. (Whether some position like this is what Wittgenstein was getting at when he claimed that "If one says 'Moses did not exist', this may mean various things" (Wittgenstein 1953, §79), is something that I'll leave to the reader to decide.)

[15] One may note similarities here to the view defended in Bilgrami (1992), which also allows for a type of metasemantic context sensitivity. However, Bilgrami distinguishes 'aggregate contents', which capture *all* of the beliefs an agent associates with a term, from the more psychologically real 'local contents' which are made up of a contextually salient *subset* of the beliefs in the aggregate contents, and thus vary from context to context. Context determines not how much weight a particular belief has in determining what we are referring to, but rather whether the beliefs in question are part of a particular 'local' content *at all*. The ultimate goal of Bilgrami's theory is precisely not to explain how our beliefs determine what we refer to, but rather to understand meaning in terms of belief rather than reference (see especially Bilgrami 1992, pp. 134–35) while preserving the intuition that meanings can be shared (because, even if the 'aggregate' contents are never shared, the local subsets contextually derived from them can be; for a discussion of this, see Jackman 2014).

reached complete agreement about such intuitions, and it has recently been sugested that nonphilosophical intuitions about such cases are generally much more variable than most philosophers had originally assumed.[16] That said, if the kind of contextualism outlined above is right, then the way in which we describe our cases will be very important, and an intuition about what a word refers to in one case need not entail that it refers the same way in others. Consequently, what are often described as "conflicting intuitions" may just be intuitions about different cases that appear to conflict when treated as context free judgments about what our terms refer to, but are perfectly compatible with each other when their context is made more explicit.

For instance, let us return to Tyler Burge's discussion of Bert and his idiosyncratic use of "arthritis." Bert uses "arthritis" much as the rest of us do but, notoriously, he also applies "arthritis" to the pains in his thigh.[17] Burge treats Bert here as still referring to *arthritis* by "arthritis," while writers such as Davidson and Bilgrami argue that Bert should be understood as referring instead to *tharthritis* (once again, a condition which includes both arthritis and similarly painful ailments in the limbs) by "arthritis."[18] This lack of consensus about what to say about Bert may reflect the fact that what Bert means by "arthritis" varies from context to context. When Bert goes to the doctor and complains "my arthritis has spread to my thigh," it may be correct to take him to be referring to *arthritis* by "arthritis." On the other hand, when he is sitting around with his brother and complains "my arthritis is too bad for me to mow the lawn today," it may be equally correct to treat him as referring to *tharthritis*.

The sort of metasemantic contextualism outlined above would explain why the extension of Bert's term "arthritis" might shift in just this way. In addition to a large set of beliefs which would be true of both *arthritis* and *tharthritis*, Bert has one set of beliefs (such as "I have arthritis in my thigh" and "My arthritis kept me from cleaning out the garage last week") which would be true only of *tharthritis*, and another set of beliefs (such as "Doctors have studied how to treat arthritis" and "The man from the insurance company said that people with arthritis should go see a doctor

---

[16] See, for instance, Weinberg, Nichols, and Stich 2001; and Machery, Mallon, Nichols, and Stich 2004.
[17] See Burge 1979.
[18] Bilgrami 1992; Davidson 1993, 1994. Davidson seems to have reconsidered his views on the example, though only if Bert "intended his hearers to take the word 'arthritis' as referring, not to what he thought it referred to, but to what it referred to when used by experts" (Davidson 2003, p. 698). Since this intention is also supposed to be "explicit," it's not clear how close to Burge's view he actually comes, because Davidson's requirement that this intention be "explicit" seems to suggest a metalinguistic understanding of the example that Burge explicitly rejects (see Burge 1979, pp. 96–97).

about it") which would be true only of *arthritis*. When he is complaining to his brother, the former set of beliefs will be given greater weight than the latter (and so he will refer to *tharthritis*), while when he is consulting his doctor, the latter set of beliefs will be given greater weight (and so he will refer to *arthritis*). What Bert means by "arthritis" shifts from context to context, and such context sensitivity may be characteristic of cases where someone's idiosyncratic usage of a word can be understood in terms of either an idiosyncratic belief or an idiosyncratic semantic value.

It would, then, not be a coincidence that Burge tends to focus on examples like visits to the doctor's office, while Davidson and Bilgrami present cases where our interests are less tied to professional standards. Each presents Bert using of "arthritis" in a context that is friendly to their views, and then generalizes from that usage to what Bert means by "arthritis" in a more context-free way.[19] Furthermore, conflicting intuitions about what Bert means may also reflect the fact that, if the comparative entrenchment of one's beliefs is part of what determines what one means, then cases like Bert's use of "arthritis" are underdescribed in a way that allows different readers of the stories to project their own sense of which beliefs should be most important on to the characters involved in them.[20] So, for instance, if we are personally disinclined to defer to expert usage even in situations where that expertise is being relied on, we may simply project those weightings on to Bert, and so, as Davidson often does, treat him as meaning *tharthritis* by "arthritis" even when he is in the doctor's office.

Much the same sort of move could be made with respect to the sometimes conflicting intutions we have about terms like "water."[21] We have

---

[19] Though the fact that Bert would come out as meaning *arthritis* even in *some* cases would be enough to establish anti-individualism, so this sort of contextualism would side more with Burge than Davidson on the larger issue at hand. Indeed, one could argue that even in those contexts where we are more inclined to say that Bert means *tharthritis*, it still may fail to be the case that those contents are individuated individualistically. If Bert wants to get out of mowing the lawn because of the pain in his thigh, but lived in a society that used "arthritis" to pick out, say, everything philosophers associate with "tharthritis" *except for* pain at the base of the spine (call it 'barthritis'), I'd expect that Bert would be correctly taken to mean *barthritis* rather than *tharthritis*, even if he happened to believe that one could get 'arthritis' at the base of one's spine. Consequently, even when an idiosyncratic concept is attributed to Bert, it doesn't follow that the concept he has is independent of how the relevant word is used in his society. (For a related discussion of why nonindividualism holds for speakers who have mastered the concepts in question, see Burge 1979, pp. 84–85.)

[20] See, once again, Jackman 2009.

[21] Though I think that the intuitions are less often in conflict for philosophers like myself who have had the importance of "water" being a natural kind term drilled into us since the beginning of our undergraduate education. The variance would be even more pronounced when one considers the use of the term before the discovery of modern chemistry.

many commitments that focus on water as a functional kind, and others that focus on it as a natural kind, and while we often presume these kinds to be co-extensive, the two would come into conflict if we were ever in a scenario like Putnam's Twin Earth case, in which we were confronted with a substance that had all of water's perceptual/functional properties (its appearance, its taste, its ability to sustain life, etc.) while having a different chemical structure. Which commitments will be weighted most heavily, and so whether "water" picks out a natural or functional kind, could vary from person to person, and with certain individuals, from context to context. Indeed, this seems to be compatible with Putnam's own analysis of the extension of "water":

We can understand the relation *sameL* (same liquid as) as a cross-world relation by understanding it so that a liquid in *W1* [World 1] which has the same **important** physical properties (in *W1*) that a liquid in *W2* possesses (in *W2*) bears the *sameL* to the latter liquid ... an entity *x*, in an arbitrary possible world, is *water* if and only if it bears the relation *sameL* (construed as a cross-world relation) to the stuff *we* call 'water' in the *actual* world. (*Putnam 1975, p. 232; boldface mine*)

Putnam claims that the 'hidden structures' determine the reference of natural kind terms not because only such hidden structures could serve in the same-kind relation, but rather because "normally the 'important' properties of a liquid or a solid, etc., are the one's that are structurally important." However, importance is, as Putnam himself goes on to stress, "an interest relative notion" (ibid., p. 239), and in some contexts the more functional properties associated with "water" may be more important to us than its microphysical ones.[22] In such contexts, it may be that the term is best seen as picking out the functional kind. Furthermore, when conversing with others, or when reading a philosopher's paper on the subject, we might not intially have a strong preference between the commitments tying to each of the two readings, and thus be willing to favor one set over another simply to 'accommodate' our conversational partners.[23]

This 'pluralistic' attitude toward the apparently conflicting intuitions outlined above bears some similarities to a view currently being proposed by Shaun Nichols, Ángel Pinillos, and Ron Mallon, who also

---

[22] This is certainly downplayed in Putnam 1975, but a sensitivity to how we can still feel the pull of the nonnatural kind reading in such cases is more evident in Putnam 1962. (For a discussion of Putnam's 'hardening of heart' on this issue, see Unger 1982, p. 165; Unger 1984, p. 124).

[23] This seems to be the understanding of such cases in Lewis 1999, pp. 313–14.

stress how our judgments about the standard externalist thought experiments are much more variable than many philosophers assumed.[24] However, they suggest that the variance between intuitions about what to say about various thought experiments in the philosophy of language should be explained by something closer to full-scale ambiguity. As they put it:

> We will argue that natural kind terms are ambiguous. In some cases, the reference of a token is fixed by a causal-historical convention; in other cases, the reference of a token of the same type is fixed by a descriptivist convention. We call this an ambiguity theory because the idea is that there are two conventions that determine the reference of natural kind terms ... (*Nichols, Pinillos and Mallon 2014, p. 7*)

While the authors take the ambiguity in question to be less extreme than the sort we see with, say, "bank,"[25] where the two semantic values are unrelated, it still seems that the ambiguity they have in mind is considerably more substantial than the sort of context sensitivity defended here. In particular, they suggest that there are two completely different ways ("two conventions") in which the referents of our terms can be determined. As they put it, their claim that natural kind terms are systematically ambiguous between descriptive and nondescriptive conventions runs against a "critical constraint on theory building in the philosophy of language," namely that "only one theory of reference will apply to a class of terms."[26]

Now the contextualist account above not only respects this "critical constraint" by proposing a "univocal theory of reference"[27] (the same function from use to meaning would determine what, say, "Arthritis" refers to in both cases, its just that the weighting of the inputs to the function changes), but also allows a good deal more flexibility than one that takes reference to simply be ambiguous between causal and descriptive notions. In particular, taking our terms to be ambiguous between the 'causal' and 'descriptive' meanings doesn't help account for contextual shifts in which both meanings seem to fall within the range of the causal. In short, the contextualist account can, in principle, explain all the cases appealed to by the ambiguity theory, and others

---

[24] Nichols, Pinillos and Mallon (2014). The authors also make the suggestion that philosophers tend to cherry pick their examples to favor those which produce intuitions favoring their preferred theory (see ibid., p. 10).
[25] Ibid., p. 26. Indeed, they also appeal to Lewis 1999 (see note 21), but they seem to treat the "accommodation" involved as deciding which of the two referential conventions to follow, rather than involving which of the commitments associated with a word should be given more stress (Nichols, Pinillos and Mallon 2014, p. 24).
[26] Nichols, Pinillos and Mallon 2014, pp. 22–23.   [27] Ibid., p. 19.

besides, so it is unclear what advantage positing the more substantial ambiguity to explain such cases would bring.[28]

'Switching' cases

Cases of contextual variation that can't be explained in terms of a simple ambiguity between 'causal' and 'descriptive' conventions arise when the source of information associated with a word that the subject is causally connected to 'switches'. We will focus on three such cases here.

Donnellan and Evans on proper names

An example of this sort can be seen in the contrasting views of Evans and Donnellan about how to understand the reference of a proper name when the source of the information associated with it changes over time. Donnellan allows that the reference of such names can vary from context to context, while Evans favors a more invariant account. I'm largely sympathetic with the general shape of Evans's theory, but he mischaracterizes Donnellan's position in a way that keeps him from seeing how his own view could be developed. In particular, Evans takes Donnellan to argue for something like what I'll call "source-dependent contextualism," which is, roughly, the view that a token of a name in a claim refers to whichever potential bearer was the source of the information that is the topic of that claim.

For the source-dependent contextualist, if our beliefs about "Napoleon" actually came from two men, one of whom ("Alpha") was the source of all of our pre-1814 information associated with "Napoleon," and another ("Beta") of whom took the original's place and was the source of the rest of our information, then claims about "Napoleon's" early life or the 1812 invasion of Russia would refer to Alpha, while claims about "Napoleon's" defeat at Waterloo or his eventual death on the island of Saint Helena would refer to Beta. By contrast, Evans argues as follows:

I think that we can say that *in general* a speaker intends to refer to the item that is the dominant source of his associated body of information. It is important to see

---

[28] The contextualist account also explains the fact (discussed ibid., p. 20) that many questions elicit a type of 'neutral' reaction rather than showing a response that clearly favors either the causal or descriptive reading. The ambiguity view might suggest that we could toggle between these two distinct sets of conventions, but the contextualist view suggests that we may face cases where the incompatible beliefs are equally weighted (or in which we have no idea what weight they have) and so have no firm idea of what is being referred to.

that this will not change from occasion to occasion depending upon the subject matter. Some have proposed [Donnellan 1970 is cited at this point] that if in the case [above] the historian says "Napoleon fought skillfully at Waterloo" it is the imposter Beta who is the intended referent, while if he had said in the next breath '... unlike his performance in the Senate' it would be Alpha. This seems a mistake; not only was what the man said false, what he intended to say was false too, as he would be the first to agree; it wasn't Napoleon who fought skillfully at Waterloo.[29]

Evans doesn't think that the reference of "Napoleon" shifts from context to context, but while he is correct to claim that Donnellan does allow for contextual variation, he doesn't present a charitable, or accurate, reading of the sort of variation that Donnellan makes room for. Indeed, Donnellan's claims about what we would be referring to in various situations seem to be a better fit with the type of contextualism defended here, than they do with the position Evans's attributes to him.[30]

We can see this by reconsidering the primary example from the paper of Donnellan's that Evans cites. In "Proper Names and Identifying Descriptions," Donnellan asks us to imagine that a student attending a party "meets a man he takes to be the famous philosopher, J. L. Aston-Martin."[31] The student has previously read a number of Aston-Martin's papers and spends an hour or so speaking with the man (but not about philosophy) over the course of the evening. Donnellan claims that if the student goes back to his seminar the next day and tells everyone "Last night I met J. L. Aston Martin and talked to him for almost an hour," he would have said something false, since the name refers to the philosopher, and not the man a the party.[32] On the other hand, if he is telling some other friends about the party and the amusing things that happened, such as when "Robinson tripped over Aston-Martin's feet and fell flat on his face," the name would refer to the person at the party, not the famous philosopher.[33]

First of all, one should note that on the account attributed to Donnellan by Evans, *both* of these utterances of "Aston-Martin" would have referred to the man at the party (while it would refer to the philosopher when the student said things like "J. L. Aston-Martin wrote 'Other bodies'"), while in Donnellan's own discussion the referent of the name *isn't* identified with the source of the particular belief that is foregrounded in the utterance. Instead, Donnellan tentatively explains the difference in who the name refers to in the two cases as follows:

---

[29] Evans 1973, pp. 16–17.
[30] For a more sympathetic reading of what is motivating Donnellan here that meshes with much of this, see Stalnaker 2008 (especially pp. 124–25).
[31] Donnellan 1970, p. 68.   [32] Ibid., pp. 68–69.   [33] Ibid., p. 69.

Perhaps the difference lies in the fact that the initial utterance of the speaker's remark would only have a point if he was referring to the famous philosopher, while in the later utterances it is more natural to take him to be referring to the man at the party, since what happened there is the whole point.[34]

The referent of a name may switch from context to context because different sources of information can, in Evans's terms, 'dominate' the total "body of information" associated with the name, and this domination may vary depending on what the point of a particular utterance is. Chances are that piece of information will bear greater weight than usual if it is the topic of the utterance, but this alone would not guarantee that other information associated with a name might carry still greater weight. If there are two sources of information associated with a name, one of which accounts for the great majority of the beliefs involved, it is quite likely that one will be 'dominant' even in cases where the sentence topic is something tied to the other (as in Evans's "Napoleon" case). By contrast, if the amount of information is more evenly split, then the 'dominant' source may often vary from context to context. Still, even if things are generally weighted heavily one way, what becomes dominant can switch. For instance, in a note to the passage quoted above, Donnellan considers a case where the student becomes good friends with the "Aston-Martin" he meets at the party, and stays so for many years without ever discovering that he is mistaken about his friend's philosophical production. In such cases, most of the speaker's "Aston-Martin" utterances will refer to his new friend, since information from the party-going Aston-Martin would typically dominate the rest, but if he claimed to know J. L. Aston-Martin "in circumstances where it is clear that the point of the remark has to do with claiming to know a famous man," Donnellan still thinks that "we would suppose him to have referred to Aston-Martin, the famous philosopher, and not to [the] man he met at the party, who later is one of his close acquaintances."[35]

Such shifts could not, of course, be explained in terms of the meaning of proper names being 'ambiguous' between a 'causal' and a 'descriptive' reading, since both interpretations of the name are equally causal. The use of "Aston-Martin" to pick out the famous philosopher rather than the party-goer isn't purely "descriptive," as should be clear when we consider the possibility that the famous Aston-Martin fabricated much of his back story and achieved his fame by taking credit for the work of one of his more retiring colleagues (and so never wrote "Other Bodies" or any of the other papers attributed to him).[36] There might, of course, be contexts in which the term is used in ways that make writing the papers more essential

---

[34] Ibid.   [35] Ibid., p. 79.   [36] See the discussion of "Gödel" in Kripke 1972/1980.

(as when a student is writing his dissertation on "Other Bodies" but cares little about the biography of the author), but that wouldn't be one of the contexts that Donnellan describes, where the "famous philosopher" and the "party-goer" are the two subjects.

Memory content

The account sketched above also applies usefully to the problem of how to ascribe thought (and memory) content in cases such as the following:[37] John is, at the age of 12, transported from Earth to Twin Earth (which is, once again, just like Earth but whose 'water' is made up of XYZ (*twater*) rather than H_2O) and he lives there for another forty years without being aware of the switch.[38] Most externalists agree that at age 12, John's use of "water" refers to H_2O but at some time over the next few years his term comes to pick out (or at least typically pick out) XYZ, so that when he asks for a glass of "water" he is talking about *twater*, and no longer talking about water. There is, however, less consensus about whether John has (1) simply acquired a *second* 'water' concept, so that he is able to have thoughts about both *water* and *twater* (the pluralistic, or "conceptual addition," view),[39] or (2) had his original *water* concept *replaced* by a *twater* concept, so that he is now unable to have any *water* thoughts (the monistic, or "conceptual replacement," view).[40]

The difference between the pluralistic and monistic views manifests itself when we try to interpret claims/thoughts of John's (at age 52) such as "I remember swimming in Lake Ontario when I was 11 and thinking 'this water was freezing!'" Defenders of the monistic view typically claim that in such attributions "water" picks out *twater* and that John has simply lost the ability to remember what he thought before. Defenders of the pluralistic view, on the other hand, may treat this as one of the cases where John was able to apply his original *water* concept, so that the recollection turns out to be a true one. Monists view even memory content to be determined by one's current environment, while pluralists typically treat

---

[37] Such cases of 'slow switching' became familiar through Burge 1988 and Boghossian 1989. For a summary of some of the discussion of such cases, see Parent 2013.
[38] This is the most familiar version of the case, but the problem can be generated around less far-fetched examples such as someone making a permanent move from Great Britain to the United States without realizing that the term "Robin" picks out different birds in the two dialects of English, and unable to tell the two sorts of bird apart.
[39] See, for instance, Boghossian 1989, 1992a, 2011; Burge 1988; Gibbons 1996; Heal 1988.
[40] See, for instance, Bernecker 2010; Brueckner 1997; Ludlow 1995, 1996, and 1999; Tye 1998.

memory content as reflecting the environment in which the thought remembered originally occurred.

The view defended here is clearly more pluralistic than monistic. However, it is in a position to allow that the monist may often be right about what we should say about particular memories. The contextualist view allows that there are a variety of 'water' concepts available to the speaker in the switching cases, and which one, say, John applies will depend upon his interests at the time. At 52, John typically refers to *twater* by "water" since most of his 'water' beliefs are tied to his contact with XYZ. However, if the purpose of his recollection were simply to reflect on his youth, most of these later water beliefs may not be relevant, while the belief that he did, in fact, experience the freezing water would be very heavily weighed. In such a case, he would plausibly be seen as thinking about *water* rather than *twater*.

On the other hand, if the recollection comes up in the context of debating whether a spot he and his family are about to visit (and which he thinks he once swam in) will be pleasant to swim in, then non *water*-friendly beliefs of his such as "there is a Great Lake full of water to the north of me that I'm thinking of vacationing at," "my children always complain when they have to swim in cold water," and so on, will be heavily weighed, and the suggestion that he refers to *twater* by the term[41] (and thus misremembers what he originally thought) will seem much more plausible.

Whether a speaker's use of "water" in a memory claim refers to H_2O or XYZ will depend at least partially on his context, and not simply on the source of the particular memory claim. In those contexts where his commitments associated with his original environment have more weight, it will refer to *water* while in those where those relating to his new environment have more weight, it will refer to *twater*. Of course, as the speaker spends more time on Twin Earth, the number and strength of his *twater* commitments is bound to grow, but the *water* commitments don't simply disappear, and in some (increasingly rare) contexts they may be important enough to outweigh the more recent *twater* commitments.[42]

There may also, of course, be contexts where "water" referred to a more 'functional' kind that picked out both H_2O and XYZ. In such

---

[41] Or perhaps a functional kind that picks out both H_2O and XYZ (see below).
[42] So, this would follow Heal in suggesting that the switch to the new contents would never be 'complete'. The original substance would be what was referred to not just because those instances of a kind that "would be the first to come to mind" in the context (Heal 1998, p. 105), but also because they would be the ones the speaker took to be most important for the point he was trying to make if questioned.

contexts, the commitments to applications on both planets would each be more heavily weighted by the speaker than any commitments to his using the term in just the way his peers do,[43] or to the term picking out a natural kind (as, perhaps, when the speaker insists that "Ever since I was 7, I've felt 'off' all day if I don't start the morning by splashing cold water on my face").[44]

Pluralistic accounts of switching cases are sometimes criticized for not suggesting any sort of "mechanism" that would determine which contents occurred in which contexts.[45] Monistic accounts have no such requirement, but the sort of contextualist account suggested above has no trouble with this extra explanatory burden. The Self-Interpretation Principle provides an explanation of why and when the contents switch, and it does so in a way that keeps self-knowledge centrally located in our account of such contents.[46] Of course what I described earlier as "source-dependent contextualism," the view that would simply tie the content of "water" in a memory claim to whatever substance was the source of that particular 'water' memory, also provides a mechanism for determining which contents appear in which contexts,[47] but that view not only makes unintuitive claims about just what the content of our memories must be in certain contexts (see the discussion of Evans and Donnellan above), but, as we shall see in the following section, it also leads to some serious tensions with some natural assumptions about self-knowledge.

---

[43] Especially since, given that the functional kind includes all of the instances of the natural kind they are talking about, his meaning something different than they do doesn't necessarily prevent them from being legitimate sources of testimonial knowledge for him.

[44] Once again, given the multiplicity of possibly readings, these switches don't lend themselves to any sort of easy explanation in terms of "water" being ambiguous between a 'descriptive' and a 'causal' reading.

[45] See, for instance, Bernecker 2010, p. 192.

[46] The predictions of such an account would be largely in line with the other account that I know of to give a plausible account of how the plurality of contents would be sorted, namely, Goldberg's (2005) account of what he calls "the defeat of the Current Face Value Presumption." Roughly put, Goldberg's view is that a speaker's term should be interpreted in accordance with the meanings of his current community unless (1) the speaker's intentions and justificatory dispositions regarding that word support a different interpretation, and (2) the speaker would, on becoming aware of this conflict with what his current society means by the term, disavow any intention to be using the word with that meaning, and correct his other beliefs accordingly. However, while Goldberg's account would make roughly the same predictions about cases (1) and (2) essentially amount to the speaker having commitments tying his use to the original context that are more heavily entrenched than those tying his use to his current context, it doesn't quite answer Bernecker's demand for a mechanism explaining why various contents appear in various contexts. That is to say, it describes how the semantic values may be distributed without giving any sort of metasemantic explanation of the distribution.

[47] Though it is less clear how the account can extend beyond direct memory reports, or reports that draw on multiple memories with multiple sources.

Externalism and inference

The understanding of the switching cases available to the metasemantic contextualist also has the advantage of allowing one to put to rest Boghossian's worry that "externalism is inconsistent with very important aspects of our intuitive conception of the mind – namely, with the a priority of our logical abilities."[48] Given that the breakdown in the priority of our logical abilities that Boghossian's argument focuses on seems to turn on our apparent inability to recognize that two concepts in our occurrent thoughts have different contents, the breakdown in our logical abilities seems tied to a breakdown in some more intuitive sense of the 'transparency' of our own thoughts, and hence suggests a serious tension between semantic externalism and our intuitive conception of self-knowledge.[49]

Boghossian argues for his conclusion by considering the following variant of the now familiar switching case: Peter is an opera fan and inhabitant of Earth. While vacationing in New Zealand he encounters Luciano Pavarotti swimming in Lake Taupo and, much to his delight, has an extended conversation with the famous tenor. Some time later, and without his knowledge, Peter is switched to Twin Earth and over a number of years most of his terms come to take on the semantic values standardly associated with Twin English, so that when he eventually sees Pavarotti's twin perform and subsequently claims that he saw "Pavarotti" sing, he is talking about *Twin* Pavarotti. However, it seems as if he can still have memory-based thoughts about the Pavarotti on Earth, and when he reminisces about the time that he saw "Pavarotti" swimming in Lake Taupo, he seems to be thinking of our Pavarotti, not his twin. Boghossian claims that this ability to access both contents could, however, result in Peter's engaging in reasoning like the following:

(1) Pavarotti once swam in Lake Taupo.
(2) The singer I heard yesterday is Pavarotti.
(3) Therefore, the singer I heard yesterday once swam in Lake Taupo.

---

[48] Boghossian 1992a, p. 17. Ludlow (1999) appeals to similar cases to undermine the pluralistic or 'conceptual addition' interpretation of the switching cases, since this particular problem doesn't arise for those who endorse the monistic or 'conceptual replacement' interpretation of such cases.

[49] Boghossian later cashes out the relevant sense of 'transparency' as: "If two of a thinker's token thoughts possess the same content, then the thinker must be able to know a priori that they do; and (b) If two of a thinker's token thoughts possess distinct contents, then the thinker must be able to know a priori that they do" (Boghossian 2011, p. 457).

According to Boghossian, "Pavarotti" refers to Earth's Pavarotti in the initial premise, but to Twin Pavarotti in the second, so that "True premises conspire, through a fallacy of equivocation that Peter is in principle not able to notice, to produce a false conclusion."[50] What would seem to Peter to be a perfectly valid inference would thus turn out not to be and so "the thesis of a priority of logical abilities is ... inconsistent with externalist assumptions."[51] This is a surprising result, and it (along with its suggestion that the identity of our concepts is not 'transparent' to us) is sure to make externalism look less appealing.

However, there is reason to be suspicious of Boghossian's claim that the references of our terms could switch mid argument in such a fashion. In particular, Boghossian's argument seems to rely on something like the 'source-dependent contextualism' mentioned earlier,[52] and thus he feels free to ignore the fact that arguments and inferences (especially those inferences meant to be introspectively surveyable) take place against the background of a single context.

In particular, just because Peter might typically utter (1) in contexts where the occurrence of "Pavarotti" refers to Pavarotti, while he typically utters (2) in contexts where the occurrence of "Pavarotti" refers to Pavarotti's twin, it need not follow that the term can support multiple semantic values in the context of an argument that involves both (1) and (2). Indeed, the contextualist account outlined above would seem to rule out the sorts of introspectively undetectable equivocation described by Boghossian.[53]

Peter has, after all, a set of 'Pavarotti commitments' that are tied to two men, and which of the two Pavarottis he refers to will depend on which subset of his commitments carries the most weight in a given context. It seems likely that a sentence like (1) would typically be uttered in the context of Peter's reminiscing about his encounter with the great tenor, and the commitments tying the term to Pavarotti will in such cases be more heavily weighted than those attached to his twin. (Of course, this

---

[50] Boghossian 1992a, p. 22. (We can assume that Pavarotti's twin never swam in either Lake Taupo or its twin.)

[51] Ibid.

[52] As he puts it, "memory-beliefs involving 'Pavarotti' or 'water' or whatever, originating in Earthly experiences, are about Pavarotti, water, and so on. And, correlatively, that memory-beliefs involving those words originating in Twearthly experiences will be about Twin Pavarotti, twin water, and so on" (Boghossian 1992b, p.42).

[53] Stalnaker (2008) also presents an account of these slow-switching cases that doesn't rely on any type of source-dependent contextualism, but his view seems to give priority to the *attributer's* context (see especially p. 131), in a way that this view does not, and thus may be open to criticism (see, for instance, Boghossian 2011, p. 465) for taking these intentional facts dependent upon other people's intentional facts, which would, in turn, face just the same need for interpretation.

need not *always* be the case, and (1) could be uttered in contexts where the commitments associated with Pavarotti's twin carried more weight.) By contrast, a sentence like (2) would be more likely uttered in contexts where the commitments tied to Pavarotti's twin are more entrenched, and in that case "Pavarotti" would refer to Pavarotti's twin. (Though, once again, there could be contexts where the occurrence of the name in (2) might refer to Pavarotti as well.)

Still, while there can be contexts where "Pavarotti" refers to Pavarotti, and other contexts where the name picks out Pavarotti's twin, these are clearly *different* contexts, and while isolated instances of either (1) and (2) can each be true in some context, there is no context in which they are *both* true. However, when (1) and (2) are incorporated into a *single argument*, they have to be interpreted in terms of *single* contexts, and so the term will need to be assigned a single semantic value in both (1) and (2).[54] Consequently, the sorts of hidden equivocation (and corresponding failures of semantic self-knowledge) that Boghossian treats the externalist as committed to allowing will not arise.

The view presented above allows both that (1) the thinker has access to two "Pavarotti" contents, and (2) those two contents will never produce an equivocation in the course of a single argument.[55] Boghossian is skeptical about the possibility of such a combination, but such skepticism seems driven by the assumption that such a combination could only be explained by a view (which he attributes to Burge and Schiffer)[56] in which the terms in an argument are quasi-anaphorically connected so that the first occurrence of a term (whose reference is determined along source-dependent contextualist lines) itself determines what the rest of the occurrences of that term refer to.[57] On such accounts (as Boghossian notes), the ordering of the premises would determine who the argument is about, so that

---

[54] See Schiffer 1992, p. 35 for a similar point and the claim that premises 1 and 2 can be compressed into something like "Pavarotti once swam in Lake Taupo, and is the singer I heard yesterday" where there is only one occurrence of "Pavarotti."

[55] For some others who deny that "Pavarotti" would have two distinct references in this case, see Burge 1998, Goldberg 2007a, and Schiffer 1992.

[56] Burge 1998 and Schiffer 1992. Note, however, that while Schiffer insists that "Pavarotti" in the second premise be interpreted in the same way as it is in the first (Schiffer 1992, p. 33), his presentation seems to leave room for the possibility that this might be a consequence of the fact that whatever determines the content of one will determine the content of the other in the context of an argument. Consequently, he doesn't seem to explicitly commit himself to the *order* of the premises determining how they are interpreted.

[57] Boghossian 2011, p. 459. For a similar argument, see Brown 2004a, pp. 177–78, and see Bernecker 2010, p. 191, and Goldberg 2007a, p. 181 for other discussions of this sort of 'anaphoric' explanation of univocality within arguments.

(1) Pavarotti once swam in Lake Taupo.
(2) The singer I heard yesterday is Pavarotti.
(3) Therefore, the singer I heard yesterday once swam in Lake Taupo.

would be a valid argument about the Pavarotti on Earth (with a false second premise), while

(1) The singer I heard yesterday is Pavarotti.
(2) Pavarotti once swam in Lake Taupo.
(3) Therefore, the singer I heard yesterday once swam in Lake Taupo.

would be a valid argument about the Pavarotti on Twin Earth (with a false second premise). That the ordering of premises should have such an effect is an admittedly unappealing conclusion, but while that presents a problem for those who respond to Boghossian's argument with such an appeal to quasi-anaphoric dependence, it should be clear that the sort of metasemantic account suggested here has no such commitment. There is no requirement that the sentence in the first premise be weighted more (or less) heavily than the sentence in the second premise, so while all of the occurrences of "Pavarotti" in the argument must be assigned the same value, that value is independent of the premises' ordering.

Conclusion

The metasemantic contextualist who relies on something like the Self-Interpretation Principle can, then, argue that a number of important debates surrounding semantic externalism arise from the fact that both sides mistakenly assume that there is a single answer to questions like "What is the semantic value of 'arthritis' in Bert's language?" or "What is the content of John's 'water' memories?", when the answers to such questions are, in fact, context-dependent. Further, while the view is motivated by a certain conception of self-knowledge as a type of 'authority' (that is, speakers' own judgments determine what they mean when their commitments conflict), it is able, once in place, to help answer the threat to self-knowledge as 'transparency' that semantic externalism seemed to present.

Bibliography

Austin, J. L. 1979. "Other Minds." In J. O. Urmson and G. J. Warnock, eds., *Philosophical Papers*, 3rd edition (Oxford University Press), pp. 76–116.
Bach, K. 1987. *Thought and Reference* (Oxford: Clarendon Press).
Bach, K. 1988. "Burge's New Thought Experiment: Back to the Drawing Room." *The Journal of Philosophy* 85, pp. 88–97.
Bach, K. 1997. "Do Belief Reports Report Beliefs?" *Pacific Philosophical Quartely* 78:3, pp. 215–41.
Barber, A. ed. 2003. *Epistemology of Language* (Oxford University Press).
Bar-On, D. 2004. *Speaking My Mind: Expression and Self-Knowledge* (Oxford University Press).
Berker, S. 2008. "Luminosity Regained." *Philosophers' Imprint* 8:2, pp. 1–22.
Bernecker, S. 2009. *Memory: A Philosophical Study* (Oxford University Press).
Bilgrami, A. 1992. *Belief and Meaning* (Cambridge: Blackwell).
Blackburn, S. 1984. *Spreading the Word* (Oxford: Clarendon Press).
Blackburn, S. 1993. *Essays in Quasi-Realism* (Oxford University Press).
Block, N. 1998. "Holism, Mental and Semantic." In *Routledge Encyclopedia of Philosophy* (New York: Routledge).
Boghossian, P. 1989. "Content and Self-Knowledge." *Philosophical Topics* 17, pp. 5–26.
Boghossian, P. 1992a. "Externalism and inference." *Philosophical Issues* 2, pp. 11–28.
Boghossian, P. 1992b. "Reply to Schiffer." *Philosophical Issues* 2, pp. 39–42.
Boghossian, P. 1994. "The Transparency of Mental Content." *Philosophical Perspectives* 8, pp. 33–50.
Boghossian, P. 1997. "What the Externalist Can Know A Priori." *Proceedings of the Aristotelian Society* 97, pp. 161–75.
Boghossian, P. 2011. "The Transparency of Mental Content Revisited." *Philosophical Studies* 155:3, pp. 457–65.
Boghossian, P. 2012. "What is Inference?" *Philosophical Studies* 169, pp. 1–18.
Brandom, R. 1994. *Making it Explicit* (Cambridge, Mass.: Harvard University Press).
Brown, J. 1995. "The Incompatibility of Anti-Individualism and Privileged Access." *Analysis* 55, pp. 149–56.
Brown, J. 2000. "Critical Reasoning, Understanding and Self-Knowledge." *Philosophical and Phenomenological Research* 61:3, pp. 659–76.
Brown, J. 2003. "Externalism and the Fregean Tradition." In A. Barber, ed., *Epistemology of Language* (Oxford University Press), pp. 431–58.

Brown, J. 2004a. *Anti-Individualism and Knowledge* (Cambridge, Mass.: MIT Press).
Brown, J. 2004b. "Wright on Transmission Failure." *Analysis* 64:281, pp. 57–67.
Brueckner, A. 1995. "Trying to Get Outside Your Own Skin." *Philosophical Topics* 23:1, pp. 79–111.
Brueckner, A. 1997. "Externalism and Memory." *Pacific Philosophical Quarterly* 78, pp. 1–12.
Brueckner, A. 2011. "A Defense of Burge's 'Self-Verifying Judgments'." *International Journal for the Study of Skepticism* 1:1, pp. 27–32.
Brueckner, A. and Ebbs, G. 2012. *Debating Self-Knowledge* (Cambridge University Press).
Burge, T. 1979. "Individualism and the Mental." *Midwest Studies in Philosophy* 4:1, pp. 73–121.
Burge, T. 1982. "Other Bodies." In A. Woodfield, ed., *Thought and Object: Essays on Intentionality* (Oxford University Press).
Burge, T. 1986. "Intellectual Norms and Foundations of Mind." *The Journal of Philosophy* 83:12, pp. 697–720.
Burge, T. 1988. "Individualism and Self-Knowledge." *The Journal of Philosophy* 85:1, pp. 649–63.
Burge, T. 1996. "Our Entitlement to Self-Knowledge." *Proceedings of the Aristotelian Society* 96, pp. 91–116.
Burge, T. 1998. "Memory and Self-Knowledge." In P. Ludlow and M. Martin, eds., *Externalism and Self-Knowledge* (Stanford, Calif.: CSLI Publications).
Burge, T. 1993. "Content Preservation." *The Philosophical Review* 102, 457–88.
Burge, T. 1999. "Comprehension and Interpretation." In *The Philosophy of Donald Davidson* (Chicago: Open Court), pp. 229–50.
Burge, T. 2003. "Perceptual Entitlement." *Philosophy and Phenomenological Research* 67, pp. 503–48.
Burge, T. 2007a. *Foundations of Mind* (Oxford: Clarendon Press).
Burge, T. 2007b. "Postscript to Individualism and the Mental." In *Foundations of Mind* (Oxford: Clarendon Press).
Burge, T. 2010. *Origins of Objectivity* (Oxford: Clarendon Press).
Byrne, A. 2003. "The Puzzle of Transparency." Unpublished MS.
Byrne, A. 2010. "Knowing that I am Thinking." In A. Hatzimoysis, ed., *Self-Knowledge* (Oxford University Press).
Byrne, A. 2011. "Transparency, Belief, Intention." *Aristotelian Society Supplementary Volume* 85:1, pp. 201–21.
Byrne, A. and Thau, M. 1995. "In Defense of the Hybrid View." *Mind* 105, pp. 139–49.
Campbell, J. 1987. "Is Sense Transparent?" *Proceedings of the Aristotelian Society* 88, pp. 273–92.
Cappelen, H. and Lepore, E. 2005. *Insensitive Semantics* (Oxford: Blackwell).
Cappelen, H. and Winblad, D. 1999. "Reference Externalized and the Role of Intuitions in Semantic Theory." *American Philosophical Quarterly* 36, pp. 337–50.
Chalmers, D. 1995. *The Conscious Mind* (Oxford University Press).

Chalmers, D. 2002. "The Components of Content." In D. Chalmers, ed., *Philosophy of Mind: Classical and Contemporary Readings* (Oxford University Press), pp. 608–33.

Chalmers, D. 2006. "The Foundations of Two-Dimensional Semantics." In M. Garcia-Carpintero and J. Macia, eds., *Two-Dimensional Semantics: Foundations and Applications* (Oxford University Press), pp. 55–140.

Chastain, C. 1975. "Reference and Context." In K. Gunderson, ed., *Minnesota Studies in the Philosophy of Science* 7, pp. 194–269.

Chomsky, N. 1992. "Explaining Language Use." *Philosophical Topics* 20, pp. 205–31.

Chomsky, N. 1995. "Language and Nature." *Mind* 104, pp. 1–61.

Cohnitz, D. and Haukioja, J. 2013. "Meta-Externalism vs. Meta-Internalism in the Study of Reference." *Australasian Journal of Philosophy* 91, pp. 475–500.

Davidson, D. 1965/1984. "Theories of Truth and Learnable Languages." In Davidson 1984b.

Davidson, D. 1967/1984. "Truth and Meaning." In Davidson 1984b.

Davidson, D. 1973/1984. "Radical Interpretation." In Davidson 1984b, pp. 125–39.

Davidson, D. 1974/1984. "Belief and the Basis of Meaning." In Davidson 1984b, pp. 141–54.

Davidson, D. 1975/1984. "Thought and Talk." In Davidson 1984b, pp. 155–70.

Davidson, D. 1977/1984. "Reality Without Reference." In Davidson 1984b, pp..

Davidson, D. 1979/1984. "The Inscrutability of Reference." In Davidson 1984b.

Davidson, D. 1984a. "First Person Authority." *Dialectica* 38:2–3, pp. 101–112.

Davidson, D. 1984b. *Inquiries into Truth and Interpretation* (Oxford University Press).

Davidson, D. 1986a. "A Coherence Theory of Truth and Knowledge." In E. Lepore, ed., *Truth and Interpretation* (Oxford: Blackwell).

Davidson, D. 1986b. "A Nice Derangement of Epitaphs." In E. Lepore, ed., *Truth and Interpretation* (Oxford: Blackwell), pp. 433–46.

Davidson, D. 1987. "Knowing One's Own Mind." *Proceedings and Addresses of the American Philosophical Association* 60, pp. 441–58.

Davidson, D. 1993. "Reply to Akeel Bilgrami." In Stoecker, R., ed., *Reflecting Davidson* (Berlin: De Gruyter).

Davidson, D. 1994. "The Social Aspect of Language." In McGuinness and Oliveri, eds., *The Philosophy of Michael Dummett* (Dordrecht: Springer), pp. 1–16.

Davidson, D. 1999. "Reply to Tyler Burge." In L. Hahn, ed., *The Philosophy of Donald Davidson* (Chicago: Open Court), pp. 251–54.

Davidson, D. 2003. "Responses to Barry Stroud, John McDowell and Tyler Burge." *Philosophy and Phenomenological Research* 67:3, pp. 691–99.

Davies, M. 1981. *Meaning, Quantification, Necessity* (London: Routledge & Kegan Paul).

Davies, M. 1998. "Externalism, Architecturalism, and Epistemic Warrant." In C. Wright, B. Smith and C. MacDonald, eds., *Knowing Our Own Minds* (Oxford University Press), pp. 321–61.

Davies, M. 2000. "Externalism and Armchair Knowledge." In P. Boghossian, ed., *New Essays on the A Priori* (Oxford University Press), pp. 384–414.

Davies, M. 2003a. "Externalism, Self-Knowledge and Transmission of Warrant." In M. Frapolli and E. Romero, eds., *Meaning, Basic Self-Knowledge, and Mind: Essays on Tyler Burge* (Stanford, Calif.: CSLI Publications), pp. 105–30.

Davies, M. 2003b. "The Problem of Armchair Knowledge." In S. Nuccetelli, ed., *New Essays on Semantic Externalism and Self-Knowledge* (Cambridge, Mass.: MIT Press).

Davies, M. 2004. "Epistemic Entitlement, Warrant Transmission and Easy Knowledge." *Aristotelian Society Supplementary Volume* 78:1, pp. 213–245.

Davies, M. 2006. "Foundational Issues in the Philosophy of Language." In M. Devitt and R. Hanley, eds., *The Blackwell Guide to the Philosophy of Language* (Oxford: Blackwell), pp. 19–40.

Davies, M. and Humberstone, I. L. 1980. "Two Notions of Necessity." *Philosophical Studies* 38, pp. 1–30.

Devitt, M. 2011. "Deference and the Use Theory." *ProtoSociology* 27, pp. 196–211.

Devitt, M. 2012. "The Role of Intuitions in the Philosophy of Language." In G. Russell and D. Graff-Fara, eds., *Routledge Companion to the Philosophy of Language* (New York: Routledge), pp. 554–65.

Donnellan, K. 1966. "Reference and Definite Descriptions." *The Philosophical Review* 75:3, pp. 281–304.

Donnellan, K. 1968. "Putting Humpty Dumpty Together Again." *The Philosophical Review* 77:2, pp. 203–15.

Donnellan, K. 1970. "Proper Names and Identifying Descriptions." *Synthese* 21, pp. 335–58. (Reprinted in K. Donnellan, *Essays on Reference, Language and Mind* (Oxford University Press, 2012).)

Donnellan, K. 1979. "Speaker Reference, Descriptions, and Anaphora." In P. Cole, ed., *Syntax and Semantics 9: Pragmatics* (New York: Academic Press), pp. 47–68.

Dretske, F. 1970. "Epistemic Operators." *The Journal of Philosophy* 67: 24, pp. 1007–23.

Dretske, F. 1981. *Knowledge and the Flow of Information* (Cambridge, Mass.: MIT Press).

Dretske, F. 2004. "The Case Against Closure." In M. Steup and E. Sosa, eds., *Contemporary Debates in Epistemology* (Oxford: Blackwell).

Dummett, M. 1975. "Wang's Paradox." *Synthese* 30, pp. 201–32.

Dummett, M. 1978. *Truth and Other Enigmas* (Cambridge, Mass.: Harvard University Press).

Dummett, M. 1981. *Frege. Philosophy of Language* (Cambridge, Mass.: Harvard University Press).

Dummett, M. 1993. "What is a Theory of Meaning? (I)." In *The Seas of Language* (Oxford University Press).

Ebbs, G. 1996. "Can we take our Words at Face Value?" *Philosophy and Phenomenological Research* 56:3, pp. 499–530.

Ebbs, G. 1997. *Rule-Following and Realism* (Cambridge, Mass.: Harvard University Press).

Ebbs, G. 2000. "The Very Idea of Sameness of Extension Across Time." *American Philosophical Quarterly* 37, pp. 245–68.

Ebbs, G. 2001. "Is Skepticism About Self-Knowledge Coherent?" *Philosophical Studies* 105, pp. 43–58.
Ebbs, G. 2003. "A Puzzle About Doubt." In S. Nuccetelli, ed., *New Essays on Semantic Externalism and Self-Knowledge* (Cambridge, Mass.: MIT Press), pp. 143–68.
Ebbs, G. 2005. "Why Skepticism About Self-Knowledge is Self-Undermining." *Analysis* 65:3, pp. 237–44.
Ebbs, G. 2009. *Truth and Words* (Oxford University Press).
Ebbs, G. 2011. "Anti-Individualism, Self-Knowledge, and Epistemic Possibility: Further Reflections on a Puzzle about Doubt." In A. Hatzimoiysis, ed., *Self-Knowledge* (Oxford University Press), pp. 53–79.
Ebbs, G. and Brueckner, A. 2012. *Debating Self-Knowledge* (Cambridge University Press).
Edgley, R. 1969. *Reason in Theory and Practice* (London: Hutchinson).
Elugardo, R. 1993. "Burge on Content." *Philosophy and Phenomenological Research* 53:2, pp. 367–84.
Evans, G. 1973. "The Causal Theory of Names." *Proceedings of the Aristotelian Society, Supplementary Volumes* 47, pp. 187–225.
Evans, G. 1975. "Identity and Predication." *The Journal of Philosophy* 72:3, pp. 343–63.
Evans, G. 1979. "Reference and Contingency." *The Monist* 62:2, pp. 161–89.
Evans, G. 1982. *Varieties of Reference* (Oxford: Clarendon Press).
Falvey, K. and Owens, J. 1994. "Externalism, Self-Knowledge, and Skepticism." *The Philosophical Review* 103:1, pp. 107–37.
Faria, P. 2009. "Unsafe Reasoning: A Survey." *DoisPontos* 6:2, pp. 185–201.
Farkas, K. 2003. "What is Externalism?" *Philosophical Studies* 112:3, pp. 187–208.
Farkas, K. 2008. *The Subject's Point of View* (Oxford University Press).
Feldman, R. and Conee, E. 2001. "Internalism Defended." *American Philosophical Quarterly*, pp. 1–18.
Finkelstein, D. 2003. *Expression and the Inner* (Cambridge, Mass.: Harvard University Press).
Fodor, J. 1975. *The Language of Thought* (Cambridge, Mass.: Harvard University Press).
Fodor, J. and LePore, E. 1992. *Holism, a Shoppers Guide* (Oxford: Blackwell).
Frapolli, M. and Romero, E. eds. 2003. *Meaning, Basic Self-Knowledge, and Mind: Essays on Tyler Burge* (Stanford, Calif.: CSLI Publications).
Gertler, B. 2011a. *Self-Knowledge* (New York: Routledge).
Gertler, B. 2011b. "Self-Knowledge and the Transparency of Belief." In A. Hatzimoiysis, ed., *Self-Knowledge* (Oxford University Press), pp. 125–45.
Gertler, B. 2012. "Understanding the Internalism–Externalism Debate: What is the Boundary of the Thinker?" *Philosophical Perspectives* 26:1, pp. 51–75.
Gibbons, J. 1996. "Externalism and Knowledge of Content." *The Philosophical Review* 105:3, pp. 287–310.
Glüer, K. 2009. "In Defence of a Doxastic Account of Experience." *Mind & Language* 24, pp. 297–327.
Glüer, K. 2011. *Donald Davidson: A Short Introduction* (Oxford University Press).

Glüer, K. 2012. "Theories of Meaning and Truth Conditions." In M. Kölbel and M. García-Carpintero, eds., *The Continuum Guide to the Philosophy of Language* (London: Continuum), pp. 84–105.
Glüer, K. and Wikforss, Å. 2013. "Against Belief Normativity." In T. H. W. Chan, ed., *The Aim of Belief* (Oxford University Press).
Goldberg, S. 1999. "The Relevance of Discriminatory Knowledge of Content." *Pacific Philosophical Quarterly* 80:2, pp. 136–56.
Goldberg, S. 2002. "Do Anti-Individualistic Construals of the Attitudes Capture the Agent's Conceptions?" *Noûs* 36:4, pp. 597–621.
Goldberg, S. 2003a. "Anti-Individualism, Conceptual Omniscience, and Skepticism." *Philosophical Studies* 116:1, pp. 53–78.
Goldberg, S. 2003b. "On Our Alleged A Priori Knowledge That Water Exists." *Analysis* 63:277, pp. 38–41.
Goldberg, S. 2003c. "What do you know when you know your own thoughts?" In S. Nuccetelli, ed., *New Essays on Semantic Externalism and Self-Knowledge* (Cambridge, Mass.: MIT Press), pp. 241–56.
Goldberg, S. 2004. "Radical Interpretation, Understanding, and Testimonial Transmission." *Synthese* 138:3, pp. 387–416.
Goldberg, S. 2005a. "The Dialectical Context of Boghossian's Memory Argument." *Canadian Journal of Philosophy* 35, pp. 135–48.
Goldberg, S. 2005b. "(Nonstandard) Lessons from World-Switching Cases." *Philosophia* 32:1, pp. 95–131.
Goldberg, S. 2007a. "Anti-Individualism, Content Preservation, and Discursive Justification." *Noûs* 41:2, pp. 178–203.
Goldberg, S. 2007b. *Anti-Individualism: Mind and Language, Knowledge and Justification* (Cambridge University Press).
Goldberg, S. 2008a. "Internalism, Externalism, and the Epistemology of Linguistic Understanding." *Communication and Cognition* 41:3, pp. 191–216.
Goldberg, S. 2008b. "Metaphysical Realism and Thought." *American Philosophical Quarterly* 45, pp. 149–63.
Goldberg, S. 2008c. "Must Differences in Cognitive Value be Transparent?" *Erkenntnis* 69:2, pp. 165–87.
Goldberg, S. 2009. "Experts, Semantic and Epistemic." *Noûs* 43:4, pp. 581–98.
Goldberg, S. 2010. *Relying on Others: An Essay in Epistemology* (Oxford University Press).
Goldberg, S. ed. 2007. *Internalism and Externalism in Semantics and Epistemology* (Oxford University Press).
Goldberg, S. and Henderson, D. 2006. "Monitoring and Anti-Reductionism in the Epistemology of Testimony." *Philosophy and Phenomenological Research* 72:3, pp. 576–93.
Graff-Fara, D. 2000. "Shifting Sands: An Interest-Relative Theory of Vagueness." *Philosophical Topics* 28, pp. 45–81.
Greco, D. 2014. "Could KK be OK?" *The Journal of Philosophy* 111:4, pp. 169–97.
Häggqvist, S. and Wikforss, A. 2007. "Externalism and *A Posteriori* Semantics." *Erkenntnis* 67, pp. 373–86.
Hahn, M. and Ramberg, B. eds. 2004. *Reflections and Replies: Essays on the Philosophy of Tyler Burge* (Cambridge, Mass.: MIT Press).

Harris, P. L. 2012. *Trusting What You're Told: How Children Learn from Others* (Cambridge, Mass.: Harvard University Press).
Hatzimoiysis, A. ed. 2011. *Self-Knowledge* (Oxford University Press).
Haukioja, J. 2005. "Hindriks on Rule-Following." *Philosophical Studies* 126, pp. 219–39.
Haukioja, J. 2007. "How (Not) to Specify Normal Conditions for Response-Dependent Concepts." *Australasian Journal of Philosophy* 85, pp. 325–31.
Haukioja, J. 2009. "Intuitions, Externalism, and Conceptual Analysis." *Studia Philosophica Estonica* 2:2 (special issue on intuitions, ed. D. Cohnitz and S. Häggqvist), pp. 81–93.
Haukioja, J. 2012. "Rigidity and Actuality-Dependence." *Philosophical Studies* 157, pp. 399–410.
Hawthorne, J. 2004. "The Case For Closure." In M. Steup and E. Sosa, eds., *Contemporary Debates in Epistemology* (Oxford: Blackwell).
Heal, J. 1998. "Externalism and Memory." *Proceedings of the Aristotelian Society, Supplementary Volume* 72, pp. 95–109.
Heck, R. 1995. "The Sense of Communication." *Mind* 104, pp. 79–106.
Heck, R. 1996. "Communication and Knowledge: A Rejoinder to Byrne and Thau." *Mind* 105, pp. 139–49.
Heil, J. 1988. "Privileged Access." *Mind* 97:386, pp. 238–51.
Hintikka, J. 1962. *Knowledge and Belief* (Ithaca, NY: Cornell University Press).
Jackman, H. 2001. "Semantic Pragmatism and *A Priori* Knowledge." *Canadian Journal of Philosophy* 31:4, pp. 455–80.
Jackman, H. 2003. "Charity, Self-Interpretation, and Belief." *Journal of Philosophical Research* 28, pp. 145–70.
Jackman, H. 2005. "Descriptive Atomism and Foundational Holism: Semantics Between the Old Testament and the New." *Protosociology 21: Compositionality, Concepts and Representations* (ed. G. Preyer), pp. 5–20.
Jackman, H. 2007. "Minimalism, Psychological Reality, Meaning and Use." In G. Preyer and G. Peter, eds., *Context-Sensitivity and Semantic Minimalism: Essays in Semantics and Pragmatics* (Oxford University Press), pp. 320–36.
Jackman, H. 2009. "Semantic Intuitions, Conceptual Analysis and Cross-Cultural Variation." *Philosophical Studies* 146:2, pp. 159–77.
Jackman, H. 2014. "Meaning Holism." *The Stanford Encyclopedia of Philosophy* (Fall edition), ed. Edward N. Zalta. http://plato.stanford.edu/archives/fall2014/entries/meaning-holism/
Kallestrup, J. 2011. "Recent work on McKinsey's Paradox." *Analysis* 71, pp. 157–71.
Kaplan, D. 1975. "How to Russell a Frege-Church." *The Journal of Philosophy* 77, pp. 716–29.
Kaplan, D. 1979. "On the Logic of Demonstratives." *Journal of Philosophical Logic* 8:1, pp. 81–98.
Karjalainen, A. and Morton, A. 2003. "Contrastive Knowledge." *Philosophical Explorations* 6, pp. 74–89.
Kripke, S. 1972/1980. *Naming and Necessity* (Berlin: Springer).
Kripke, S. 1977. "Speaker's Reference and Semantic Reference." *Midwest Studies in Philosophy* 2:1, pp. 255–76.

Kripke, S. 1979. "A Puzzle About Belief." In A. Margalit, ed., *Meaning and Use* (Dordrecht: Reidel), pp. 239–83.

Kripke, S. 1982. *Wittgenstein on Rules and Private Language* (Oxford: Blackwell).

Lewis, D. 1983. "Languages and Language." In *Philosophical Papers*, volume I (Oxford University Press), pp. 163–88.

Lewis, D. 1984. "Putnam's Paradox." *Australasian Journal of Philosophy* 62, pp. 221–36.

Lewis, D. 1996. "Elusive Knowledge." *Australasian Journal of Philosophy* 74, pp. 549–67.

Lewis, D. 1999. "Reduction in Mind." In *Papers in Metaphysics and Epistemology* (Cambridge University Press), pp.

Loar, B. 1988. "Social Content and Psychological Content." In R. Grimm and D. Merrill, eds., *Contents of Thought* (Tucson: University of Arizona Press), pp. 99–110.

Lormand, E. 1996. "How to be a Meaning Holist." *The Journal of Philosophy* 93:2, pp. 51–73.

Ludlow, P. 1995. "Social Externalism, Self-Knowledge and Memory." *Analysis* 55:3, pp. 157–59.

Ludlow, P. 1996. "Social Externalism and Memory: A Problem?" *Acta Analytica* 14, pp. 69–76.

Ludlow, P. 1999. "First Person Authority and Memory." In M. De Caro, ed., *Interpretation and Causes: New Perspectives on Donald Davidson's Philosophy* (Dordrecht: Kluwer), pp. 159–70.

Ludlow, P. 2008. "Cheap Contextualism." *Philosophical Issues* 18:1, pp. 104–29.

Ludlow, P. 2014. *Living Words* (Oxford University Press).

Ludlow, P. and Martin, N. eds. 1998. *Externalism and Self-Knowledge* (Stanford, Calif.: CSLI Publications).

McDowell, J. 1986. "Singular Thought and the Extent of Inner Space." In J. McDowell and P. Pettit, eds., *Subject, Thought, and Context* (Oxford: Clarendon Press).

McDowell, J. 1991. "Intentionality and Interiority in Wittgenstein: Critical Comments on Crispin Wright." In K. Puhl, ed., *Meaning Scepticism* (Berlin: De Gruyter), pp. 148–69.

McDowell, J. 1998. "Response to Crispin Wright." In C. Wright, B. C. Smith and C. MacDonald, eds., *Knowing Our Own Minds* (Oxford University Press).

McGinn, C. 1977. "Charity, Interpretation, and Belief." *The Journal of Philosophy* 74, pp. 521–35.

McGinn, C. 1982. "The Structure of Content." In A. Woodfield, ed., *Thought and Object* (Oxford University Press).

Machery, E., Mallon, R., Nichols, S. and Stich, S. P. 2004. "Semantics, Cross-Cultural Style." *Cognition* 92, pp. B1–B12.

McKinsey, M. 1991. "Anti-Individualism and Privileged Access." *Analysis* 51:1, pp. 9–16.

McKinsey, M. 1994a. "Accepting the Consequences of Anti-Individualism." *Analysis* 54:2, pp. 124–28.

McKinsey, M. 1994b. "Individuating Beliefs." In J. Tomberlin, ed., *Philosophical Perspectives 8: Logic and Language* (Ridgeview, Calif.: Atascadero).

McKinsey, M. 1995. "Anti-Individualism and Privileged Access." *Analysis* 55, pp. 9–16.
McKinsey, M. 1999. "The Semantics of Belief Ascriptions." *Noûs* 33:4, pp. 519–57.
McLaughlin, B. and Tye, M. 1998a. "Externalism, Twin Earth, and Self-Knowledge." In C. Wright, B. Smith and C. Macdonald, eds., *Knowing Our Own Minds* (Oxford University Press), pp. 285–320.
McLaughlin, B. and Tye, M. 1998b. "Is Content-Externalism Compatible with Privileged Access?" *Philosophical Review* 107:3, pp. 349–80.
Marcus, R. B. 1961. "Modalities and Intensional Languages." *Synthese* 13:4, pp. 303–22.
Marcus, R. B. 1971. "Essential Attribution." *The Journal of Philosophy* 68:7, pp. 187–202.
Marcus, R. B. 1972. "Quantification and Ontology." *Noûs* 6:3, pp. 240–50.
Melnyk, A. 2008. "Conceptual and Linguistic Analysis: A Two-Step Program." *Noûs* 42, pp. 267–91.
Millikan, R. 1993. *White Queen Psychology and Other Essays for Alice*. Cambridge, Mass.: MIT Press.
Moore, G. E. 1939. "Proof of an External World." *Proceedings of the British Academy* 25, pp. 273–300.
Moran, R. 2001. *Authority and Estrangement: An Essay on Self-Knowledge* (Cambridge, Mass.: Harvard University Press).
Morton, A. and Karjalainen, A. 2008. "Contrastivity and Indistinguishability." *Social Epistemology* 22, pp. 271–80.
Nagasawa, Y. 2002. "Externalism and the Memory Argument." *Dialectica* 56, pp. 335–46.
Nichols, S., Pinillos, A. and Mallon, R. 2014. "Ambiguous Reference." Unpublished MS.
Nozick, R. 1981. *Philosophical Explanations* (Oxford University Press).
Nuccetelli, S. ed. 2003. *New Essays on Semantic Externalism and Self-Knowledge* (Cambridge, Mass.: MIT Press).
Owens, J. 1990. "Cognitive Access and Semantic Puzzles." In *Propositional Attitudes: The Role of Content in Logic, Language, and Mind* (Stanford, CA: CSLI Press), pp. 147–73.
Pagin, P. 2006. "Meaning Holism." In E. Lepore and B. Smith, eds., *The Oxford Handbook of Philosophy of Language* (Oxford University Press), pp. 214–32.
Pagin, P. 2012. "Transparency and Structured Meanings." Unpublished MS.
Parent, T. 2013. "Externalism and Self-Knowledge." *The Stanford Encyclopedia of Philosophy* (Summer edition), ed. Edward N. Zalta. http://plato.stanford.edu/archives/sum2013/entries/self-knowledge-externalism/
Patterson, S. 1990. "The Explanatory Role of Belief Ascriptions." *Philosophical Studies* 59, pp. 313–32.
Pettit, P. 1996. *The Common Mind* (Oxford University Press).
Pryor, J. 2000. "The Skeptic and the Dogmatist." *Noûs* 34, pp. 517–49.
Putnam, H. 1962. "It Ain't Necessarily So." *The Journal of Philosophy* 59:22, pp. 658–71.
Putnam, H. 1973. "Meaning and Reference." *The Journal of Philosophy* 70, pp. 699–711.

Putnam, H. 1975. "The Meaning of 'Meaning'." In A. Pessin and S. Goldberg, eds., *The Twin Earth Chronicles: Twenty Years of Reflection on Hilary Putnam's "The Meaning of 'Meanin'"* (New York: M. E. Sharpe), pp. 3–52.
Putnam, H. 1996. "Introduction." In A. Pessin and S. Goldberg, eds., *The Twin Earth Chronicles: Twenty Years of Reflection on Hilary Putnam's "The Meaning of 'Meaning'"* (New York: M. E. Sharpe).
Recanati, F. 2012. *Mental Files* (Oxford University Press).
Ryle, G. 1949. *The Concept of Mind* (University of Chicago Press).
Sainsbury, R. M. and Tye, M. 2012. *Seven Puzzles of Thought: And How to Solve Them: An Originalist Theory of Concepts* (Oxford University Press).
Sawyer, S. 1998. "Privileged Access to the World." *Australasian Journal of Philosophy* 76, pp. 523–33.
Sawyer, S. 2001. "The Epistemic Divide." *The Southern Journal of Philosophy* 39, pp. 385–401.
Sawyer, S. 2002. "In Defence of Burge's Thesis." *Philosophical Studies* 107, pp. 109–28.
Sawyer, S. 2003. "Sufficient Absences." *Analysis* 63, pp. 202–8.
Sawyer, S. 2004. "Absences, Presences and Sufficient Conditions." *Analysis* 64, pp. 354–57.
Sawyer, S. 2005. "Contrastive Knowledge." In T. Gendler and J. Hawthorne, eds., *Oxford Studies in Epistemology*, volume I (Oxford University Press), pp. 235–71.
Sawyer, S. 2006. "Externalism, Apriority and Transmission of Warrant." In T. Marvan, ed., *What Determines Content? The Internalism/Externalism Dispute* (Newcastle upon Tyne: Cambridge Scholars Publishing).
Sawyer, S. 2007. "Closure, Contrast and Answer." *Philosophical Studies* 133, pp. 233–55.
Sawyer, S. 2008. "The Contrast-Sensitivity of Knowledge Ascriptions." *Social Epistemology* 22, pp. 235–45.
Sawyer, S. 2011. "Internalism and Externalism in Mind." In J. Garvey, ed., *The Continuum Companion to the Philosophy of Mind* (London: Continuum).
Sawyer, S. 2014. "Contrastive Self-Knowledge." *Social Epistemology*
Schaffer, J. 2004. "From Contextualism to Contrastivism." *Philosophical Studies* 119, pp. 73–103.
Schaffer, J. 2005. "Contrastive Knowledge." *Oxford Studies in Epistemology* 1 (ed. T. Gendler and J. Hawthorne), pp. 235–71.
Schaffer, J. 2007. "Closure, Contrast and Answer." *Philosophical Studies* 133, pp. 233–55.
Schaffer, J. 2008. "The Contrast-Sensitivity of Knowledge Ascriptions." *Social Epistemology* 22, pp. 235–45.
Schaffer, J. and Knobe, J. 2012. "Contrastive Knowledge Surveyed." *Noûs* 46, pp. 675–708.
Schantz, R. ed. 2003. *The Externalist Challenge: New Studies on Cognition and Intentionality* (Berlin: Walter de Gruyter).
Schiffer, S. 1992. "Boghossian on Externalism and Inference." *Philosophical Issues* 2, pp. 29–38.
Schroeter, L. 2007. "Illusion of Transparency." *Australasian Journal of Philosophy* 85:4, pp. 597–618.

Schroeter, L. 2013. "Two-Dimensional Semantics and Sameness of Meaning." *Philosophy Compass* 8:1, pp. 84–99.
Searle, J. 1967. "Proper Names." *Mind* 67:266, pp. 166–173.
Searle, J. 1983. *Intentionality* (Cambridge University Press).
Segal, G. 2000. *A Slim Book About Narrow Content* (Cambridge, Mass.: MIT Press).
Sellars, W. 1956/1997. *Empiricism and the philosophy of mind* (Cambridge, Mass.: Harvard University Press).
Shoemaker, S. 1994. "Self-Knowledge and 'Inner Sense': Lecture I: The Object Perception Model." *Philosophy and Phenomenological Research* 54:2, pp. 249–69.
Snowdon, P. 2012. "How to Think About Phenomenal Self-Knowledge." In A. Coliva, ed., *The Self and Self-Knowledge* (Oxford University Press), pp. 243–62.
Soames, S. 2002. *Beyond Rigidity. The Unfinished Semantic Agenda of Naming and Necessity* (Oxford University Press).
Sorensen, R. A. 1998. "Logical Luck." *The Philosophical Quarterly* 48:192, pp. 319–34.
Speaks, J. 2011. "Theories of Meaning." *The Stanford Encyclopedia of Philosophy* (Summer Edition), ed. Edward N. Zalta. http://plato.stanford.edu/archives/sum2011/entries/meaning/
Spicer, F. 2009. "On Always Being Right (About What One is Thinking)." *Canadian Journal of Philosophy* 39, pp. 137–60.
Spicer, F. 2011. "Two Ways to be Right about What One Is Thinking." *International Journal for the Study of Skepticism* 1:1, pp. 33–44.
Stanley, J. and Williamson, T. 2001. "Knowing How." *The Journal of Philosophy*, pp. 411–44.
Stalnaker, R. 1993. "Twin Earth Revisited." *Proceedings of the Aristotelian Society* 93, pp. 297–311.
Stalnaker, R. 1997. "Reference and Necessity." In B. Hale and C. Wright, eds., *A Companion to the Philosophy of Language* (Oxford: Blackwell).
Stalnaker, R. 1999. *Context and Content* (Oxford University Press).
Stalnaker, R. 2008. *Our Knowledge of the Internal World* (Oxford: Clarendon Press).
Stampe, D. 1977. "Toward a Causal Theory of Linguistic Representation." *Midwest Studies in Philosophy* 2 (*Studies in the Philosophy of Language*), pp. 43–63.
Stanley, J. 2007. *Language in Context: Selected Essays* (Oxford University Press).
Tye, M. 1995. "A Representational Theory of Pains and their Phenomenal Character." *Philosophical Perspectives* 9, pp. 223–39.
Tye, M. 1998. "Externalism and Memory." *Proceedings of the Aristotelian Society, Supplementary Volume* 72:1, pp. 77–94.
Tye, M. 2000. *Consciousness, Color, and Content* (Cambridge, Mass.: MIT Press).
Unger, P. 1982. "Toward a Psychology of Common Sense." In *Philosophical Papers*, volume I (Oxford University Press).
Unger, P. 1984. *Philosophical Relativity* (Oxford: Blackwell).

Warfield, T. A. 1992. "Privileged Self-Knowledge and Externalism are Compatible." *Analysis* 52, pp. 232–37.
Warfield, T. A. 1998. "A Priori Knowledge of the World: Knowing the World by Knowing our Minds." *Philosophical Studies* 92, pp. 127–47.
Weinberg, J., Nichols, S. and Stich, S. 2001. "Normativity and Epistemic Intuitions." *Philosophical Topics* 29:1–2, pp. 429–59.
Wittgenstein, L. 1953. *Philosophical Investigations*, 3rd edition (Oxford: Blackwell).
Wiggins, D. 2012. "Practical Knowledge: Knowing How To and Knowing That." *Mind* 121:481, pp. 97–130.
Wikforss, Å. 2001. "Social Externalism and Conceptual Errors." *The Philosophical Quarterly* 51:203, pp. 217–31.
Wikforss, Å. 2004. "Externalism and Incomplete Understanding." *The Philosophical Quarterly* 54, pp. 287–94.
Wikforss, Å. 2006. "Content Externalism and Fregean Sense." In T. Marvan, ed., *What Determines Content? The Internalism/Externalism Dispute* (Newcastle upon Tyne: Cambridge Scholars Publishing), pp. 163–79.
Wikforss, Å. 2008a. "Self-Knowledge and Knowledge of Content." *Canadian Journal of Philosophy* 38:3, pp. 399–424.
Wikforss, Å. 2008b. "Semantic Externalism and Psychological Externalism." *Philosophy Compass* 3:1, pp. 158–81.
Williamson, T. 2000. *Knowledge and its Limits* (Oxford University Press).
Wright, C. 1986. "Facts and Certainty." *Proceedings of the British Academy* 71, pp. 429–72.
Wright, C. 1998. "Self-Knowledge: The Wittgensteinian Legacy." In C. Wright, B. C. Smith and C. MacDonald, eds., *Knowing Our Own Minds* (Oxford University Press).
Wright, C. 2000. "Cogency and Question-Begging: Some Reflections on McKinsey's Paradox and Putnam's Proof." *Philosophical Issues* 10, pp. 140–63.
Wright, C. 2001. *Rails to Infinity* (Cambridge, Mass.: Harvard University Press).
Wright, C. 2003. "Some Reflections on the Acquisition of Warrant by Inference." In S. Nuccetelli, ed., *New Essays on Semantic Externalism and Self-Knowledge* (Cambridge, Mass.: MIT Press), pp. 57–77.
Wright, C. 2011. "McKinsey One More Time." In A. Hatzimoysis, ed., *Self-Knowledge* (Oxford University Press).
Wright, C., Smith, B. and MacDonald, C. eds. 2000. *Knowing Our Own Minds* (Oxford University Press).

Index

2D semantics, 13, 197, 198, 203–4, 212

access
  access transparency, 145, 146–48
  accessibilism, 119–41
  differential dubitability, 120–21, 129–41
  explicatory access
    rationality and, 124–27
    thesis, 122–24
    transparency and, 127–28
  externalism and, 121–29
    externalism v internalism, 119
    incompatibility with introspective access, 121–24, 197
  privileged access, 8–9, 49–74, 75–76, 78–79, 119, 121
achievement problem, 3–6, 79
anti-individualism
  Burge, 21, 41–42, 84, 170–71, 191
  comprehension, self-knowledge and, 184–94
  individualism and, 76
  McKinsey paradox and, 79, 80–81, 84–85
  thesis, 76–78
anti-luminosity argument, 7–8, 19–40
attitude externalism, 3–6, 8
Austin, J.L., 173

Bach, Kent, 176, 193
Bar-On, Dorit, 52
belief transparency, 157–62, 167–69
Berker, Selim, 7–8, 21, 24, 25, 35
Bilgrami, Akeel, 233, 234, 235
Blackburn, Simon, 55
Boghossian, Paul
  belief transparency, 157
  externalism and inference, 244–47
  influence, 5
  'memory argument,' 13, 197–200
  minimal self-knowledge, 168–69, 174
  Pavarotti argument, 104, 106–7, 110–11, 114, 118, 128, 152, 203, 244–47

switching argument, 99–101, 107, 111–12, 113–18, 122, 200–1, 208–11, 241
transparency, 5, 9–11, 15, 97–112, 113–18, 127–28, 144, 146, 148–51, 152–56, 158–62
Brown, Jessica, 3, 128, 150–51
Brueckner, Tony, 8, 41–48, 165, 175
Burge, Tyler
  anti-individualism, 21, 41–42, 84, 170–71, 191
  'arthritis,' 229, 234–35
  basic self-knowledge, 4, 8, 11, 175
    memory argument, 198–202
  Boghossian and, 198, 246
  cogito-like judgments, 4, 5, 8, 11, 41–42, 46, 193
  cohabitation, 101
  comprehension and self-knowledge, 184, 191–93
  on differential dubitability, 133–36, 137–41
  explicatory knowledge, 122, 123–24
  externalism, 98–99, 120
  memory, 198–202, 206, 211
  on neo-Russellianism, 176
  self-verifying judgments, 8, 41–48, 199
  switching, 42, 99–101, 200–1, 241
  thought attribution, 169, 170–71
  transparency of mental content, 10
Byrne, Alex, 6

Campbell, J., 112
Cappelen, H., 218
Cartesianism, 19–22, 42, 51, 52
Chalmers, David, 139, 204
cogito-like judgments, 4, 5, 8, 11, 41–42, 46, 193
Cohnitz, Daniel, 214, 217–19
comprehension
  anti-individualism, self-knowledge and, 184–94

Index

doxatic diversity of knowledge communities, 187–88
Conee, Earl, 119
consequence problem, 3–6, 79
content judgments, 151–57
content preservation, 185
contextualism
 ambiguity and externalist intuitions, 233–38
 self-interpretation principle, 228–33, 243
 semantic contextualism, 14
 source-dependent contextualism, 238–41, 243
 switching cases, 238–47
  inference, 244–47
  memory content, 241–43
  proper names, 238–39
contrastive self-knowledge
 McKinsey paradox and, 88–93
 meaning, 85–88

Davidson, Donald, 14, 175, 229, 234, 235
Davies, Martin, 3, 79, 82, 228
denoting, 224–25
Descartes, René, 19–22, 42, 51, 52
Devitt, M., 218
Dickens, Charles, 67
differential dubitability
 Burge's modification, 134–36, 137–41
 defending, 136–39
 deference and indexicality, 139–41
 explicatory access thesis and, 136
 Frege, 11, 120–21, 132–34
 survey, 129–41
 thesis, 132–34
Donnellan, K., 238–39
doxatic diversity of knowledge communities, 187–88
Dretske, Fred, 28, 81, 82, 85–86, 87
Dummett, Michael, 25, 146, 151, 152

Ebbs, Gary, 11, 165–83
Elugardo, Ray, 193
Evans, Gareth, 6, 166–67, 176, 188, 238–39
explicatory access
 differential dubitability and, 136
 internalism and, 140, 141
 rationality and, 124–27
 thesis, 122–24
 transparency and, 127–28
expressivism, 52, 202
externalism
 See also specific aspects
 development, 3–6

first-order/second order, 13–14, 214–27
meaning, 197
revolution, 2–3

Falvey, Kevin, 149, 211
Faria, P., 101
Farkas, Kati, 141, 194
Feldman, Richard, 119
Fernandez, Jordi, 13, 197–213
Finkelstein, D., 52
Fodor, J., 153
Frege, Gottlob
 differential dubitability, 11, 120–21, 132–34
 theory of reference, 1, 103–4
Fregeanism, 43–44, 98, 120, 130–31, 145, 150–51, 158–64
functional transparency, 145, 146–48

Gertler, Brie, 11, 15, 119–41, 167
Gettier cases, 36
Goldberg, Sanford, 1–15, 122, 123–24, 134, 148, 156, 171, 202, 243
Greco, Dan, 39

Häggqvist, S., 223
Harris, Paul, 173
Haukioja, Jussi, 13–14, 15, 214–27
Heal, J., 242
Hintikka, Jaacko, 27

individualism, meaning, 76
inference, contextualism, 244–47
internalism
 accessibilism and, 119
 explicatory access and, 140, 141
 externalism and, 119, 129
 Frege, 120–21
 meaning, 119
introspective knowledge of comparative content (IKCC), 98–99, 113

Jackman, Henry, 14, 228

KK principle
 anti-luminosity argument, 7–8, 19–40
 defending, 27–40
 margins of error, 22–23, 30–37
 phenomenal states, 23–27
Kripke, Saul, 1, 98, 139, 151, 157, 203–4, 217, 219, 222, 225–26

Lewis, D., 43
Loar, B., 98
Ludlow, Peter, 200, 218, 231, 244

Index

McGinn, C., 216
McKinsey, Michael
  consequence problem, 3–6, 79
  explicatory access and, 122
  paradox. *See* McKinsey paradox
McKinsey paradox
  1991 furore, 50
  argument, 75, 216–17
  contrastive self-knowledge and, 9, 79–93
  metainternalism and, 13–14, 215, 220–25, 241
McLaughlin, B., 224
Macmillan case, 179–83
Mallon, Ron, 236–37
Marcus, Ruth Barcan, 1
margins of error, 22–23, 30–37
Martin, C.B., 68
memory argument
  basic self-knowledge and, 198–202
  content and memory, 202–12
  debate, 13, 197–213
  revisiting, 208–12
metaexternalism
  externalism and, 217–20
    content, 219–20
    reference, 217–19
  first-order externalism and, 13–14
  meaning, 214, 218
metainternalism
  answer to McKinsey, 13–14, 215, 220–25
  denoting v aiming to denote, 224–25
  embracing, 214
  explanation of content externalism, 221–22
  explanation of knowledge of content externalism, 222
  knowledge of content and, 225–27
  meaning, 219
  about thought, 220
Millianism, 98, 144–45, 148–49, 158–64
minimal self-knowledge
  Evans argument, 166, 176
  meaning, 166–69
  minimalism about, 165–66, 169–76, 184
  survey, 165–83
  transparency constraints, 168–69
Moore, G.E., 81
Moran, R., 167

Nichols, Shaun, 236–37

Owen, David, 157
Owens, Joseph, 149, 211

Paderewski argument, 10–11, 98, 105, 107, 108, 113–18, 151
Parent, Ted, 50
Pavarotti argument, 104, 106–7, 110–11, 114, 118, 128, 152, 203, 244–47
perceptual knowledge
  contrastive understanding, 87
  externalism, 3
  McKinsey paradox and, 82–83
  mechanism, 72
  model of introspection, 20
  normal functioning, 38
Pettit, Philip, 222–24
phenomenal states, 23–27
Pinillos, Ángel, 236–37
privileged access, 8–9, 49–74, 75–76, 78–79, 119, 121
Putnam, Hilary, 78, 139, 169, 170–71, 216, 217, 219, 236

Recanati, François, 147
reduction response, 142–43
relevant alternatives theory, 85–86, 199, 201, 209–12
Rochford, Damien, 29
Russell, Bertrand, 43–44, 176–78, 181, 183
Ryle, Gilbert, 52, 53

Sainsbury, Mark, 7, 10–11, 15, 97–98, 101–12, 113–18, 151, 160
Sawyer, Sarah, 4, 9, 75–93
Schiffer, S., 246
Schroeter, Laura, 107
Segal, G., 80
self-blindness, 20
self-interpretation, 228–33, 243, 247
self-knowledge
  access. *See* access
  anti-individualism, comprehension and, 184–94
  Burge, 4, 8, 11
  content externalism and, 215–16
  contrastive, 88–93
  KK principle. *See* KK principle
  memory argument and, 13, 197–213
  minimal self-knowledge, 165–83
  memory argument and, 198–202
  self-verifying judgments, 8, 41–48, 199
Sellars, Wilfred, 25
Shoemaker, Sydney, 19–21, 125
Sidelle, Alan, 132
Snowdon, Paul, 8–9, 49, 50, 53–56, 57, 59–61, 62–74
Sorensen, R.A., 101

Index

Spicer, Finn, 8, 41, 43–48
Stalnaker, Robert, 7–8, 19–40, 43, 153, 154, 175, 245
Stampe, Dennis, 30
Stanley, J., 174
switching scenario
  Boghossian. *See* Boghossian, Paul
  Burge, 42, 99–101, 200–1, 241
  contextualism, 238–47
  externalism and, 144
  Oscar, 149, 151, 155–56
  Pavarotti. *See* Pavarotti argument
  slow-switching, 122–23, 200–1, 208–11, 241
  Switching Response, 142

thought attribution and word identification constraint, 170–83
transparency
  See also access
  access transparency, 145, 146–48
  belief transparency, 157–62, 167–69
  Boghossian v Sainsburty and Tye, 9–11, 97–112, 113–18
  content judgments, 151–57
  epistemic transparency, 127–28, 147, 175
  explicatory access and, 127–28
  functional transparency, 145, 146–48
  insignificance, 11, 142–64
  opposing theories, 148–51
  paradox, 101
  rejecting logical rationality, 101–9
  relevance, 14–15
  thesis, 97–100
  Transparency Constraint, 168–69, 178–79
triple identity, 185
Twin Earth, 41–42, 76–78, 89–92, 151, 162, 199–203, 209–10, 216, 218, 220, 223, 236, 244
Tye, Michael, 7, 10–11, 15, 97–98, 100, 101–12, 113–18, 151, 160, 224

Wang's paradox, 25
Wiggins, D., 174
Wikforss, Åsa, 11, 15, 121, 131, 142–64, 193, 223
Williamson, Timothy, 7–8, 19–40, 174
Winblad, D., 218
Wittgenstein, Ludwig, 49, 51, 52, 53, 54–56, 60, 63, 74, 233
Wright, Crispin, 8–9, 49–74, 82